NAMING THE GODS

Cy Twombly's Passionate *Poiesis*

GARY D. ASTRACHAN

www.ChironPublications.com

Interior and cover design by Cornelia Murariu
Printed primarily in the United States of America.

ISBN 978-1-63051-736-6 paperback
ISBN 978-1-63051-737-3 hardcover
ISBN 978-1-63051-738-0 electronic
ISBN 978-1-63051-739-7 limited edition paperback

Library of Congress Cataloging-in-Publication Data Pending

Names: Astrachan, Gary D., author.
Title: Naming the gods : Cy Twombly's passionate poiesis / Gary D.
    Astrachan.
Description: Asheville, N.C. : Chiron Publications, [2019] | Includes
    bibliographical references. | Summary: "Naming the Gods: Cy Twombly's
    Passionate Poiesis concerns itself with the contemporary art work of Cy
    Twombly as seen against the deep background of classical Greek
    mythology. In particular, the two entwined figures and images of
    Orpheus, lyre player, lover and journeyer to the underworld, and
    Dionysos/Bacchus, god of wine, ecstasy and madness, are taken up as the
    two principal thematic leitmotifs which animate and overarchingly inform
    Twombly's entire artistic oeuvre across all the mediums in which he
    worked, both literally and symbolically, from the early 1950's until the
    last series of brilliantly colored paintings he made just before his
    death in 2011. His preoccupations with the rhythms of language, poetry
    and writing on the one hand, and his tendencies towards wildly
    expressive gestural abstraction on the other, ultimately combine in his
    creation of a genuinely new and original performative aesthetic which
    unites and connects the powerful impulses of mark-making, painting and
    assembling with the basic human needs for individuation, realization and
    redemption"-- Provided by publisher.
Identifiers: LCCN 2020005173 (print) | LCCN 2020005174 (ebook) | ISBN
    9781630517366 (paperback) | ISBN 9781630517373 (hardback) | ISBN
    9781630517380 (ebook)
Subjects: LCSH: Twombly, Cy, 1928-2011--Criticism and interpretation. |
    Mythology, Greek, in art.
Classification: LCC N6537.T96 A88 2019 (print) | LCC N6537.T96 (ebook) |
    DDC 700/.47--dc23
LC record available at https://lccn.loc.gov/2020005173
LC ebook record available at https://lccn.loc.gov/2020005174

When rhythm has become the sole and unique mode of thought's expression, it is then only that there is poetry. In order for mind to become poetry, it must bear in itself the mystery of an innate rhythm. It is in this rhythm alone that it can live and become visible. And every work of art is but one and the same rhythm. Everything is simply rhythm. The destiny of man is a single celestial rhythm, as every work of art is a unique rhythm.

— **FRIEDRICH HÖLDERLIN**

In the time of distress which is ours, the time when the gods are missing, the time of absence and exile, art is justified, for it is the intimacy of this distress: the effort to make manifest, through the image, the error of the imaginary, and eventually the ungraspable, forgotten truth which hides behind this error.

— **MAURICE BLANCHOT**

CONTENTS

PREFATORY NOTE

IMAGES GIVE BIRTH TO WORDS. In the long course of writing this book, I have been sustained and held in the embrace of a vast body of images. These images contain in themselves everything that could possibly be conveyed by the words—and considerably more. Everything, including all speech, language and writing, returns to images. Of course words are images too, and in their weight and solidity, they carry the dark traces of the depths from whence they come. In reading, we retrace the steps of the words back down to their origins in the underworld of images.

Each of the gods of Greek mythology comprise an entire world, whole constellations of multi-faceted images, and these images are what we can see and know of them. With their roots deep in Hades, and their eternal dwellings on Mount Olympos, the gods blossom into vision in our own human world. There they reveal themselves through their signs, traces and tracks.

Since the publication of this book entailed limiting the printed number of images to a maximum of thirty, I have created a website:

www.namingthegods.com

This site is a visual supplement and picture gallery to accompany you, dear reader, on this journey into images. I have tried to include as many of the images specifically referred to in the written text as possible. They correspond and are linked to the actual page numbers of the book, and they hopefully provide an affective counterpoint and amplification of the thematic narratives at play within this theatre of the imagination.

Koinos Hermes!

Gary D. Astrachan
Spring 2019

LIST OF IMAGES

1. Cy Twombly, *Untitled*, Gaeta, 1984.

2. Cima da Conegliano, *Orpheus Playing for the Animals*, c. 1505-10.

3. François Perrier, *Orpheus in the Underworld Playing Before Pluto and Persephone*, c. 1647-50.

4. Cy Twombly, *Orpheus*, 1979.

5. *Orpheus Singing to the Thracians*, detail, c. 450 B.C., Orpheus Painter.

6. Cy Twombly, *Winter's Passage: Luxor*, Porto Ercole, 1985.

7. *Death of Orpheus*, detail, c. 440 B.C., Phiale Painter.

8. Odilon Redon, *Orpheus*, c. 1903-10.

9. Cy Twombly, *Untitled (Say Goodbye, Catullus, to the Shores of Asia Minor)*, 1994.

10. Cy Twombly, *Untitled (Say Goodbye, Catullus, to the Shores of Asia Minor)*, detail, 1994.

11. *Orpheus and Eurydice*, detail, Roman copy of 420 B.C. Greek original by Callimachos.

12. Robert Rauschenberg, *Cy Twombly with a musical instrument*, 1953, Rome.

13. *Dionysos in Ecstasy*, detail, c. 490 B.C., Kleophrades.

14. Cy Twombly, *Dionysus*, 1975.

15. Cy Twombly, *Fifty Days at Iliam, Part IV: Achaeans in Battle*, detail, 1978.

16. *Zeus and Dionysos*, detail, c. 460 B.C., Altamura Painter.

17. *Raving Maenad with Panther and Snake in Hair*, detail, c.490-80 B.C., Brygos Painter.

18. Cy Twombly, *Bacchus*, Part II, detail, 1981.

19. Cy Twombly, *Naxos*, 1982.

20. Tiziano Vecellio, called Titian, *Bacchus and Ariadne*, c. 1520-23.

21. *Dionysos and Ariadne*, detail, c. 340 B.C.

22. Cy Twombly, *Untitled*, installation view Parts I and II, 2005.

23. Cy Twombly, *Untitled (Bacchus 1ˢᵗ version)*, 2004, installation view, 2008.

24. *Dionysos Diasparagmos, Paroxysm of the Ecstatic Crisis*, detail, c. 450 B.C.

25. Cy Twombly, *Vengeance of Achilles*, Rome, 1962.

26. Cy Twombly, *Fifty Days at Iliam, Part V: The Fire That Consumes All Before It*, detail, 1978.

27. Cy Twombly, *Suma*, 1982.

28. Cy Twombly, *Untitled*, installation view Parts VII and VIII, 2005.

29. *Dionysos and Ariadne*, detail, c. 400 B.C.

30. Cy Twombly, *Untitled (Camino Real)*, Part II, 2011.

I

Caesura-ing the Visible

IN THE VOLUME OF THE COLLECTED *Writings on Cy Twombly,* there is an arresting piece on Twombly's sculpture entitled "Beauty that falls," written by Giorgio Agamben originally in 1998, and here reproduced in its entirety:

> There comes a point in the creative course of every great artist or poet, when the image of beauty, which, up to that moment he had pursued in a seemingly continuous upward movement, suddenly reverses direction and becomes visible vertically, in its fall. It is the movement that Hölderlin defined, in the notes to his translation of Sophocles, as the "caesura" or "anti-rhythmic interruption": when the word, as if checked in mid-flight, for a moment reveals not what it says, but its own nature. And it is the vulnerable moment at the end of the poem where—as Dante wrote in *De vulgari eloquentia*—the verses seem to fall hugging each other in the silence.
>
> It is just the same fixed fall, that makes Caravaggio's angels' wings quiver in the *Opere della Misericordia* ("Works of Mercy") or that infuses life into color's darkening matter in Titian's late paintings—like the San Salvador "Annunciation" in Venice or the "Apollo and Marsia" in Prague. He had to sign these canvases *fecit fecit* in the awareness that he had not made them as much as he had really unmade them.

This is what Twombly's gesture is like in those extreme sculptures where it is as if every ascension has been inverted and broken, almost thresholds between doing and not-doing: beauty that falls.

It is the point of de-creation, when the artist in his unparalleled style no longer creates but decreates—that untitled messianic moment in which art stays miraculously still, almost astounded: fallen and risen in every instant.

(Agamben 2002, p. 283)

This marvelously poetic passage includes, in its relatively short breadth, references to quite a number of important figures in the course of Western culture: Sophocles, playwright of Oedipus and Antigone; Dante, traversing heaven and hell meting out literary justice; Caravaggio, glowering darkly in chiaroscuro; and Titian, long-lived master of painted coloratura. This evocative single page, notwithstanding all of the above-mentioned eminent notables, is particularly striking for our theme, however, for its stunning conjunction of the very first and the very last-named individuals who appear in its far-flung though compact embrace: Friedrich Hölderlin and Cy Twombly. Now what could Hölderlin, the early nineteenth century German poet and prose writer, entirely mad for nearly the whole second half of his life, from about 1806 until his death in 1843—living in the tower of the carpenter Ernst Zimmer on the Neckar River in Tübingen—possibly have to do with the temporally disparate Twombly, a vital and productive contemporary American artist, born in 1928 in Lexington, Virginia, and until his death in 2011, residing since the 1950s, for the most part, both in Italy and in the United States? What could conceivably bring together these two historically, culturally, and characterologically separated and distinctive artistic personages?

The answer, we propose, would seem to lie somewhere in the region of ancient Greece, in the fertile soil and subterranean springs of Hellenic culture as they bubbled up and spread from the Mediterranean basin throughout all of Europe. It is, in fact, precisely in Hölderlin's powerful prose work, the *Remarks* on the translation of Sophocles' "Oedipus," written in 1803, that he introduces the notion of the "caesura," or "anti-rhythmic interruption," to characterize the epiphanic moment in tragedy when the words, images, and actions of the dramatic spectacle, suddenly come to a complete halt; and then, in a blinding flash, reveal not only what the tragic representation or word "says, but (instead) its own nature" (ibid.). It is this still point, this dizzying pause and absence of movement, as defined by Hölderlin, that Agamben compares to the extreme sculptural gestures of Twombly, that in their continuous artistic rising, abruptly stop and begin to fall—"fallen and risen," as he writes, "in every instant" (ibid.). And there, in that still void, in that vertiginous spiraling, like Sophoclean tragedy, these sculptures, paintings and poetic and prose works reveal their innermost tragic essence, *through* and *in* their drama, through their presentation of an *event*, and in the terms of the experienced and experiential processes they actually *make happen*. This is an art that reveals its inner dynamic core, its being, through the performative gestures, which in those delimited moments are enacted to unveil it. *Aletheia*, "unveiling" in Greek, and translated through the centuries as "truth," presents the rhythmically beating innermost heart within these acts of creating and de-creating. These sublimely poetic gestures, continuously and with abandon, perform their dance on the razor's edge between being and non-being.

With this deft metaphorical move, Agamben gathers up the corpus of Twombly's artwork within the folds of Hölderlin's poetic discourses on the very nature of representation itself. And then, going even further back in time, he also implicitly includes the creations of both Hölderlin *and* Twombly within the sudden and tragic reversal and recognition precipitated through the horror-struck gaze of Oedipus. This most mortal man, Oedipus of Thebes, who seeing into the terrible truth of his own actions and behaviors, furiously raises the sharpened knife and puts out his own eyes. This instant, this instantaneous moment, as Hölderlin deliberately charts it out (Hölderlin 1988, p. 96), subjecting it to minute psychological analysis, is the soul-wrenching break or rupture of all tragedy, of all tragic art—when the ill-fated protagonist looks into the daimonic abyss created by the immortal gods who dwell beyond this world, on the other side of this great rift torn open within us, mere humans. The gods live on the other side of this cleft. *They* inhabit the realm of infinity, while our own fractured, finite, and fatal bodies remain rooted to this earth. This unbridgeable division and apportioned lot which runs through all of human life constitutes the very basis and precondition for tragedy.

Agamben, via Hölderlin, thus points us back to a quintessentially aesthetic moment and movement enfolded within both the creation and reception of art which suddenly opens up to, or allows for, a perception into these roiling depths of being and not-being. It is the moment when everything comes crashing down, leaving a stillness and eerie quiet once the rubble settles. Only then do the wails, moans and cries slowly begin to rise with the clouds of dust from the ruins. This radically transformative experience both underpins, and at the same time, annihilates all works of art. Agamben describes a chasm, a chiasm, a crisscrossing or fissure, which unexpectedly cracks open within the material artwork itself, to unveil the work's nameless, bottomless and faceless roots and sources. The 'end' of painting and thus of art, in the words of Maurice Merleau-Ponty, is "to attend internally at (this) fission of Being" (Merleau-Ponty 1993, p. 360).

This performative moment, as acknowledged, expressed and portrayed by Hölderlin, Sophocles and Twombly, Agamben suggests, is the ground, perhaps even the groundless ground, of all sublime and tragic art. He refers to this constellation of events as an art that also 'falls' at least as much as it rises. He circumscribes an art that is definitely no longer heroic, and in fact, is more often openly anti-heroic. It is a kind of art that is indeed created perhaps even after the 'end of art.'

This foundational experience of tragedy consists in this sense then, in a precise moment when the representation detaches itself from its production, or product, whether in image, word, gesture, deed, spectacle or sound, and lays bare the innermost nature of the representational process itself, its birth, as it were—out of death—out of the psychical pall of death which enshrouds life. This art tears to shreds the veil of *māyā*, the illusion and appearance of ordinary reality, which in the tragic or sublime aesthetic experience, is "now merely fluttering in tatters before the mysterious primordial unity" (Nietzsche 1967, p. 37).

What is addressed here is a particular quality of aesthetic experiencing, which, as we know from both Hölderlin's writings and Twombly's artworks, has the consistently astounding capacity to totally transfigure our own representational subjectivity. It is an art that alters the very ways we see, think, and experience the world and our selves. During the timelessly unnameable moments opened by these works, we become witness to a presence which emerges paradoxically, out of the presentation of an absence, a divestment, out of privation, loss and disappearance; and which furthermore, produces its effects through disarticulation, dismemberment, and destruction. This is an art that runs exactly counter to all of our usual expectations and needs from art—for comfort, solace, beauty, or reassurance. This is an art that seeks to create "new presentations, not in order to enjoy them, but in order to impart a stronger sense of the unpresentable" (Lyotard 1984, p. 81). This is a downward going path of art, and life, that creates via a descent. This is an art that falls. This art makes its connections through disintegration, disruption, sexuality, chaos, breakdown, loosening, loss, trauma, and madness.

II

THIS MATTER OF SPACE/MAKING SPACE MATTER

Further pursuing the striking parallels between Greek tragedy, Hölderlin and Twombly, all within this context of the 'disruptive turn of art,' we come next to this one sentence, also from Agamben, this time from his book, *The Man Without Content* (1999). Referring to Aristotle's discussion of "(the) arts as beginnings, especially the architectonic arts," he writes:

> That art is architectonic means, etymologically: art, *poiesis,* is pro-duction of origin, art is the gift of the original space of man, *architectonics* par excellence.
>
> (Agamben 1999, p. 101)

In our desire to wend our way back to the sublimely liberating visitation of god's absence, and to the Hölderlin-Twombly connection hinted at in Agamben's first long quote, and thus to also return to a discussion of the performative process and moment of artistic representation, or decreation, in poetry and in painting, we need to first begin to unpack, explicate, and amplify this passage of Agamben's. Our chosen text above is this series of short, concise statements, really one sentence, which Agamben first wrote in Italian in 1970, when he was 28 years old (and six years earlier had already played the role of Philip the Apostle in Pier Paolo Pasolini's film, *The Gospel According to St. Matthew,* and after that had then studied with Martin Heidegger in France) (Morris 2004, pp. 12- 15). This quote, concerning as it does the sense of space that art both creates and inhabits in its presentation, affords us a stage or platform on which to perform our own present inquiry into Twombly's lifelong and extensive project of *mythopoiesis* in relationship to these notions of space, time and matter touched upon by Agamben. Art, it would seem, both collates and confabulates aspects of all three of these basic concepts of space, time, and matter for its own uniquely special stagings and effects.

Despite its extreme brevity relative to the quote with which we began this exploration, the ideas of the 'origin' and 'space' of art raised here provide an orientation within which we may try to descend into this immaterial matter of both painting and language, even as it disappears before our eyes. This passage appears in a chapter which he titles, "The original structure of the work of art." He begins the section with a quote transcribed from Hölderlin's period of so-called "incoherent speech" (Agamben 1999, p. 94), during the late phase of the poet's life when he actually was often quite 'mad':

> Everything is rhythm, the entire destiny of man is one heavenly rhythm, just as every work of art is one rhythm, and everything swings from the poetizing lips of the god.
>
> (Hölderlin in ibid.)

In addition to the two major topics of space and matter that emerge from Agamben's quote for our primary considerations, we must thus also mention a third concept, glimpsed as it were between the other two and alluded to here by Hölderlin. For without this *tertium non datur,* we could well imagine that the entire project of art would itself founder and fail. The third element not necessarily 'given' in either the material creation of art, nor in the space or environment of its reception, is the indispensably reciprocal gaze which is exchanged between an artwork and its viewer—*in time.* It is this gaze, the world of the visible with which we are inextricably enmeshed through vision, that constitutes the unique aesthetic 'place,' or *topos,* for the relationship between the created work of art and its beholders. The gaze, which can also be a listening, is thus the relational medium, both the mix and the setting, in which and by which artistic experience takes place. The 'look,' or 'hearing,' an attentiveness and quickening, rhythmically happening, mediates between the space and time of the artwork itself in its enclosed materiality, and in its subsequent manifestation in the world, as it participates with an environmental context and an 'other.' Jean-François Lyotard writes:

> There can be no work of art if the seer and the seen do not hold one another in an embrace, if the immanence of one for the other is not manifested and glorified, if the visual organization does not make us feel that our gaze has been seen and that the object is watching.
>
> (Lyotard 1989, p. 224)

Here in this experience of art there is thus a reversibility, an intertwining, an overlapping, a conjoining and interweaving between the seer and the seen. "(The) seer is caught up in the midst of the visible, that in order to see, the seer must in turn be capable of being seen" (Johnson in Merleau-Ponty 1993, p. 48). We are in this sense then, of one 'flesh' with this visible world. Things are, and the world itself is, made of the very same stuff as the body. "'It is first of all by the world that I am seen or thought.' The seer is seen while he sees, and thus there is vision in things" (Lyotard 1993, p. 330). In the beginning we are all to start with, *seen beings.*

Returning now to the passage of Agamben's quoted above, he first states that art is essentially synonymous with *poiesis. Poiesis,* that resonant word from the Greek that gives us our poetry, poetics, and poetizing, also means in its original sense, simply man's *doing,* "pro-ducing," he says, making, fabricating, and creating. As opposed to *praxis,* 'practice,' practical work, or *téchnē,* 'skill,' *poiesis* is a bringing forth from concealment, hiddenness and non-being into the 'light of presence.'

Plato writes that "any cause that brings into existence something that was not there before is *poiesis*" (Agamben 1999, p. 59). *Poiesis,* however, derives exclusively from man, not by contrast, from nature. *Poiesis* is inherent in the human soul's capacity for *aletheia,* the 'unveiling' that pro-duces things, leading them from occlusion and form-lessness into being and presence. The task of *poiesis* bequeaths to the poet, whether working with words, images, movements, sounds, materials, or pigments, the vocation of creatively re-figuring both the subject him or herself, and the natural world. *Poiesis* bears within itself as its original mission this compelling desire for a complete transfiguration of our natural state. As the alchemists would have it, creation quintessentially involves an *opus contra naturam,* a working not only despite, but *against* nature.

On a quite literal level then, *poiesis* aims at and intends to radically reno-vate both our material condition, and our specular, speculative, and spectacular relationship with the world, both inwardly and outwardly. It disrupts our ocularocentric, or vision-centered, relationship with the world. *Poiesis* seeks nothing less than the total transformation of our inner and outer natures.

Agamben goes on further to claim that "art, *poiesis,* is pro-duction of origin" (ibid., p. 101). Art, he implies, leads us forth, *pro-ductus,* and brings us out of our usual, everyday selves—to our origins—(back) to our original starting place. It is a going out, a being led outward, and a coming back. Its trajectory includes a turning around, a pause, either at the apex or nadir, and a reversal of direction—again a 'falling,' a falling back into the world, a going back to beginnings, and maybe even before beginnings. *Poiesis,* in short, produces a kind of ecstasy, a swooning, allowing us to stand outside of and beside our usual selves, *ek-stasis*—and to gaze at our commonplace selves from this trans-figured state. We become beside ourselves. Art pro-duces a divinely-backed madness—a madness which is supported by a god.

Art exists in order to lead us out of our normally constructed selves, and therewith to bring us back to where we have come from. While reminding us of and deriving from our original home, it simultaneously, however, seems to be also leading us toward the soul's true home, which is, in fact, somewhere out in front of us, out ahead of us, outside of us, still unfulfilled. In its creation and "pro-duction of origin" and beginnings, art reveals not only where we are coming from, our native sources and origins, but also who and what we are as human beings, *and* most importantly of all perhaps, where we are going. *Poiesis* and art perform an 'anamnesis,' a re-membering and a re-collecting. "Anamnesis is *recognition* itself; it is a matter of the *destination of the subject*" (Lacoue-Labarthe 1994, p. 21). Art imaginally leads us into the messianic future about which we have always dreamt.

In thus bringing us back to our unique and individual origins, *poiesis* bears the immense capacity to convey to us our destination as well, showing us *to what* we are destined by virtue of our human birthright and inheritance. Composed as we human beings are, of both *soma and psyche,* body *and* soul, our Orphically conjuncted nature, art re-calls us to just this brutally simple fact, our tragic, fatal and irreducibly limited condition, our own death. This *is* tragedy - this fact that our precarious physical mortality is conjoined with an aspect of divinity, timelessness, and immortality. We are led to the realization that we have god, gods, and even many gods, within our selves.

Poiesis recollects us to our origins, while pointing at the same time toward the future and what awaits us.

Sublime or tragic art thus traverses in its wide arc the whole body of time, pointing to a messianic future which is yet to arrive, has yet to come, and furthermore, needs *us* for *its* realization. And all this while tragic art deposits us there—in that future. We are dislocated, dis-placed, in different places at once, all over the place. Existence may, in fact, be, learning how to be in several places at the same time, easy for a god, but how can *we* truly *be* in different places at once?

Human beings thus bear within themselves not only a 'god-likeness,' but the task of facilitating and fulfilling the impersonal fates of the gods *themselves* who live within us. This is our legacy. The god within us bears *its own* fate. We are, or must become, the Hephaistian midwives of this god, or gods, whom we bear within our selves. This *is* then the poet's vocation, the task of *poiesis*: to birth the gods who speak through us, to fulfill *their* mission. "This attitude," Agamben says, "this reverse embrace of memory and forgetting which holds intact the identity of the unrecalled and the unforgettable, is vocation" (Agamben 1995, p. 45).

Art, in extending its range in this same sense and direction, therefore points also to a *space*, to a kind of dwelling and *place* that awaits us, that is somewhere out there just beyond our view or grasp, further along this overgrown, winding path, which in our wandering, twists and turns out of sight. Art clairvoyantly peers into this spiraling underbrush of a future so that we might fulfill the destiny of this being that eludes us. "That we know not how to name what awaits us," Lyotard writes, "is the sure sign that it awaits us" (Lyotard in Rajchman 1985, p.112).

Poiesis thus facilitates the creation of the actual and imagined space for which we have been born. It has the power to concretely and figuratively reconstruct for us a kind of world to which we have always belonged, a world and environment with which we know at a deep level we are, in fact, kin. It is a *topos* that is strangely familiar, like 'home,' our original home and habitation, our authentically human dwelling place.

In its pro-duction of origin, art also, however, paradoxically, produces an 'otherness' in us, an awareness of the 'other' from which we have become alienated and separated in space and time—and since birth. Art thereby creates too, a homesickness *(Heimweh),* a longing and nostalgia for this 'other,' which while it is the closest and most natural of feelings and things for us, is also the most distant, unknown, uncanny *(unheimlich),* often frightening, and definitely most foreign of feelings. *Poiesis* produces this *déja vu* experience, which is as if we are recalling something heard perhaps while *in utero.* Longing and language come together in this search for our own original mother tongue, our own voice and song, which is at every turn and every time a foreign language to us, because it is still *un-*conscious. Longing for the lost language of our beginnings, our genesis and origins, is the impetus for all art.

Poiesis also opens up a terrible gulf of aloneness and presents this 'other,' through the presentational experience itself. *Poiesis is,* in fact, just this presentation and production of 'otherness.' In its creation of an alterity, strangeness and alienation, including a separation with and from our own selves, it therefore makes us feel incomplete, fragmented, partial, broken and vulnerable. Yet in that feeling of weakness and lack, loneliness and separation, there is often still an exhilarating freedom and power, an autonomy—to create, to make, to do. Despite touching nothing, we are liberated. Through division and separation, we step out of historical time in order to *re-enter* it more fully at another point. Agamben writes:

> By opening to man his authentic temporal dimension, the work of art also opens for him the space of his belonging to the world, only within which he can take the original measure of his dwelling on earth and find again his present truth in the unstoppable flow of linear time.
>
> (Agamben 1999, p. 101)

This kind of poetic representation arising from emptiness, absence and loss, does not then simply re-present for a second time what is known, comfortable, soothing, simple or satisfying; rather, it presents what is difficult and unpresentable. It yearns to represent what may even, in fact, be ultimately, not at all representable. It thus also often, though not always, demands actions of disturbance, upset, and even violence. Maurice Blanchot writes: "Only if it is torn unity, always in struggle, never pacified, is the work a work." He calls it: "torn intimacy" (Blanchot 1982, p. 229). It is an art that first of all unsettles, dis-organizes, and then frustrates assumptions, beliefs and culturally established values and securities. It produces discordance, division and dissension. It is multiple, heterogeneous and polyvalent. It frankly and openly reveals the failure, wreckage and ruin of our current state of affairs, while at the same time, it accepts this condition of dis-integration and catastrophe as the unavoidable ground, beginning and ferment indispensable for any further creative work, or life, for that matter. This is an art that flourishes in the obvious and acknowledged decline and breakdown of all great representational art. This is a *praxis* in perpetual revolt. Breaking free of traditional narratives and conventional representational themes, it is a subversive and anarchic art that creates in order to see where it will go. It does not and can not have preconceived goals.

"Art," Agamben writes, "is the gift of the original space of man" (Agamben 1999, p. 101). In pro-ducing origin, art gives back to us our "original space." But what kind of "original space" is this? What kind of space do we have 'originally' that can be given back to us? In returning us to proximity with our origin, art restores us to our own originality, our individuality. Art, the creation of meaning, *poiesis*, is the *via regia* of the individuation process, that is, the process of becoming whoever or whatever it is that we are supposed to be in this life. And each and every one of our points, or moments of origin, are furthermore not reproducible. Art is the pro-duction that comes into being from these attempts to re-produce and re-present our unrepresentable, irre-producible, and unique originality, that 'other' and transformed being we now are to ourselves.

Additionally, that which is most original in us and about us, is also at the same time, the most impersonal and strangest aspect of our being altogether. In the choral ode of Sophocles' *Antigone*, as mediated and translated by Hölderlin and more than a century later by Heidegger, we find the passage that: "the uncanniest of the uncanny is the human being" (Heidegger 1996, p. 68). That which is given in a flash, out of time, this original state of being, is also instigated and precipitated, or at least furthered and encouraged, by the making and presentation of sublime art. *Poiesis* makes us strangers to our selves. It rocks and ruptures our world. This is an art which must, of necessity, derange the senses.

A circle and cycle of gratitude, debt and re-payment is established through this extraordinary gift; a gift by the way, which the visible and aural world, and nature herself, also constantly, freely and openly presents. Hölderlin writes in his poem, "The Poet's Vocation" (1800-01):

> O all you heavenly gods
> And all you streams and shores, hilltops and woods,

> Where first, when by the hair one of you
> Seized us and the unhoped-for spirit
>
> Unforgettably came, astonishing, down
> Upon us, godlike and creative, dumbfounding
> The mind, every bone shook
> As if struck by lightning -

(Hölderlin 1972, p. 33)

The poet's vocation as established here through a wrenching fear and holy terror, comes at the exorbitant expense of the poet's entire further life. The moment of vocation signals both a beginning and the end of all ordinary human life. It is the coincidence of both abandonment, loss, and decline, as well as growth, gain and presence.

As a medium in which we see, hear, feel, move, and breathe, the *topos* of art could only be a space created out of an arduous working in and on, soul, a working with *psyche*. It is a space composed of actual soul stuff, or soul *matter*. It *is* the melding and admixture of inner with outer nature in the co-creation of something authentically new. *Poiesis* is thus the creation of a radically re-novative, innovative and changed *materia,* as well as a completely overturned thought and feeling. The status of matter itself is hence transfigured. Antonin Artaud speaks of this "phosphorescent point at which all reality is recovered, but changed, transformed" (In Larratt-Smith 2014, p. 22).

Here we begin arriving with Agamben's quote at a bifurcation in the paths of art, where it theoretically divides into the two separate though related modalities of space and matter. As a "gift of the original space," art is also thus *some thing*. And *some thing* must have the quality of space to it, around it, and about it. This *thing* we call art, an 'art work,' produces out of itself, out of its own reality, matter and materiality, the quality of a soul space—a space for soul, a room for *psyche*. It is an actual place in the world, made, manifested and modeled, where the soul can finally breathe freely and dwell. It is this space for soul which is restored to us in art, returned to us, given back as a gift, offered, set apart, and sacred. Certain real things, in life, events, experiences, environments, relationships, attitudes, actualities, things that really matter about this world, thereby then hold open the possibility of becoming truly redeemed and transformed. Rainer Maria Rilke tells us that:

Transcience everywhere plunges into a deep being. And so all forms of this earth are not only not to be used in a time-limited way only, but, so far as we are able, to be given place in those superior significances in which we have a part.

(Rilke 1942, p. 133)

The vocation of sublime art calls the artist to re-create just this all-inclusive space where all things once again, can, and do, matter. Art is the glorification and apotheosis of matter and the materiality of life itself.

In the Homeric "Hymn to the Earth," the anonymous eighth century B.C. poet begins by giving voice to:

> The mother of us all,
> the oldest of all,
> hard,
>   splendid as rock
> Whatever there is that is of the land
>   it is she
>   who nourishes it,
>   it is the Earth
>   that I sing

(In Boer 1979, p. 1)

Art is thus the redemption of soul in and out of matter. Soul, which has fallen into matter, needs *us* for *its* redemption. *Poiesis* effects this transubstantiation of matter into soul. *Poiesis* thereby also enacts the transformation of the visible world into the invisible. It is made visible in its invisibility by art. *Poiesis* has this power to restore and present this invisibility *in* its visibility. Rilke again writes of this ongoing reciprocal relationship between the inner and outer worlds of the artist:

> It is our task to imprint this temporary, perishable earth into ourselves so deeply, so painfully and passionately, that its essence can rise again, "invisibly," inside us. We are the bees of the invisible. We wildly collect the honey of the visible, to store it in the great golden hive of the invisible.

(Rilke 1989, p. 316)

The space created and given by art, pro-duced thus out of soul and matter, is an original space. It is thereby akin to the space from which we originate, the space before we were born. It is a space which both predates and postdates the world.

Art creates and restores to us an altered and alternative space where we can also dwell *in the world*. Yet, art is created and exists explicitly in bold resistance to the world, that is, in opposition to the world as 'given,' as nature, or natural, unredeemed, inert, soul-less. Art provides us with the means to produce an actual transubstantiation of matter, an alchemical de-material-ization of so-called 'reality,' in order to produce a parallel reality, an altered, changed, and transfigured reality, a metamorphosed material reality redeemed by soul, and only therefore meaningful, restored, and glorified. It is this project that deserves to be called 'art'—perhaps even: 'sublime art'—since it is an art produced from the sublimation of matter. It is through this endeavor that the world is thereby relieved or taken out of its fallen state and re-collected to its original space and matter. Here again in the domain of Rilke, the Orphic poet laureate of the dual realm, we read the last line of his famous poem, "Archaic Torso of Apollo" (1908): "*Du musst dein Leben ändern*," "You must alter your life," "You must change your life," or literally, "You must make your life other-ed" (Rilke 1989, p. 60-1).

Blanchot tells us that the work is always a beginning, a commencement. It originates and initiates something new, and yet, it remains anterior to all beginnings. Quoting Hölderlin, he says: "Poetry always inaugurates *something else*" (Blanchot 2003, p. 238). Sublime art, like the great Greek temples of the ancient world, is "*the abode of the gods*' absence" (Blanchot 1982, p. 231). They are no longer there. They have fled. The work of *poiesis* stimulates this risky search for origins, otherness and presence.

> Through the work there takes place in time another time, and in the world of beings that exist and of things which subsist there comes, as presence, not another world, but the other of all worlds, that which is always other than the world.
>
> (ibid., p. 228)

This "gift of the original space of man" that "art" provides, Agamben finally refers to in this same quote with which we started this section, as: "*architectonics par excellence*" (Agamben 1999, p. 101). This is the original, primordial, or perennial construction of space: 'architectonics.' 'Architectonics' derives from the two Greek words, *arche* and *tektonikós. Arche* is what is first, the first principal, the originary model. It refers to what is primary or primal, the beginning form. Heidegger translates *arche* as, "at once beginning, point of departure, origin, rule" (Heidegger 1996, p. 100). *Arche* means, he says,

> that from which something proceeds, namely, such that that from which something proceeds is not left behind but determines and prevails in advance out beyond everything proceeding from it.
>
> (ibid.)

The concept of the 'archetype,' in Jungian terms, in the language of 'analytical psychology' created by Carl Jung, denotes the first form, or primordial 'imprint.' The word 'archetype' derives from *typos*, the mold or imprinted blows and patterns used in type-making, which in this case structure the human psyche in both the formal sense, the archetype *per se*, and in its contents, the archetypal images, patterns, behaviors, or symbols which appear phenomenally. The archetype is that psychological structure in us which allows and creates the possibility for us to have, to shape, and to organize our specifically human experiences.

For Jung, the archetype belongs to the 'objective psyche.' It is what he refers to as a 'psychoid factor.' The archetypes comprise and compose the dynamically moving and formative contents of the collective unconscious, whose boundaries remain unchartered, and therefore extend to the nethermost known and unknown points of both psyche *and* matter. *Arche* as 'origin,' 'original form,' 'first principle,' 'beginning genealogy,' and 'essence,' coming together with *typos,* 'type,' 'blow,' or 'imprint,' leads Jung to write, that an "archetype presupposes an imprinter ... We simply do not know the ultimate derivation of the archetype, any more than we know the origin of the psyche" (In Adler 1978, p. 49 and Jung 1953/1968, p. 14). Who or what does the 'imprinting' we call god, intelligence, genetics, design, evolution, or entelechy.

Tektonikós, from which we get the word, 'tectonic(s),' pertains to the art and science of building and construction, especially as in architecture.

Archi-tectonics thus refers to the science, basic principles and original designs for creating structure, shape and organization out of matter.

A second meaning of tectonics, however, refers "to the structure of the earth's crust and to the forces or conditions within the earth that cause movements of the crust such as earthquakes, folds, faults", and rock formations (Barnhart 1962, p. 1243). Finally, tectonics also designates the results of such movements, like tectonic valleys or mountains. As a noun, tectonics is "the science or art of assembling, shaping or ornamenting materials in construction" (ibid.). It refers to the constructive arts in general, and again, secondarily, to structural geology specifically.

Another word altogether, which makes its presence felt nevertheless, in the word *architectonics,* and needs to be included here to flesh out our exposition, is the Greek word *téchnē. Téchnē,* which gives us technic, technique, technical, and technological, refers to the art and skill involved in making, creating and crafting, especially in the arts and sciences, but also in any industrial, mechanical, professional, or trade sense. For the Greeks, the *téchnē* of art was to be found in the artistic, skillful, or even clever and crafty imitation, *mimesis,* of nature. That is, 'nature,' *physis* itself, the physical, material world, reveals the *téchnē* of operations, the how, why and wherefore of the making, doing and transforming of things. The artist, scientist, or craftsperson must therefore devote themselves to the careful observation and comprehension of nature, that is, to studying and understanding the inner and outer workings of the external natural world. We can recall that up until at least the twentieth century, art was considered to be essentially the skillful imitation and reproduction of nature, and thus the representation of the truthfulness within nature itself. An artist was carefully trained as an apprentice in a guild, or in an academy, shop or school, in closely examining and analyzing the works of nature, whether in anatomy, still life, landscape, optics, perspective, or draftsmanship, in order to be able to faithfully and objectively re-produce them. To make a copy of nature, as it were, that could fool the eye into believing it to be an objectively 'real' work of nature herself, was for many centuries and essentially up to the modern period, the guiding and determining vision of all artistic education and training.

Art, in this context, is then seen as an apprentice and handmaiden to nature herself. It exists in order to intuitively further nature's own innermost desires or goals *(teloi).* In this scheme too, the *teloi,* the 'goals,' 'targets,' 'ends,' or 'purposes' of nature, therefore need *us* for the seeking, fulfilling, or perfecting of *their* own desires, designs and destinies. This is again the project of both alchemy and analytical psychology, or psychoanalysis, as well as it is of all sublime artistic practice.

Amongst all these different etymological strands, what we nevertheless hear repeated over and over again, is that architectonics clearly designates a primordial construction and proffering of a space that we recognize as familiar and inherently belonging to us, as belonging to the human soul. Architectonics provides the fulfillment of an extremely long-held and deeply-felt dream, vision and promise. It both contains and reveals meanings of ultimate significance for our basic human condition.

Art in giving back to us our own true space, a quintessentially *psychic* space wherein we can breathe freely and dwell, also returns to us a renovated relationship with matter. That is, art renews our connection both with the actuality of the material, physical, sensuous world, as well as with what authentically 'matters.' In reconfiguring our priorities, art confronts us with what matters to us and to the world, as well as it candidly diagnoses 'what the matter is' with both us and the world. Art reflects back what matters within us and to us, specifically in our *connecting* with the world. With brutal honesty, it lays bare the nature of our own unique, individual relationship with the world. It may therefore, like dreams, often not be either especially attractive or appealing. This is thereby an art that is not made to *please*, but to unsettle and jar.

Architectonics returns to us our place and space in being-in-the-world, in our bodies, in our 'homes,' families, communities, countries, cultures, and on this earth's crust or surface. *Poiesis* reveals a way that human beings are destined to live on the earth, in this space that we have been given. Art shows us why and how we have been created to live in the world, in relationship to this 'nature' which has preceded us, and with and out of which we have developed as a unique animal species, *homo sapiens, homo faber*—this nature which, though rapidly changing and disappearing, will still long survive us. Architectonics points us towards an original soul geography, "the Earth as *Ur-Arche*", "a unity of time-space... 'which brings out the carnal *Ur-historie*'" (In Merleau-Ponty 1993, p. 362).

Tectonics as the primal topography of the world as given, also provides us with an image, sensibility and sense of the world, things, objects, landscape, as a phenomenal, *visible* reality. This is the skin, texture and flesh of the world, its body and bones as contained within the *visible*. This 'natural' or given world, hides within itself, however, the *invisible*. The painter Paul Cézanne says, that actually, "Nature is on the inside" (ibid., p. 47). "What is proper to the visible is...to be the surface of an inexhaustible depth: this is what makes it able to be open to visions other than our own" (Merleau-Ponty 1968, p. 143). Architectonics, *poiesis* and painting, seek to draw this invisibility out of its hiddenness in the world and to restitutionally present it as our original space—within the visible—"celebrating" it as the "enigma of visibility" (Silverman 1993, p. 267).

The visual world, that is, "what *is* simply and fully...as a texture..."

> is the concretion of a universal visibility, of one sole Space that sep-
> arates and reunites, that sustains every cohesion (and even that of
> past and future, since there would be no such cohesion if they were
> not essentially parts of the same space). Every visual something, as
> individual as it is, functions also as a dimension, because it is given
> as the result of a dehiscence of Being. What this ultimately means
> is that the hallmark of the visible is to have a lining of invisibility
> in the strict sense, which it makes present as a certain absence.
>
> (Merleau-Ponty 1993, p. 147)

The hallmarks of an art or *poiesis* that would offer 'architectonics,' and present this 'intercorporeality' of vision, would therefore appear to entail certain formal properties, qualities and elements that wrench us away from our usual habits, modes and conventions of perceiving and experiencing the world. This kind of art, in order to re-place and re-novate our typical modalities of thinking and relating, would of necessity, stimulate, provoke, confront, and interrogate us as viewers. Rather than providing answers or solutions, this disarticulative art instead asks questions, dis-solves structures and demands responses. It challenges, disorients and disturbs. It alienates us from our everyday selves and our usual ways of feeling and being.

An art that grabs us by the scruff of the neck and makes us want to look more deeply, become engaged, lose track of time, and grapple with the material and materiality of its productions is a sublime art. It is an art that takes us into its *own* expansive space and eradicates *our* normal boundaries of both space and time. It erases the conventional limits of thinking and experiencing. It takes us outside of ourselves. This art creates a "feeling of mutation within the relations of man and Being" (ibid., p. 347). It is outside of us. It is an art that envelops us in the mystery of its making, and furthermore provokes us to determine how it is made. We ask: 'where does this come from?,' 'what is this?,' or, 'how does this happen?'

It sets us on the interminable track of attempting to resolve questions which can sometimes hardly be formulated, and/or perhaps never be answered. These works precipitate an unending quest for the ineffable source(s) of, in a sense, joy. We are forced into a kind of blissful submission by them as we embark upon a journey of gratitude. We wish to bestow thanks upon the source of these gifts of artistic enthusiasm and inspiration. Unlike much reflective, contemplative, or beautiful art, these works prompt us into action, and make us want to *do* things ourselves, to make and create things, to further, enact, and perform these dimly apprehended artistic meanings before us. They are messages, signals and beckonings to another place, outside of our selves. They point toward, convey, and transport us to the *outside* in general. This is an art that does not have any unifying strategies, identifying traits, or typical characteristics. What is, in fact, at stake in the making of this art, is that it preserves its indeterminacy. Sublimity produces indeterminacy. Sublimity is committed to creating indeterminacy.

As we gaze into the vortex of jostling, swirling matter, which *is* both art and nature, we momentarily perceive the constant flux, instability, restlessness and agitation in the *materia*, in matter itself, as in the painted strokes, slashes, splashes, drips and spatters before us in Twombly's gestural markings. We become aware of the tireless movement of atoms and molecules in everything, *and* within our own bodies. Everything, as the pre-Socratic philosopher Heraclitus says, is in flux. It is all flowing, becoming. Everything in the material world is in motion, and exceeds our grasp. Sublime art performs this reality of matter itself, the reality of our materiality, our bodies, both the most determined and un-determined aspect of human being, since our bodies contain a finite end, our deaths, the abolition of our being, about which we know nothing.

It is thus an embodied gaze that comes into play in the experience of sublime art, revealing that the visual *is* the corporeal; that vision is of the body and not just of the eyes or mind, though the eyes and ears may be surely among the main portals of perception, the doors and windows of the soul. The painting is an extension and projection of the artist's flesh, and it then becomes part of the world's own contoured, folded, flexing and fleshy body as well. If it is truly alive, this work of art, then it too breathes. The rhythms of art affect both body and soul. We hear and feel what we see, and we see and feel what we hear. Both body and soul speak in their own respective languages, which though foreign to us, we *must* learn to hear, translate, interpret and understand.

This specific kind of art which delineates, fuses and ultimately transcends our different senses, attempts to work "without rules in order to formulate the rules of what *will have been done*" (Lyotard in Carroll 1987, p. 156). Painting, sculpture, cinema and poetry speak in this context in order to find out what they will have to say, and what will have been said. The "*post modern*," Lyotard refers to, as what "would have to be understood according to the paradox of the future" (ibid.). We arrive at our sublime destinations, wherever they are, only by not being there yet.

Poiesis is thus finally, not the creation or representation of 'some thing,' but rather an ongoing, impassioned experiment and vital interaction with matter and space, to see what *will have been* created. Moving ever more deeply into the present, the future slowly reveals and presents itself to us. *Poiesis* creates in order to invoke a presence, to birth the child of the future who is yet to come, to hasten the messianic radiance which is our destiny.

"The space of modern painting," Merleau-Ponty says, quoting the artist Jean Paulhan, is "space which the heart feels." It is, he continues:

> "space in which we too are located, space which is close to us"... and to which we are closely and organically connected by our sensory perception... "(O)ur relationship to space is... that of a being which dwells in space relating to its natural habitat."
>
> (In Jacobus 2012, pp. 32-3)

Poetry and painting are the materializations and realizations of the soul's space in time, the forms of psyche's true *topos*. Blanchot, paraphrasing Mallarmé, writes that poetry "endows our stay with authenticity. We stay authentically only where poetry takes place and gives place" (Blanchot 2003, p. 237). He says further:

> A temporal dimension different from the one of which the time of the world has made us masters is at play in language when

language lays bare, by the rhythmic scansion of being, the space of its unfolding.

(ibid., p. 239)

Heidegger, in his writings on Hölderlin, discusses this same space opened by poetry and tragic art as the realm of what he calls 'being' (or Being), *Dasein* itself, Being-in-itself, which the poet and the poem discloses, reveals, and brings into presence.

> The word of poetizing, in terms of what it poetizes and the way in which it poetizes, is determined from out of that which is itself to be poetized, because it "is" only as something poetized.
>
> (Heidegger 1996, pp. 123-4)

This is in a way the hidden secret of performative art in every single one of its countless events and manifestations taking place right now, throughout what we call 'time' and 'space,' in the world, and in the universe, with which we are wildly and swiftly spinning. *Poiesis,* the art of the sublime, exists in its being performed. And we cannot say *only* in its being performed, thus confining and limiting it to just those temporally and site-specific performances—while at the same time condemning ourselves to the necessity of recreating them—since it *is* always and everywhere being performed in infinite variations of breath and pulse, ebb and flow, rhythm and rest. *Poiesis* is this work which we enjoin and fling ourselves into, basically, in order to die, and perhaps, be reborn—and perhaps not. The faint and vanishing traces etched by this inexorable and relentless effort onto and into matter we call art, *poiesis,* the attempted articulation, testimony and witnessing of what it is to be for a while, for a brief time, in this human life.

III

ORPHEUS DESCENDING, FALLING

Eight years after Agamben's piece, "Beauty that falls," originally appeared as an introductory essay for a catalog of Twombly's sculptures shown in Rome in 1998 (In Twombly 1998, p. 5), and then again in *Writings on Cy Twombly* (2002), he published a slightly longer introductory essay in a catalog for another exhibition of Twombly's sculptures which was held in Munich in 2006. This essay, entitled "Falling beauty," is about twice as long as the first piece with which we began, and though covering and especially concluding with much of the exact same content and textual ground, as its extremely similar title would suggest, it begins with a long prelude of new material concerning the poetry of Rainer Maria Rilke in connection with Twombly's art. He focuses in particular on an "Untitled" sculpture located and dated "Gaeta 1984," on which Twombly has directly written the last stanza from Rilke's tenth and final "Duino elegy" in an English translation: "And we, who have always thought /of happiness climbing, / would feel the emotion that almost startles / when happiness falls" (Rilke 1939, p. 85; Agamben 2006, p. 13).

Agamben, in pursuing his theme of the movement of falling beauty, as he did in the earlier essay, makes the unique connection here between the metrically ruptured, broken and shattered lines of this last stanza of Rilke's, which Twombly literally copied onto the scrolled base of his sculpture, and the inverted ascension and suspended moment of falling which takes place in the actual form and materials of the "Untitled" sculpture itself. Twombly's piece actually looks as if it is broken in the middle, with the top half toppled down at an acute angle and pointing to the Rilke inscription, which is written on a piece of loose notecard resting on the sculpture's base (Twombly 2000, p. 89).

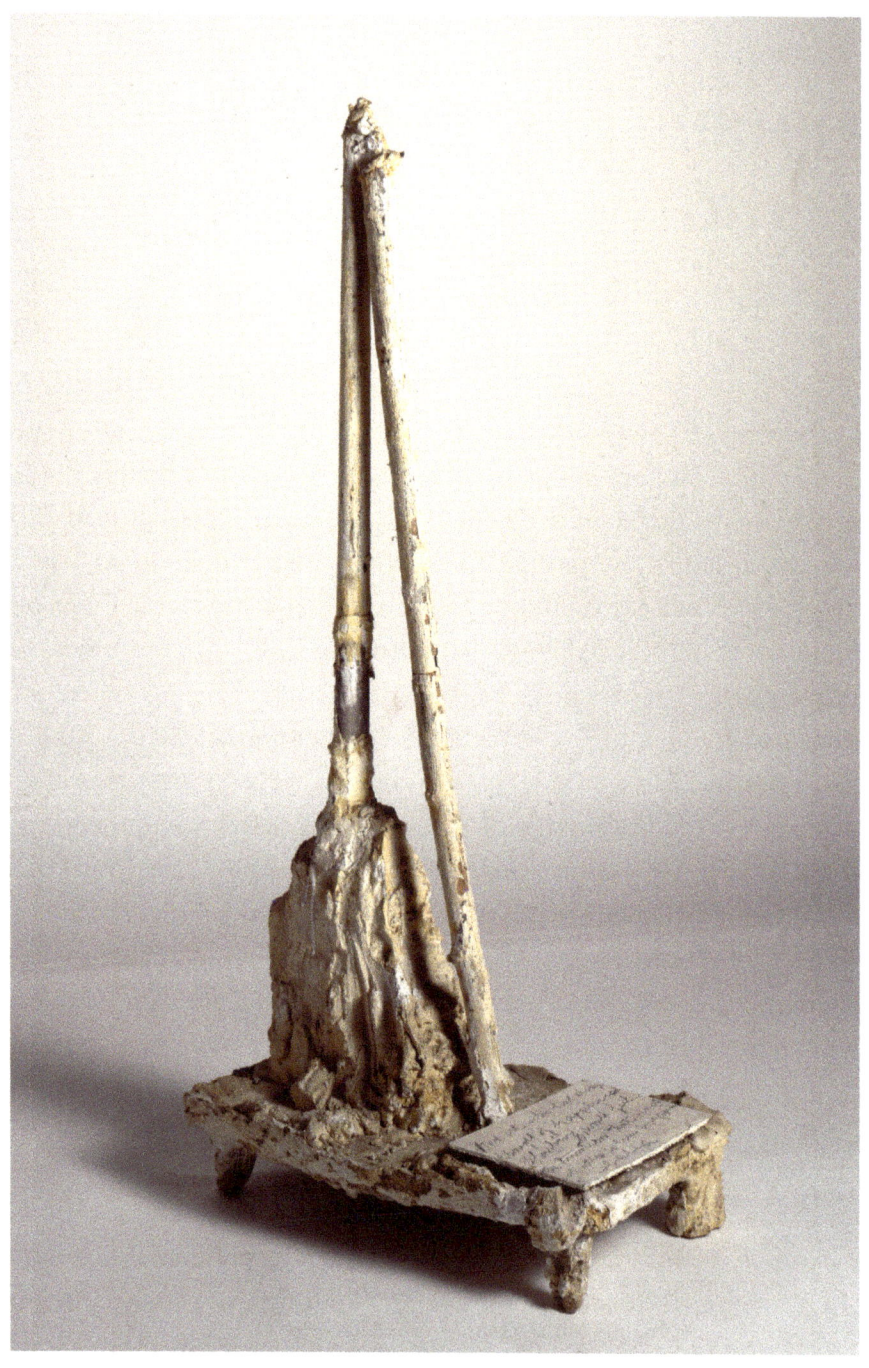

1.   Cy Twombly, *Untitled*, Gaeta, 1984.

And then, toward the end of this essay, Agamben once again introduces Hölderlin's notion of the 'caesura,' the 'anti-rhythmic suspension' and 'pure word,' which forcefully disrupts the 'alternating of representations' and the 'successive movement of the subject and the sense,' all in order to blindingly reveal the sublime nature of representation itself. This is the central point and nexus for us. This is for us now the main event: that our entire way of thinking, perceiving and experiencing, our very identity and innermost subjectivity, as well as the orderly flow of the tragic drama, aesthetic performance, perceived object, or phenomenal presentation before us, no matter what it is, a production of *Oedipus Rex,* a tree, a sunset, a sculpture or a painting, in short, our grasp of the world as it is, is completely smashed and destroyed by this 'caesura.' Here, there occurs a complete break. It is only this obliterative and annihilating action which opens us up into a totally 'other' reality, one that is uncontrolled, uncontainable, and abyssal.

Agamben further claims that Twombly, in "this visionary sculpture... has succeeded in giving form to a caesura, in displaying its sculptural equivalent" (Agamben 2006, p. 15). The artwork itself that appears in "the shattering and breaking of the upward movement" is not, he says, "simply a representation of the caesura, but is the caesura itself, in its movement" (ibid.). In other words, this particular piece of sculpture, and Agamben would undoubtedly say, most if not all of Twombly's sculptures, each in their own way and with their specifically original plastic means, forms and vocabulary, actually perform and present in themselves the unrepresentable subject matter of art, the sublime, the inward nature of the frenzied representational process itself, though obviously perhaps not with all of the works in equal degrees of strength. This particular sculpture, in being literally broken, smashed and purposefully ruptured, clearly presents an ascension which is suddenly snapped, fractured, inverted and purposefully reversed. The artistic gesture in which a dramatic ascension is reversed and suspended, and/or enters into a fall, finds literal expression in many of these sculptural works of Twombly's, and as we shall attempt to elaborate, becomes manifest symbolically as well, in his paintings, drawings, collages, photographs and graphic print works—particularly in regard to certain mythological motifs which themselves contain images of reversal, brokenness, abjection, and descent. And furthermore, we hope to illustrate that it is these very same networks of distinguishing features and underlying mythologems and patterns, especially of ascending and descending, and rising and falling, which have thematically guided his work and imagery over his lengthy artistic career. It is specifically as we shall see, through his lifelong explorations of the sustained mythemes of Orpheus and Dionysos/Bacchus, that Twombly has uniquely and consistently evolved an artistic style of 'de-creating,' 'un-doing,' 'dis-solving', and 'de-mythologizing,' in order to birth the presence of the gods, to name them into being, albeit most frequently in their absence, tentativeness, occlusion, and exile.

Looking for a time at any of Twombly's paintings, it could easily also be contrarily hypothesized and argued, that he actually hides, secretes, effaces, erases, camouflages, conceals, and disguises, at least as much content of the gods, of their substance and experiential and aesthetic history in his works, as he leaves revealed. These two conjectures are in fact both true. His is a project of appearances *and* disappearances, traces and suggestions, hints and allusions. The gods, when they show themselves, appear in the gaps, ruptures, smears, and smudges. Though their names are sometimes scrawled as titles on the works, more often they poke through only obliquely, in cast-off blobs of paint and deposits of plaster, forlorn, and rejected. His is a project of private revelations, discrete epiphanies, and a tactful honoring of intimate hierophanies.

As we have previously argued that the caesura is conveyed in the words of Hölderlin's poetry and prose, and as Hölderlin proposes that it is communicated, perhaps even originarily, in the decisive moments of Sophoclean tragedy, and as we are now initiating, that the caesura, the tragic break, is an ever-present leitmotif in Twombly's major artistic productions, so too do these sublime depths hovering on the edge of being and not-being, and life and death, present themselves, incredibly, time and time again, in one of the singularly great accomplishments of twentieth century art, in Rilke's own relatively slim, though poetically full-to-bursting volume, the *Sonnets to Orpheus*. Rilke completed writing this amazing collection of 55 sonnets, from start to finish, with almost no changes in their final form whatsoever, within the space of three weeks. Part One of the book, which comprises the first 26 of the sonnets, he wrote in what he himself calls, "a single breathless act of obedience, between the 2nd and 5th of February 1922, without one word being doubtful or having to be changed" (Rilke 1942, p. 7). He furthermore wrote them out and had them all published in the precise order in which they appeared to him during those miraculous days. Those "few days," as he declares, were "a nameless storm, a hurricane in the spirit...everything that was fiber and fabric in me cracked" (Rilke 1984, p. 337). In a subsequent letter, he said further that,

> Even to me, in the way they arose and imposed themselves on me, the Sonnets to Orpheus are perhaps the most mysterious, most enigmatic dictation I have ever endured and achieved.
>
> (ibid., p. 336)

During this same astounding burst of enthusiasm in which he wrote 26 sonnets in four days, Rilke also completed the second part of the Orpheus poems, 29 additional sonnets, within the following two weeks, by the 20th of the same month. Simultaneously, he brought to fruition his other most famously celebrated and majestic work, the *Duino Elegies*, which he had begun in the winter of 1910-11, and had not even really looked at in their only half-completed state in more than seven years, since 1915, finishing them in a week, by the eleventh of that same month, February, 1922. "Betweenwhiles," his translator drily records, "sundry late and fragmentary poems had also come into being" (In Rilke 1942, p. 7). In fact, many of the most incredibly depthful of the 500 uncollected poems Rilke wrote over the course of his relatively short life, are also among these "late and fragmentary poems" (ibid.) from these same three or four wintry alpine weeks of transport. This is surely a pinnacle of any artist's production, in any medium, from any period of history—this one month's laboring in dedication and devotion to a single, very particular, overriding image which called out to him from every cell of his body and resulted in such a monumental legacy of work.

What appears most decidedly in this unprecedented maelstrom of inspired creativity, however, is that Rilke, throughout this extraordinary time, uses the mythical figure of Orpheus himself, lyrical singer of the known and the unknown realms, of the visible and the invisible, as his psychopomp, muse, and mediator, as the image of the artist who 'goes down,' and as the emblem for his own astonishing collection of sonnets. It is with the postcard reproduction of Cima da Conegliano's Renaissance drawing of "Orpheus" on the wall next to his writing desk in the small Château de Muzot, that Rilke transcribes the *Sonnets* "which stormily imposed themselves" upon him (ibid., p. 132). For it is, after all, Orpheus, and Orpheus alone in Greek mythology, who descends to the underworld unaccompanied and by himself, and therefore comes to embody the fractured fate and dismembered destiny of a mortal being, like all of us, who, risking everything, exists in this disjointed gap between life and death, daring to descend. Orpheus *is* that timeless human/god imago, who out of the excruciatingly torn and separating tension of body and soul, nevertheless wrenches from that abyss in himself songs of praise: to his beloved Eurydice; to the natural world resplendent in its transient glory; and to the immortal Olympians who dwell on high.

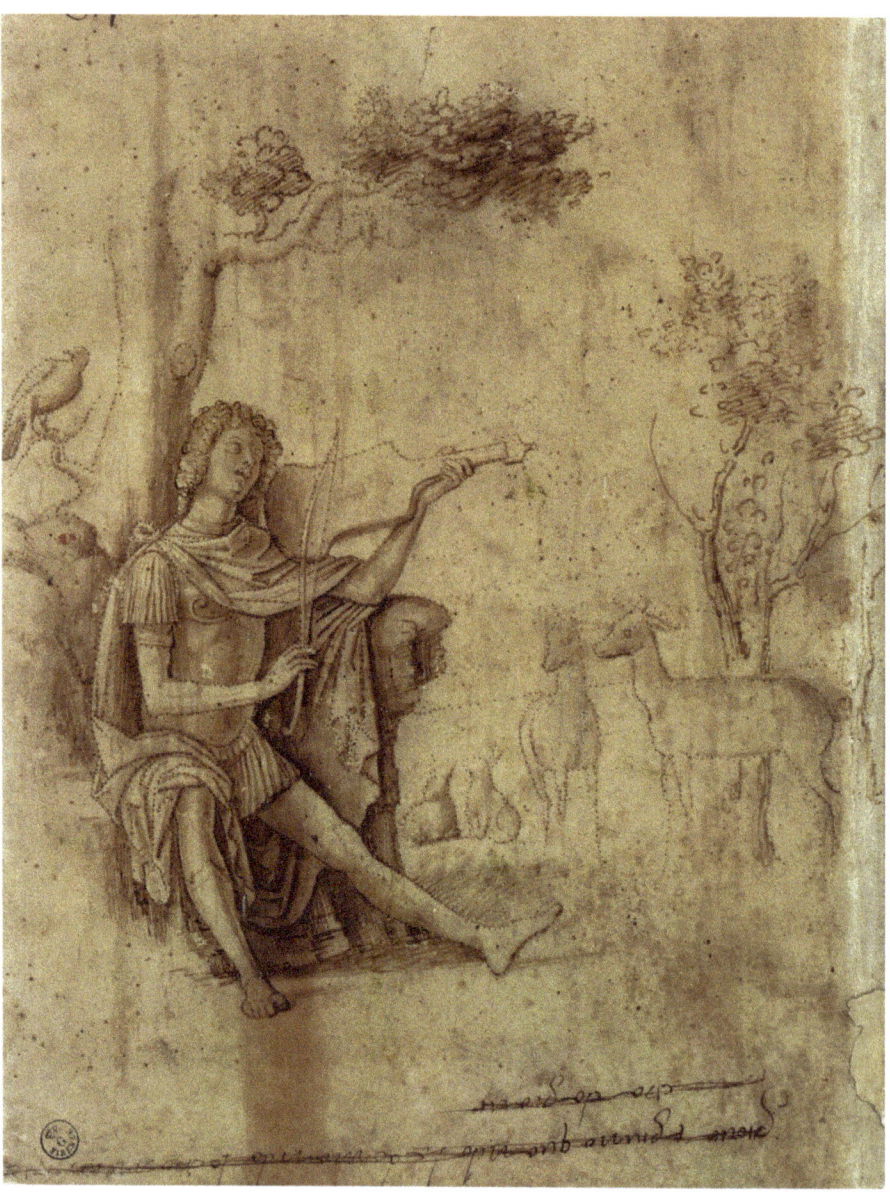

2.   Cima da Conegliano, *Orpheus Playing for the Animals*, c. 1505-10.

Blanchot, writing in 1955 as if describing Orpheus or any one of his significant acolytes, any one of those artists for example whom we are considering: Sophocles, Hölderlin, Rilke, and Twombly, says, that the poet must keep

> the two spheres distinct, by living the separation purely, by being the pure life of the separation itself. For this empty and pure place which distinguishes between the spheres is *the sacred,* the intimacy of the breach which is the sacred.
>
> (Blanchot 1982, p. 274)

It is thus as he suggests, that only by holding, occupying and maintaining that excruciatingly bounded liminal space that the voice of the poet may in fact even aspire and hope to poetize at all. For it *is* only in the words, speech and language of poetry and prose, and *in* the materials, shapes, forms, movements, sounds, gestures and colors of artworks, that the unrepresentable becomes, through *poiesis,* presentable and presented. Heidegger says that, "Hölderlin poetizes purely from out of that which, in itself, essentially prevails as that which is to be poetized" (Heidegger 1996, p. 165). Also reflecting on this same crucial point, Philippe Lacoue-Labarthe writes that Hölderlin's poetry is "thought as poem":

> The question is not to know if thought can give rise to poetry. The real question is if thought, if it really thinks (in truth), is not un-avoidably poetic.
>
> (In Lernout 1994, p. 106)

Poiesis solicits from out of the realm of non-being that which has not yet ever until then, come into existence before, and, summons it in the only form in which it *can* appear, that is, as the unthought which remains to be thought, as poetry, as a verbal or pictorial language crying out to be voiced, expressed, and heard.

This journey, this epic, terrifying downwards track, this *katabasis* to Hades, the poet's path towards that which is to be poetized, indefatigably retraces, each time, the steps of Orpheus' immortal descent to the under-world. *Orphne* in Greek already means the "darkness," the depths towards which Orpheus is ineluctably drawn (Kerenyi 1959, p. 281). As the lyre player once upon a time boldly ventured down to those gloomy halls, went once and for all time to that place of depth and death, to stand helplessly before the lord and mistress of the shades, trying solely with the naked power of his song to win back his belovéd wife, bitten by a poisonous snake on their wedding day, Orpheus, against all odds, actually succeeds. He triumphs over death. He completes and does what essentially cannot be done. And he *undoes* what has never before been undone—the pall of death itself. He charms all of death's dark denizens with his song. They grant him

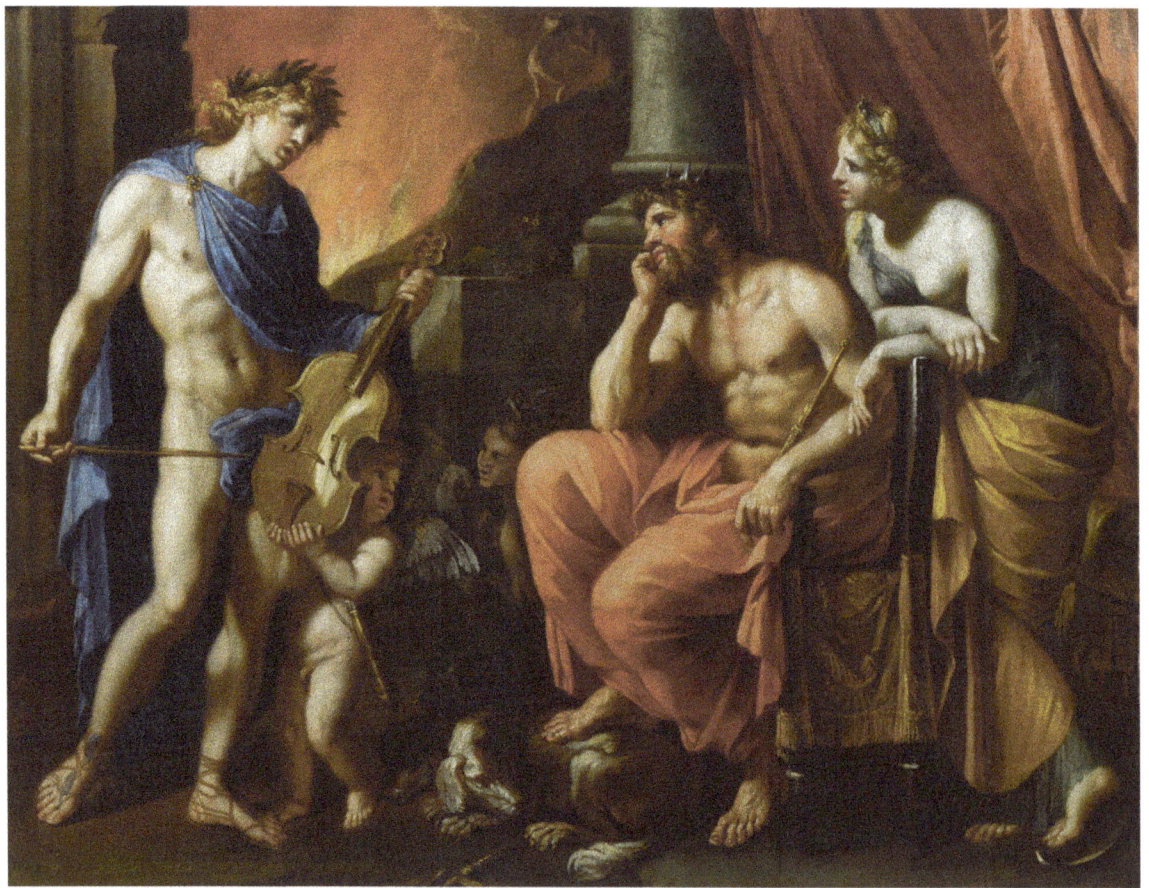

3.   François Perrier, *Orpheus in the Underworld Playing Before Pluto and Persephone*, c. 1647-50.

his paramount wish, his overwhelming desire. Eurydice is actually restored to him, given back, on the one condition and with the singular injunction, however, that he not under any circumstances, look behind and gaze upon her, that is, at least not until they have again both gained the upper daylight world of mortal beings. Then, when Orpheus, in the end, only a man after all, and, one maddened by his passion, turns around to look at his belovéd, perhaps to see if she really is following him along the winding track—he is mistrustful, insecure, frantic, uncertain, angry—he loses her completely. He looks upon her for this last time now—as he must, as he has been fated to do from the beginning of time. And she dies away from him—again—for this second time—and now truly forever. She is no longer there. She is evaporated, gone, a receding wraith. She fades away like a mist. As he re-verses his gaze, she has already re-versed her path and deeper direction away from him, veering away from life and love and back towards death and non-being.

Destined throughout all eternity to look back, he fatally trespasses death's dire laws of binding necessity. Determined to gaze upon Eurydice one more time, to grasp her with his seeing, his eyes, his looking, to once again possess his belovéd, she vanishes from him, along with all other women, all hope or possibility of union, and perhaps even along with love itself, all now gone, forever. Wishing to surpass the gods, he loses all that he has had and known, his everything.

So now it is still left for us to ask, what Eurydice is this? Who is she? What love? What knowledge? What beauty? What desire? What most intimate secret tempts him to risk losing everything, his all, the work of a lifetime, even the allotted time of his life itself?

Is it that Eurydice is the most belovéd of all women for whom he *must* build his monument of ultimately sorrowful songs? Is he more in love with an idea of her, her *eidos,* an image or form of her, than with the woman Eurydice herself? Is she the mystery of life itself, the innermost jewel of life and death, the center of the lotus? Is she the riddle of existence and art revealed, incarnate in feminine form? Or is she even more impossible to imagine than all these pitiful parables or allegories could ever suggest? Is she beyond-ness or other-ness itself?

These are the questions that haunt all of the Orphic poets. These are the still-vibrating questions taken up by tragedy, romance, the whole operatic tradition initially birthed by Orpheus and Eurydice, all grand artistic spectacle and *Gesamtkunstwerk,* as well as all the initiatory rituals of every one of the religious mystery traditions since time immemorial.

Their love became the subject matter for all of the earliest and boldest experiments in putting together drama, dance, music, recitation, and text in performances which begin trying to comprehend the enigmatic and riddling nature of their relationship, to each other and to the gods, to the archetypal, immortal powers that be. Their tragic story became a new modality of attempting to artistically express the inexpressible. The very first three operas ever written as a new form of expression, are all entitled "Orfeo," or "Euridice," one by Jacopo Peri in 1600, another by Giulio Caccini also in 1600, and the famously still-popular version by Claudio Monteverdi in 1607. In attempting to re-create early Greek drama, the ideal for these Florentines became what opera still remains to this day: a desire to "represent the meaning of the text—what Peri in his foreward to *Euridice* describes as 'following the passions'" (McGee 1982, p. 179). Their tragic theme and complicated love story continued to have a further tremendous efflorescence in the French court also during the Baroque era, with operas and cantatas composed by Charpentier, Clérambault, Courbois, and Rameau. The much later opera by Gluck in the eighteenth century on the same theme (1762), where Orpheus became the Incarnation of Music, is referred to by nearly everyone discussing the mythologem of Orpheus whether mythologically, musically, or literarily. Since then, there have continuously been musical variations on the theme of these two star-crossed lovers created by Haydn, Liszt, Offenbach, Stravinsky, Milhaud, Foss, Henze, Birtwistle, and Glass, just to name a very few.

Throughout the centuries, the poets, priests and prophets, and now we ourselves, continue to seek this renewing source and origin of song. For always and everywhere, as Rilke writes, it *is* Orpheus singing when there is song. There is tuneful sound and remembered rhythms only when and where there is sublime poetry.

> Set up no stone to his memory.
> Just let the rose bloom each year for his sake.
> For it is Orpheus. His metamorphosis
> in this one and in this. We should not trouble
>
> about other names. Once and for all
> it's Orpheus when there's singing. He comes and goes.
> Is it not much already if at times
> he overstays for a few days the bowl of roses?

O how he has to vanish, for you to grasp it!
Though he himself take fright at vanishing.
Even while his word transcends the being-here,

He's there already where you do not follow.
The lyre's lattice does not snare his hands.
And he obeys while yet he oversteps.

(Rilke 1942, p. 25)

We can see, read and hear throughout the vast body of Cy Twombly's artistic *oeuvre* of the past sixty years, how he, perhaps more than any other artist besides Rilke himself, in any medium, has consistently, and even explicitly, returned to pick up the Orphic thread and melody, dangling and unfinished though still sounding, weaving and whispering its lines and tones into the very fabric and textures of his own artworks, ranging from huge, wall-sized canvases, to small, discursive, script-like drawings on single sheets of paper. In his constant and single-minded poetic striving to arrive at the revivifying origins of art, the name 'Orpheus' itself, and his songs, stories, memories, adventures, passions, poetry, and myths, his actual image and fate too, trembles and resonates in the strokes, smears, swirls, smudges and spatters that Twombly has so vibrantly strewn across the surfaces of his art. Sowing and scattering the Orphic seed syllables and wispy melodic strains into his vast corpus of materials, they continue to germinate there in the streaks and folds and shoot forth new sprouts and blossomings of the lyre player's legacy. Twombly's works appear as if created 'under the spell of Orpheus' (Bernstock 1991), possessed by that magical name whose soulful resonances have accumulated over millennia. At times, seemingly attempting to exorcize himself of this poet's ghost, he scrawls the name 'Orpheus' large and repeatedly across paintings, sculptures and drawings, but instead, in that very effort, he ends up bewitching probably himself as well as us, his viewers. He cannot, however, rid himself of the deeply etched tracings of that precarious name, hidden as they are, in his own soul. And so, it keeps recurring, as a leitmotif, maintaining a deep steady pulse and rhythmic throbbing in his work which arches over the last half of the twentieth century and continues up into his most recent exhibitions regularly occurring now around the world well into the twenty-first century.

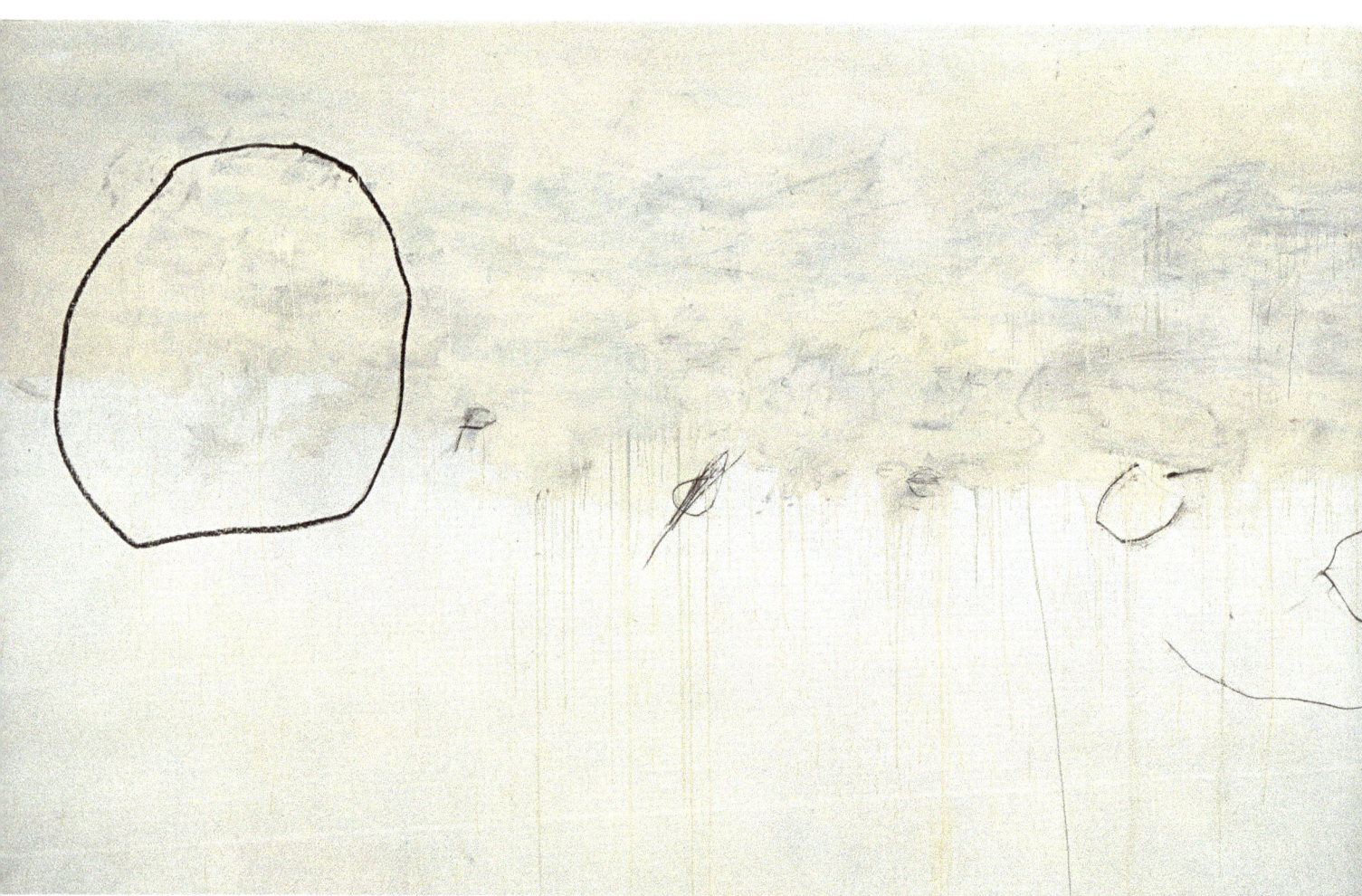

4. CY TWOMBLY

Orpheus, 1979

Oil based house paint, [paint stick], wax crayon on canvas

77 x 131 3/4 inches

195.6 x 334.6 cm

© Cy Twombly Foundation

We could possibly view Twombly's entire artistic output as the unful-filled desire to pronounce that name *out* of himself, sometimes murmured or just thought out loud, sometimes shouted; to exteriorize it and make positively manifest the restless and wandering spirit, the *Geist,* of Orpheus; to express and utter that name so completely, in paint and color, in line and letter, in form, feeling and thought—to portray him with such vigorous arm and hand movements so thoroughly, that the debt to the sorrowful soul singer would finally, this time, be repaid. This is how Twombly appears to approach each and every work, from sketched draft to completed canvas, as if it were the last, and the first piece, beginning again, every time perhaps 'the one,' to now portray and definitively capture the fleeting form and essential nature of the renowned lover, lyre player, prophet, and poet, Orpheus.

'Famous Orpheus,' as he was called in the first ever written convo-cation of him by the mid-sixth-century B.C. poet, Ibycus (Robbins 1982, p. 5), hovers in the washes and shadowings of Twombly's pale gray and whitish backgrounds, the melancholy twilights of distant Mediterranean lands and shores. Twombly's fascination with the figure of Orpheus, from the tragic and somber musician and journeyer to Hades of the ancient Graeco-Roman world, to the priest and preacher of the early Christian era, through to the Renaissance viol or lute player at home in nature and joyfully singing surrounded by animals and trees, to the English romantic poets' lyrical obsessions with classical ruins and the Greek and Italian light, to the evanescent psychopomp who finally inhabits Rilke's poetry and prose in the high Alps of southern Switzerland—this whole montage of tradition becomes powerfully depicted in his numerous articulations of that legendary lover's ecstasy and anguish, his exultations and his ulti-mate agonies.

The artist first began to unravel the skein of Orpheus' far-flung mythologem in a concerted way in the 1960s, in a series of drawings and paintings, at times variously dedicated to either the poet Rilke or to Orpheus himself. Well into the 1970s, Twombly continued to mine the rich veins of original classical and mythological material, as well as and particularly, Rilke's *Sonnets to Orpheus*, as sources, employing phrases, lines, or transfer-ring and writing out whole stanzas and passages from Rilke's poetry onto the surfaces of his artwork; sometimes creating pieces simultaneously on paper, canvas, linen, wood, found materials, and plaster, Orpheus spilling over from medium to medium, a continuing line of musical meaning stretching out, sounding and unfolding over time. In two series of drawings, from 1975 and 1979 respectively, most of which were done in Italy, in Gaeta, Sperlonga, Naples, Capri, Rome, and Bassano, literally dozens of sheets of paper are covered with

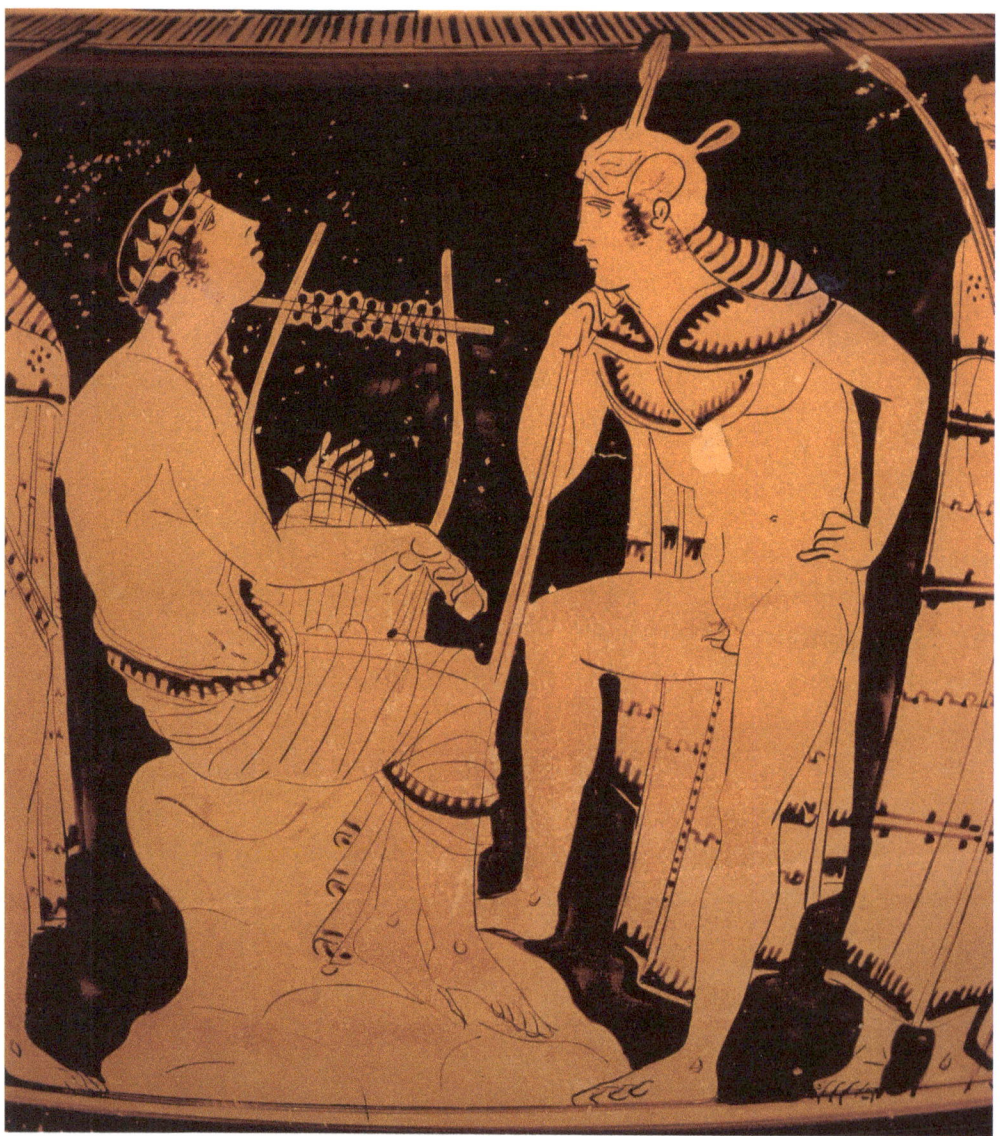

5.   *Orpheus Singing to the Thracians*, detail, c. 450 B.C., Orpheus Painter.

scrawling, calligraphic, awkward variations on the name 'Orpheus' itself. With the 'O' overly large and accentuated, he traced the letters of the rest of the name, trailing and tailing away across and down the sheets of paper. Sometimes he spells the name out in Greek letters, and just as often he writes it in Italian, German, or English. Sometimes he even draws out the name on the backside of another artwork. It is all the same when Orpheus sounds and his name *is* being sung and recited out loud. He is invoked.

Despite the different languages in which the name is rendered, and for this artist the process of creation is all about words, sounds and languages, as well as about the nature of all language itself, the large omnipresent 'O' of Orpheus' name in Twombly's representations mirrors and mimics the many instances where the poet Rilke has used the letter 'O' to start a crucial line in the sonnets, either praising and rapturous, or woeful and doleful; as in the earliest operas, Orfeo and Euridice exclaim "O-hime," "Alas," the grievous cry of sorrow welling up and out into the air. In the first two lines of the volume's very first sonnet (I: 1), we find: "O pure transcendency! /O Orpheus singing! O tall tree in the ear!" In the second, sonnet I:2: "O will you yet invent ..." In sonnet I:4: "O you tender ones .../O you who are blessed, O you who are whole." Sonnet I:5 poignantly exclaims: "O how he has to vanish for you to grasp it!" In I:7, we read the beautiful: "O ephemeral press/ of a wine that for men is unending." In sonnet I:9, three out of the four stanzas begin with the word "Only," again an 'O' in the English translation. In I:12 we hear: "O music ..." In I:13, the final line begins with: "O experience ..." In I:17, we find the line: "One! o climb ... o climb ..." I:23 begins with: "O not till the time..." And in one of the most powerful of all the sonnets, to end Part One, I:26, lamenting the death and absence of Orpheus, he writes: "O you lost god!" The spoken 'O' is a fervent expiration of breath, a monosyllabic exhalation of soul from deep within, a mournful wail, a total submission to and encompassing embrace of the 'outside,' a longing for and love of the desirous god and his Eurydice *in the world.* It is an aerial, pneumatic performance of the body's ecstasy and anguish, its passions and losses.

The 'O' reverberates throughout these poems as itself a sung invocation and prayer call to the guiding presence *and* disappearances of Orpheus. In the protohistorical period of ancient Greece, Orpheus was regarded not only as a coeval of Heracles and Peleus, born in the generation before the Trojan War, but as a forefather and ancestor of both Hesiod and Homer. That is, he was seen to predate the very founders and symbols of official Greek religion, theology, poetry, and culture themselves. He is an even more venerable teacher from *before* the famous stories of Troy, when the gods and heroes still made their usual rounds. Besides being imaged as a very ancient heroic poet and originator of Greek spiritual belief, he also came to be viewed as a fabled guide from well beyond the strictly Greek classical world who could transport expired souls to a life outside of death and mortality. This in itself is a very non-Greek idea, and was seen to be imported into the Hellenic mainland culture from Orpheus' native Thracian, 'northern,' barbarian birthplace (contemporary Bulgaria), where these more mystical, archaic, older, chthonic, and subterranean cult practices held sway, since in traditional Greek religious practice, all deceased souls were consigned for eternity to Hades. Period. No exceptions. There was no notion of salvation, redemption or afterlife in the ancient Greece of Homer's time. Orpheus startlingly reemerged in Greek religion and culture with the exciting and brand-new possibilities for direct, more immediate and ecstatic spiritual experiences, and he additionally brought with him an entire eschatology, belief system and rituals, which included with them, the promises of a life after death for the initiates (Astrachan 1992).

In one of Orpheus' earliest portrayals on a fragment of ancient pottery, he is seen in the bow of the boat 'Argo' singing and playing the lyre, shamanically leading Jason and the other Argonauts to the legendary land of Colchis and to the golden fleece they are seeking. Fish rise up out of the sea to hear his voice, and birds fly over his head to listen to his song. "His actual office was that of *Keleustes*, singer of the chanties which gave the rowers their time" (Guthrie 1952/1993, p. 28). As Orpheus leads these warriors, seekers and searchers to the 'other' worlds, so too does he lead the artists and poets to their 'other' world, the underworld of dreams and visions. Like Hermes, Orpheus is a psychopomp, a 'guide of souls,' leading the creative individual and mystagogue into the beyond and into regions of depth.

Orpheus guides the Argonauts with his voice, calling out with his supplicating song from the front of the vessel, singing out to the furthest reaches of space and time spreading endlessly and expansively before these seafaring adventurers. His chanting and lyre playing helps carve their way through the waves into the unknown. As the crew of rowing oarsmen stroke, pull, and stretch behind him, Orpheus' tuneful voice sounds out in counterpoint to their unified bending, bowing, and flexing rhythmical movements.

The song of Orpheus is, in fact, once again, the caesura itself, floating in the air, the *counter-rhythmical* interruption punctuating the regular rhythmical sweep of the oars.

In his 1912 essay, "Concerning the poet," written in Duino, Italy shortly after his own formative trip to Egypt, Rilke tells us that the "position," and nothing less than the "meaning of the poet was revealed to him on board the large sailing vessel with its sixteen oarsmen which conveyed him up the Nile to the island of Philae" (Jacobus 2008, p. 2). The rhythmic call and response between the Orphic lead singer in the prow and the chorus of oarsmen behind him provided Rilke with an allegory of the "position of the poet, his place and effect within time" (Rilke 1954, p. 66). This man sitting in the front of the boat, Rilke says, seemed to be influenced only by "the pure movement of his feeling when it met the open distance, in which he was absorbed in a manner half melancholy, half resolute" (ibid.). Those moments when he sang, coming as an "unpredictable intervention":

> felt by all of us in a most peculiar manner, not only helped (the rowers) rhythmically, but quite perceptibly transformed the powers within them, as it were, so that, being eased, they brought fresh, still untouched sources of strength into play.
>
> (ibid., p. 65)

The song of the Orphic guide-as-mediator and shaman in the prow, leading the way into the unknown, came suddenly, at quite irregular intervals, and yet, Rilke continues, "even then it was the right thing...appropriate" (ibid.).

> In him the forward thrust of our vessel, and the force opposed to us were continually held in counterpoise—from time to time a surplus accumulated: then he sang. The boat overcame the opposition; but what could not be overcome (was not susceptible of being overcome) he, the magician, transmuted into a series of long floating sounds, detached in space, which each appropriated to himself. Whilst those about him were always occupied with the most immediate actuality and the overcoming of it, his voice maintained contact with the farthest distance, linking us with it until we felt the power of its attraction.
>
> (ibid., p. 66)

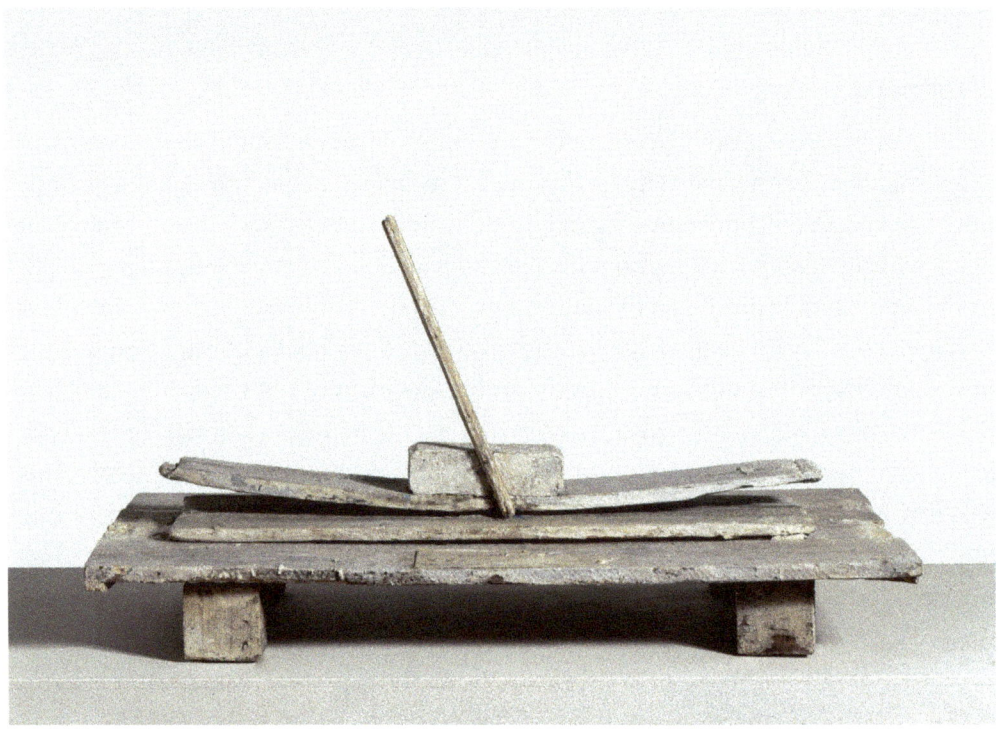

6.   Cy Twombly, *Winter's Passage: Luxor*, Porto Ercole, 1985.

Rilke's own voice, singular, 'detached' and 'floating,' its counter-rhythms set against the deep silence and surround of eternal unending time in this underworldly land of the dead by the Nile, undoubtedly came back to haunt Twombly as well, when he himself visited for the second time and then spent the winter of 1984-5 in Egypt, staying in the Old Winter Palace in Luxor. Among the immense monuments and sepulchral tombs of long-gone Pharaohs, built in stone amidst shifting desert sands, and nourished by the rhythm and diurnal flow of ships and goods plying their leisurely courses up and down the life-giving waters of the Nile, both artists seemed to be able to find, or re-find, their own singular place and space as poets, orienting their souls to the infinite points on the horizon, their selves now *embodying* the caesura, embracing this rupture as their unique destiny within this vast backdrop of deep and timeless history. Both artists lifted their floating voices and raised them up in counterpoint against the limitlessly arching vault of a sun-whitened sky spreading soundlessly and atemporally over the desert temples, tombs, statues, and great pyramids.

The 'O's roll on and on in Rilke's sonnets as Twombly's own looping 'O's also fill canvas after canvas during certain periods of his long artistic career. For decades, the painter adds line upon line of curling, circling, repeated 'O's, especially in the so-called 'gray' ground or 'blackboard paintings,' creating more than a hundred of them between 1967 and 1971. Frequently noted critically, most of these paintings are highly reminiscent of the Palmer method of handwriting development exercises used extensively in the 1940s and '50s in school systems throughout the United States. The curlicues, slantings and circles continue tilting endlessly, row after row, re-versing direction after each line, starting all over again, lasso lines of writing, an obscure poetic verse nevertheless imbued with a continuous, flowing, rhythmical poise and pulse. In this connection R.B. Onians tells us that "for the earliest Greeks, time and fate were circles. The process of time was the movement of the circle around the earth" (Onians 1987, p. 251). The thousands of Twombly's O-shapes echo signifiers for zero, null and nullity, infinity, emptiness, nothingness, and wholeness, as well as the sheer repetition and endlessly repeating movements and tasks of those sojourning in the underworld, like Sisyphus, Ixion, Tantalus and others. This was, it would seem, a period for Twombly of a deep underground incubation, a slow, subtle mining within the earth, a careful, compulsively repetitive looking for an exit or spark during a time of otherwise apparent stasis and near blockage. The 'blackboard paintings,' in their uniform grays, whites and blacks, appear in the context of Twombly's whole *oeuvre* as an underworld journey, a waiting in limbo, or even a diabolical punishment from the gods, consigning the artist to a kind of monotony and boredom in order to strengthen and test his endurance and resolve in his vocation as a mark-maker. They are the winter times, the darkening and *nigredo* of his own four seasons, and his Demeter-like wandering and mourning for the lost feminine, love, excitement and exuberance of his youth. It was as if he needed to begin again, not this time, however, with the more primitive marks of his actual artistic beginnings, as in the very early pictographs, or in the all-over paintings of the mid-late '50s, but instead spiralling onward with the elementals of handwriting, cursive script, learning in a new way, how to write once again, by hand—and by heart. What was once in his work a build-up of singular discrete lines, marks and impulsive gestures and forms scrawled all over on paper or canvas, now become with the gray or black background pieces, continuously repeating lines of movement, rhythmically crossing the surface like waves across the sea, like the real lines of a text, a true hand-writing, a visual and visible chant, both poetic and musical, scrawled and scribbled over vast backgrounds of receding space, though curiously emptied of emotion; a writing over and against the deep and empty background of an echoing inner space.

Nine of Rilke's Orpheus sonnets begin with the single word 'O,' and there are 44 uses of the declaiming, longing 'O' in the 55 sonnets. Besides the explicit rolling, tumbling, looping 'O's of Twombly's blackboard paintings, variations of which still strongly continued vibrantly renewed with color until he could no longer paint, until just shortly before his death, Twombly performs the shape of the 'O' endlessly throughout much of his other, both earlier and later, work: the 'O' of wheels, chariot wheels with spokes, in flames, rolling through Homeric epics, wheeled sculptures and drawings of carts, solar barges and wagons; as testicles accompanying an heroic phallus or a warrior's thrusting motions; globular breasts; numerous sun symbols; Hindu or Buddhist prayer wheels; in numbering systems, calculating, counting, dividing, marking out time and space as zero or a beginning point; materialized in the faces of flowers and blossoms, hugely circular, bursting in air; and even appearing in the chanted mantra of 'OM' written onto paintings and sculptures. In these contexts, the rounded exclamation of the 'O' seems to denote the open singing mouth of Orpheus, who even as he is brutally destroyed and dismembered by the vengeful Maenads, his head severed from his body, continues sounding, calling out his lover's name, 'O Eurydice,' as his head, thrown into the Hebrus River by the maddened women, rolls in the swells across the Aegean Sea, the head still singing through Virgil and Ovid: 'O my beloved, O Eurydice.'

According to the ancient myths, the disembodied, still-lamenting head of Orpheus eventually washed up on the island of Lesbos. Preserved and revered by the local inhabitants there, the talking head of Orpheus became a famous oracle at a shrine in Antissa. In yet another tale, the head is buried in the Bakcheion on Lesbos, the shrine of Dionysos there, and his lyre was preserved in a temple of Apollo; thus rendering tribute both to his Dionysiac fate and to his Apollonian nature. In any event, it is this same island of Lesbos (Lesvos) which later becomes so famous throughout antiquity for the unusually great number of singers and poets it actually produces.

In other tales of Orpheus' sad end, it is recounted that the Muses, the sisters of his mother, Kalliope, gather the scattered parts of his body and bury them at Leibethria, on Mount Olympus. Having no one to whom to give his lyre,

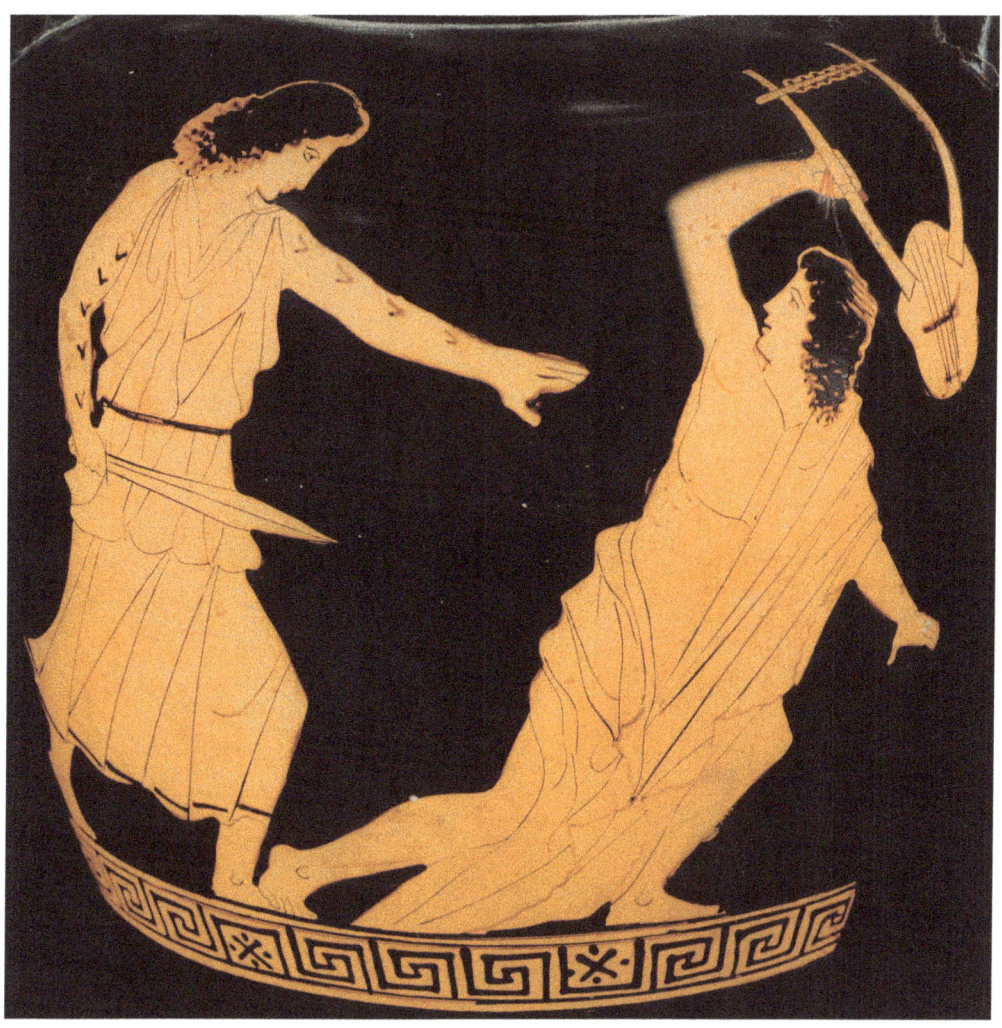

7. *Death of Orpheus*, detail, c. 440 B.C., Phiale Painter.

one legend relates that they then asked Zeus to set it among the stars as an
unchanging memorial to him and to themselves. There it exists to this day
as the constellation 'Lyra.' The theme of his oracular head and magically
resounding lyre was extremely popular in antiquity for the vase-painters and
tragedians—Aeschylus is said to have written an entire trilogy on the subject—
but it also became a widespread motif much later for the Romantic poets
and artists, particularly for many of the French symbolist painters. Indeed
one of them at that time in the late 19th, early 20th centuries, Odilon Redon,
created at least six different artistic versions of the severed, still-singing head
of Orpheus, with and without his lyre, and made in a number of mediums,
including paint, pastel, pencil, and etching (Kosinski 1989).

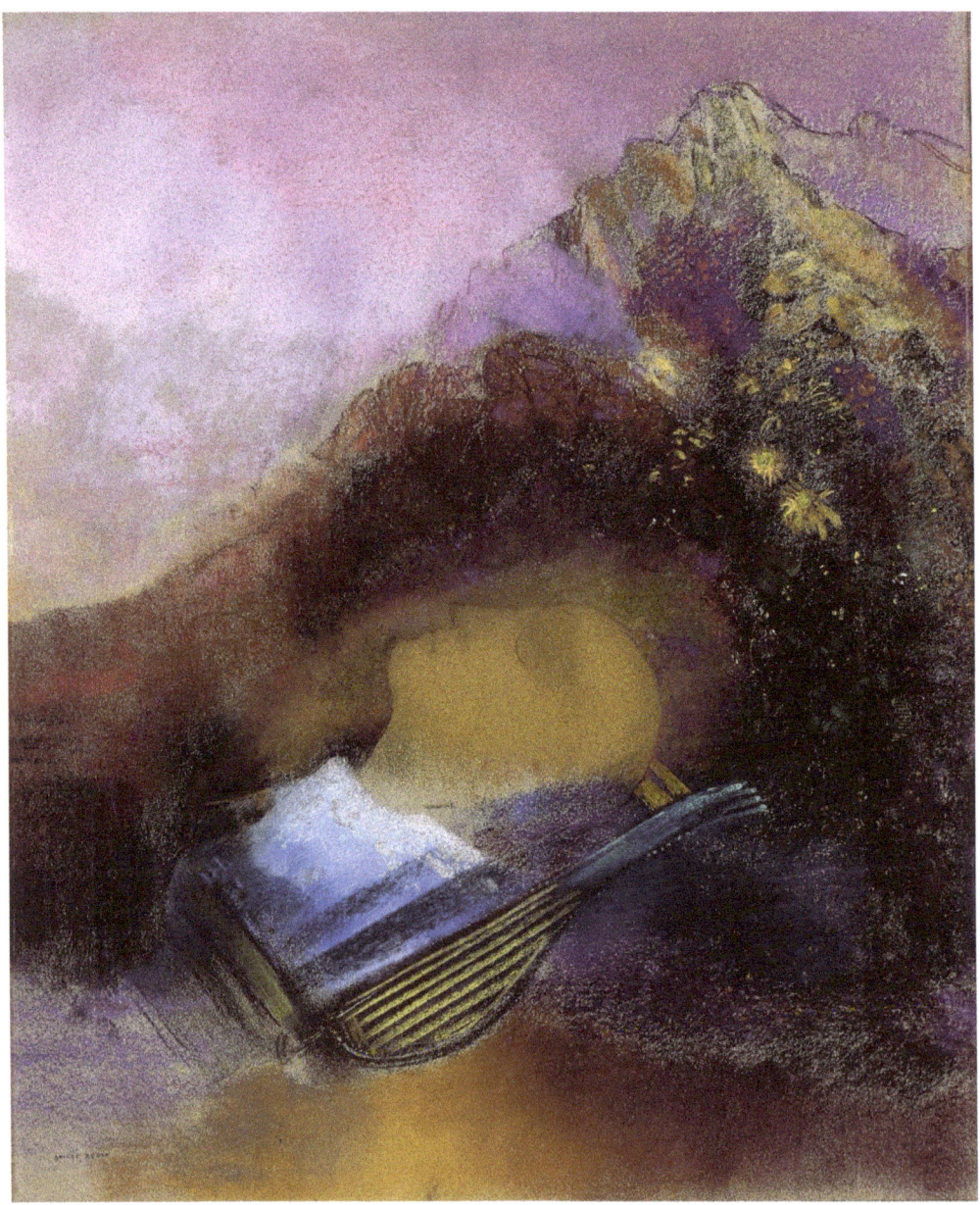

8.   Odilon Redon, *Orpheus*, c. 1903-10.

In several of his clearly mythologically influenced drawings and paintings on paper, Twombly accompanies the name of Orpheus with fragments of
Rilke's sonnets (Twombly 1975, 1979), again sometimes written or drawn out in
their original German, or in an English translation. In these pieces, he puts
language and words into a kind of play with other forms and images through
a wide variety of highly suggestive graphic expressions. Pairing a stanza of the

sonnets, written out at the bottom of the page, with an ascending or descending relatively simple straight-ruled line, sometimes broken or angled in the middle, in the center of the sheet, he leaves the viewer with both a sense of the image's intuitive 'rightness,' as well as with the need to somehow relate the name of Orpheus, the fragment of poetry, and a geometric form darkened against a scumbled, painterly background, to an emotional experience of movements upwards and/or downwards, that is, to transcendences and/or falling and failures. In one sculpture, "Untitled," made in Rome in 1983, there is the exact same sparely ascending/descending trajectory in white-painted wood which captures Rilke's phenomenon of rising and falling in one, while mirroring the precise unending angle of the drawings which also stretch achingly on forever upwards (Twombly 2000, p.62). Even with their severely minimalist notation, these pieces still manage to poignantly evoke Orpheus' longing and yearning, *his* rising and falling, and *his* tragically broken body and still-aspiring, desiring heart and soul. The most frequently repeated passage in this body of Twombly's 'Orpheus' works he takes from Rilke's sonnet II:13:

Be ever dead in Eurydice, mount more singingly,
mount more praisingly back into the pure relation.
Here, among the waning, be, in the realm of decline,
be a ringing glass that shivers even as it rings.

(Rilke 1942, p. 95)

In other related thematic works on paper, plywood or canvas, Twombly titles the top of the sheet with the poet's name, 'Rilke,' or 'To Rilke' (1975, 1984, 1988), written in his characteristic opposite-handed meander. There are further several whole series of paintings that he develops as an homage to Rilke or to his poetry, fragmentarily quoting poems on the surface in dark script.

Of the many pieces on paper which are dedicated either to Orpheus or to Rilke himself, sometimes, as in a series of 21 drawings done in Naples in 1975: "Orpheus," "Untitled," "Narcissus," "Allusion (Bay of Napoli Part II)," "Allusion (Bay of Napoli Part I)," and to "Dionysos" as well, many of these also incorporate other words and terms, epithets, and mythological aspects and attributes, as well as the place names where the pieces were created, dates, the artist's initials or signature, dedications, and other barely legible or half-erased notations, letters and words. The sheets of paper with their fairly elemental scriptural and graphic content notwithstanding, also include numerous overpaintings, rubbings, smudgings and effacements which give them the appearance of fully-formed, worked-on and worked-over painterly pieces which have a certain solidity and permanence, despite the fleeting, fragile and fragmentary processes they bear. They carry the whole history of their making on their marked surfaces. That is, they record in their Orphic tracings, signs, passages of time, the passing of time, the weathering effects of sheer duration, as well as, and most importantly, Twombly's artistic concentrations of detail and thoughtful interventions, all layered and displayed right out there *on their surfaces*. They are themselves witnesses to the passing of time. They are in a way, their own self-sufficient historical objects, incised and inscribed with the minute recordings and incidents of particular passings of time, both long past and vividly present, conjoined with the bodily movements of their making. They are visual journal and diary entries, sites, which seem to autobiographically transcribe the events, incidents and actions that take place in the experiential accompanying of a myth downwards, and the crisis of descending to an emotional resolution which takes place over a specific period of time, in the dimension of depth, and in a particular locale, grounded in a poetically-charged, highly specific *topos*. Twombly begins here to map out a distinctive and characteristic geographical and psychological *topos* all his own, an Orphic landscape and refuge of the soul. The images, words, myths, and memories all seek shelter there in the confines of the paper. Like a magic papyrus, the austere works guide the viewer to a protected, sacred space of 'just seeing,' bare witnessing, presided over by the fabled figure of Orpheus himself.

Beyond their apparently simple means, these works on paper support and convey a powerful emotional and psychological content that through their surface presentations, echoes and amplifies a variety of mythopoetic associations, archetypal memories, and both personal and universal feelings of a surprising profundity. One's response to these sheets seems entirely disproportionate to what is actually being presented in such sparely economic terms, through such subtle shifts and moods, and fleeting gradations of feeling recorded for the most part, in transient graphite. One's breath is taken away and replaced by astonishment before a piece of paper with barely anything on it, sometimes just one word, and some slight modulation of a background tone or *sfumato* in rubbed lead pencil. That a single word written or drawn across a sheet of paper has the power to evoke such a rich network of mythical, poetic, artistic, and aesthetic thoughts, feelings, and fantasies, indeed an entire cultural world of historically grounded meanings and values, stands as the singularly remarkable achievement of these materially modest pieces on paper. They continue reverberating with the legacy of the classical world hugely resonant behind them.

Throughout Twombly's body of work, we will see that his use of actual words, names, fragments of poetry, particular people and places both historical and imaginal, but especially the written phrase, pregnant with meaning, becomes increasingly important for him to set off aspects of the paintings themselves, and as he said, to 'kickstart' and inspire a creative process. This working method, also more significantly, becomes a way for him to powerfully identify with a deeply and intuitively grasped poetically rhythmical movement and sensibility of soul contained within the language of verse itself. He goes on from there, from the poetry, words and names, to the non-verbal pictorial image, developing his own painterly and sensuous vocabulary of color and forms to convey the entire experience.

> The act of writing out the words of others in his own hand is a way of claiming them as his own and of passing them through his anatomy.
>
> (Larratt-Smith in Twombly 2014a, p. 21)

The poetry itself becomes part of the fabric and fiber of both his own body and muscle memory, as well as of his consequent art productions through materially re-creating and owning the recurring memory and physical rhythm of the actual words used through mindfully drawing them out.

Twombly seamlessly joins language, words, poetry and painting into a unique configuration of mark-making which is then registered by the viewer at several different levels at once. Adriana Bontea suggests that his scribbling and handwriting directly into his works could be considered a kind of response to Paul Klee's concept of form-making, *Gestaltung*, a process characterizing both visual arts and writing. Klee says:

> When I write the word wine with ink, the ink does not play the primary role but makes possible the permanent fixation of the concept wine. Thus ink helps us to obtain permanent wine. The word and the picture, that is, word-making and form-building, are one and the same.
>
> (Klee 1961, p.17)

Twombly carries on through his own poetics of mark-making the epistemological desires and responsibilities of the Orphic initiate: to continue, to renew and to transmit the songs and teachings of mother nature herself, her landscapes and soulscapes, the mythopoetic interiority of the natural world. His use of language, poetry and the eventual development of his own calligraphic script all testify to his commitment to the embodied rhythms inhering in the spoken, sung and written words of our ancestors.

Marcel Detienne, the classical mythologist, writes that:

> The song of Orpheus produces writing; it becomes a book; it is written down in hymns and incantations, and in cosmogonies and theogonies...(T)he writing of Orpheus is an open-ended text. His speech continues through exegesis—that is, through the commentaries that it prompts educated initiates to write... The song of Orpheus generates interpretations, gives rise to exegetic constructions that become or are an integral part of the Orphic discourse. This is polyphonic writing, a book with several voices... (I)n the space of Orpheus and the writing of his disciples, the sole purpose of the eschatological vocation that prompts them to write is knowledge, real knowledge of the genesis of the gods and of the world, knowledge that extends to the extreme isolation of the individual.
>
> (Detienne 2003, pp. 135-6)

Leaping in scale now to some of Twombly's very large, wall-sized paintings, we again see the name 'Orpheus' appearing in dark pencil, paint, oil stick, or crayon, somewhat monumentally at times, in two instances covering nearly the whole canvas or paper (1975, 1979). There the name Orpheus hovers against ghostly gray and white painterly depths, emerging through creamy drips and textures, and in the piece on canvas, beautifully tinged with bluish haze and drips.

Among these bigger paintings taking up the Orphic theme, there are also several long, linear, dark ground works done even earlier, with one or two white horizontal lines drawn straight across the canvas in what looks like chalk on a blackboard, segmented at intervals by numbers, counting, marking out time, distances and space, as if in a mechanical diagram, or a kind of cryptic calculation, or in an esoteric Platonic or Pythagorean measuring system. The use of numbers in these poetic-scientific, self-contained 'systems' created by Twombly as sprawling tableaux of time-lines set over against deep space, these "wanderers from mathematics,"

> give an aura of exactness only to elude definition... (T)he numbers draw the mind's eye into the vast expanse of the Orpheus canvas to participate in Twombly's speculations on measurable and infinite space and space's coefficient, time.
>
> (Delehanty in Del Roscio 2002, p. 70)

These pieces are titled: "The Veil of Orpheus" (1968), which is a whitish house paint ground with lead pencil and wax crayon on four joined canvasses; "Treatise on the Veil" (1968), done over six linked panels with white wax crayon over black, oil-based house paint; and, "Treatise on the Veil (Second Version)" (1970), the largest, 'a time line without time,' Twombly says, which runs to nearly 10 feet high and 33 feet long, on one stretched canvas, also done with white crayon over a dark ground. There are also 12 smaller, collaged drawings done as studies and related to the two later 'Treatises,' 10 of which were done over two days in 1968 (Twombly 1973, pp. 65-7).

The sources for these monumental works, all of which seem to be occupied with intervals, segmentations, and movements in, of, and through both time and space, as in a traced geography of feelings travelling through a musical score or composition, are extremely varied. They range from the artist's investigations into the nature of speed, simultaneity and the representing of dynamisms in the modernist paintings of the Italian Futurists, Balla and Boccioni in particular, as well as in Marcel Duchamp's famous depictions of moving figures, especially his 1912 "Nude Descending a Staircase." Going even farther back in time, Twombly had long been interested in Leonardo da Vinci's numerous studies, drawings and diagrams of natural and mechanical forces, while the notion of the veil seems to derive in equal parts from Leonardo's notebook studies and drawings of folded draperies and materials, and from a photograph of Eadweard Muybridge's, entitled, 'the veiled bride' passing in front of a train (Cullinan in Twombly 2008, p. 123). The strongest origin of the veil metaphor comes, however, according to Twombly himself, from the influence of hearing the *musique concrète* cantata, "Le Voile d'Orphée," "The Veil of Orpheus," from the ballet *Orphee 53* by Pierre Henri (1951-3).

> The work, which consisted of a recording of the sound of a piece of cloth being (continuously) torn apart, echoes and conflates the legend of Orpheus raising the veil of Eurydice and also anticipates him being torn apart.
>
> (ibid.)

In many versions of the ancient myth from both Greek and Roman art, we can actually see Orpheus not only turning around, but lifting Eurydice's veil to look at her for a fatal last time.

Even more recently and simply, however, Twombly recalled in conversation that the painting's title originated in a visit to Sicily. Once while standing on the crest of a hill, he "saw a bridal procession below. The bride wore a long veil, and that sight later inspired the title of the painting" (Mancusi-Ungaro in Twombly 2013, p. 73).

Many of these works which bear a strong resemblance to musical notation and a transcribing of sound through time, albeit in a highly abstract and minimalist mode, can also be traced to Twombly's influences from John Cage and his conceptual experimentations with both music and performing. Both Twombly and Cage were at Black Mountain College at the same time, from 1951 to 1953, and both actively participated in the rich and diverse alternative art forms that were being pioneered there by Charles Olson, Franz Kline, Robert Rauschenberg, Robert Motherwell, Jack Tworkov, Aaron Siskind, and Ben Shahn, as well as numerous others.

Temporal progression and duration, a stretching out and punctuating of life's chronologies, as well as the bodily feel of the long lines being applied to canvas by hand and arm, as empathically recapitulated by the viewer in these intensely unique pieces, present a literal experience of following highly specific sensations through the actual space of their own unfolding and being definitively marked out. He draws out the lives of Orpheus and Eurydice in attenuatingly long lines of mournfully singing materials. As a whole, the 'veil' paintings present a visual analogue to the experience of reading an abstract musical score, following a life's path and hearing music—a hushed, minimal, richly enigmatic music, hovering on the edges of inaudibility, separation, emptiness, and silence. These works make us equally conscious of all the vast spaces that surround the lines of sound and time drawn across the surfaces of the paintings, as well as of our own physical bodies as we visually and corporeally traverse the extensive spaces that the Orphic 'veil' pieces latitudinally and longitudinally create and chart out. They are mysterious maps of the soul's itineraries, fibrous nerve endings and rambling mind journeys into the empyreans of inner and outer worlds of sensation, reverie, profound silence and deep space.

In an unusually large sculpture, done in Rome in 1979, clearly related to this series of paintings in form and style, Twombly has used a long, gently-curving lath describing the Orphic movements of both rising upward and curving downward, as well as alluding to the lyre's shapely arc. On either side of the plinth or base, he has written the name Orpheus in widely-spaced Greek letters running in opposite directions. Complementing the whole multi-directional figuration of the piece with its ongoing ascending and descending vectors which continue on into infinite space, is its title, again quoting from Rilke's *Sonnets to Orpheus,* "Orpheus (Thou unending trace)" (Twombly 2000, pp. 48, 61-2). In viewing the sculpture, we too are left with a 'trace,' a hint or sign, a subtle scent, an elusive aroma of an ancient receding world with its own cosmically coded and organized universe and arcane and vanishing systems of meaning.

In these elongated and puzzling pieces, the viewer is, in a sense, invited or forced to attempt to reconcile at least two entirely different modalities of mark-making and meaning-making, which though colliding and clashing with each other on a rational level and remaining endlessly and logically contradictory even on the canvases, nevertheless perfectly and harmoniously cohabit within the fabricated mythology of the image's own world, the newly demarcated spaces of soul created by Twombly. The precise and finely-drawn lines, the geometrical and mathematical notation, numbering and lettering systems, all conceived and executed in the context of an ungraspably analytic and crypto-scientific framework, are ranged and *occur* against a hugely abstracted background of vague, amorphous and indefinitely painted and scumbled surfaces made with sweepingly and muscularly large and impulsively gestural strokes. Clouds, deep space, a night sky, an astronaut's view of the earth from the moon, as in the many photographic images coming back from the Apollo space explorations taking place at that time, an unformed world of possibility contains and enfolds these spindly time lines of Twombly's and the viewer's individual life, fragilely spun out within and over against an endless and gravity-less immensity. An autobiographical simplicity and innocence are maintained throughout the paintings' complicating matrices and expanses.

There are also two paintings, entitled "Duino" (1967, 1971), in a similar horizontal format from the same period which refer to Rilke's *Duino Elegies,* named after the Italian castle on the Adriatic coast where he began writing the series of poems. There is a feeling especially to all of these very large, long works that some abstract arithmetical and mystical problems and pathways are being haltingly worked out and charted through, with their continuously rising and notated and numbered lines, and all in the context of a personalistic, diagrammatic sacred geometry, or occult and musical numerology. Despite their tensile and vibratory rhythmical energies, most of the 'Orphic' pieces from this period nevertheless emit a cloaked and powerful hush of solemnity, a strong sensation of loss, and a deepening meditative quietude against which the noises of the world slowly disappear.

There is one painting that Twombly, at his most epic, worked on from the early 1970s in Italy until its final unveiling in a New York City art gallery in 1994, which coincided with a major retrospective of his work held at the Museum of Modern Art there, that apotheosizes the Orphic thematic. Its first public appearance was as one of two smaller side shows held in New York City galleries to complement the impressively generous and comprehensive retrospective going on at the same time at MoMA. Each one of these two adjunctive

9.   Cy Twombly, *Untitled (Say Goodbye, Catullus, to the Shores of Asia Minor),* 1994.

side exhibits also offered, however, their own kind of miniature retrospective, including even the one very big painting, since it spanned and displayed a 20-year range and cross-section of Twombly's artistic painterly styles and techniques, themes, images, concerns, content, and changes in palette, emotional tone and colorings, all on one vast multi-sectioned canvas.

As the only work in the cavernous, post-industrial cement and steel gallery space, a former garage, which appeared in this context 'made' for the piece, setting it off in an almost theatrical dramatic 1960s 'art happening' casualness which contrasted with the work's sober formality and grandeur, the large painting ran along one entire far wall opposite the entrance. Amply filling the space, it also bore its fourth title over the 24 years of its making. The painting, which is now in the Menil Collection in Houston, a museum designated at least in part specifically to house the largest publicly-displayed collection of Twombly's work in a building of galleries specially designed and meticulously collaborated on by Twombly himself and the architect Renzo Piano, measures 157 by 624 inches, that is approximately 13 feet high by 52 feet long—big enough to take a few decent strolls along, to slowly walk back and forth in front of its substantially looming expanse. It confronts and overwhelms with its sheer incorporative size and quietly majestic and grandly classical scale.

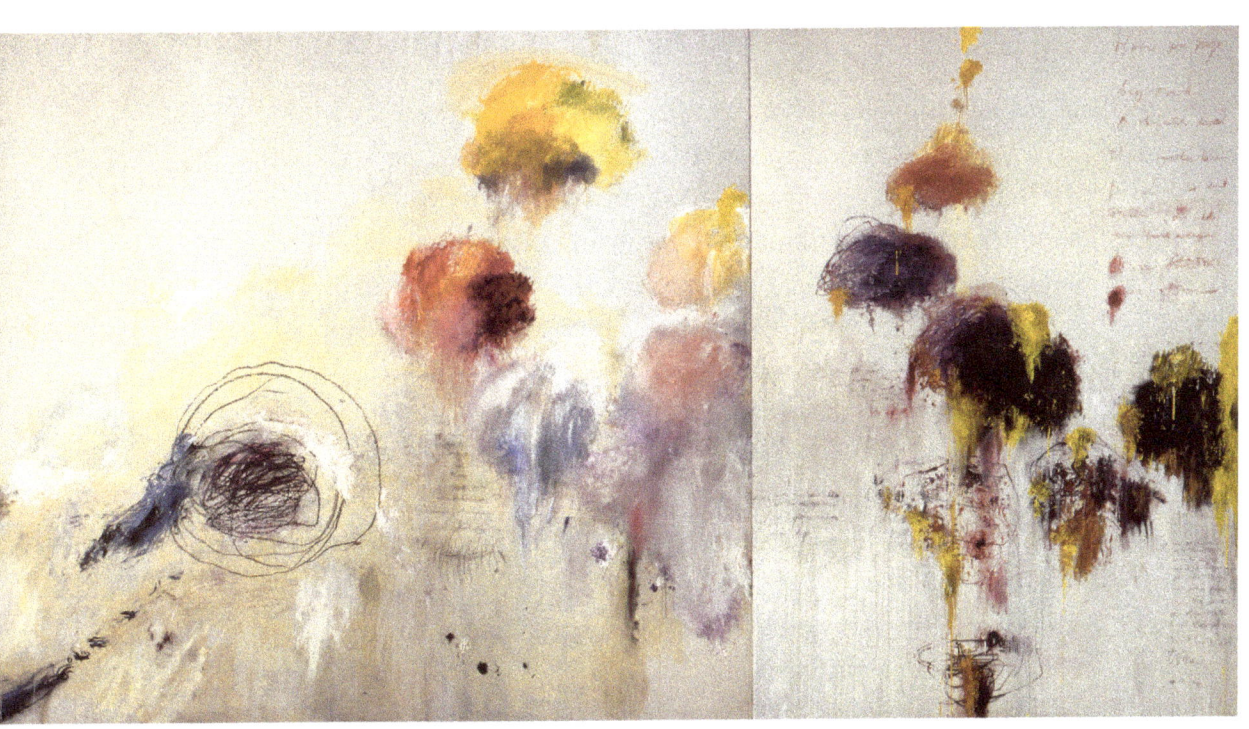

Its first title, "The Anatomy of Melancholy," actually inscribed over a large portion of its second quartile in the '70s, refers to Robert Burton's encyclopedic volume on grief and sorrow written in 1621. For a short while, during its display in Twombly's Rome studio in 1982, the artist considered calling it, "On Mists in Idleness," from part of a line in John Keats' poem, "The Human Seasons" (1818). The line with that phrase occurs at a moment in the poem which takes place during the human soul's autumn, when: "his wings he furleth close: contented so to look / on mists in idleness …" (Leeman 2005, p. 269). During a period when he made scores of drawings and paintings concerning different images and passages from Keats' poetry, Twombly also did a series of three drawings in 1960 entitled, "On Mists of Idleness," and, in fact, many of the works from this period until the last years are indeed suffused with autumnal whitish mists and atmospheric clouds and seas of fluidly luminous paint.

Shortly after the work's completion in 1994, the painting bore the noncommittal name, "Untitled", or "Untitled Painting"; and it was only at its showing at the Gagosian Gallery in Soho that it finally received its full and definitive title, "Untitled, Say Goodbye, Catullus, to the Shores of Asia Minor." This valedictory salute derives from an altered line of Catullus' first century B.C. poem written on the occasion of the lyric poet's leaving his dead brother's body buried on the plains of Asia Minor, in what is now contemporary Western Turkey by the Aegean Sea, to sail back to his native Rome.

In this veritable journey of a painting itself which traverses sizable spans of historical, physical and imaginal time and space, the name 'Orpheus,' spindly and stretched, is no less than three times faintly repeated in paint and floats languidly in, on, and across the sprawling central portions of the densely painted surface, covered by a white glaze, the letters, O-R-P-H-E-U-S, spaced far apart. 'ORPHEUS' reverberates in this hushed atmosphere more as a gentle whisper, or as a benevolently presiding patron deity, benedictory, than as an exclamation, declaration of content, or as a label, title, or explanation for anything that actually appears in or on the washed and textured passages of paint. In fact, the name 'ORPHEUS' has to be picked out and discerned beneath surface layers, as it is woven like broadly gestured graffiti on a faded, peeling, and warmly weathered Roman wall, already in the process of being covered over by other marks, remnants, and signs left by time's deposited signatures, so that underpaintings and pentimenti glint and seep through the many layers here and there. The name, though softly drawn or written so that it blends into the subdued, muted tones of the ground, nevertheless unites, animates and irradiates the whole towering painting, as Orpheus himself invites and knits together wildly divergent themes: elegiac loss, absence, separations, death and mourning, as well as the reveries, dream journeys and landscapes of the soul which knows and sings the secrets of nature and can burst into effusive joy and ecstatic bodily vitality. Orpheus is present in this huge work as a figure of mortality, mutability and a quietly organizing power of order in the midst of chaos. His thrice-repeated name signifies the possibilities of transformation and metamorphosis inherent within the project and endeavor of art-making itself. He is the inspiring guide leading us toward *poiesis,* the desire and urge to create with the languages of art in the looming face of nothingness, to enliven and rapt with song even the shades of the underworld, to resurrect and transmit images of memory, desire, eternity, and history, the rich traditions and cultures of the distant past with speech, song, and words, to continue on and attempt to redeem Orpheus' own sadly dismembered destiny, to try now through *poiesis* and our own efforts, *to ourselves bring back Eurydice*, the *anima mundi*, soul, into the world.

The darkly stitched and scarred sailing vessels in the painting, Egyptian, Phoenician, Venetian, or Celtic funerary barks, or ferries of Charon, which glide, drift and navigate endlessly pale, grayish seas, resonate and rock with the waves. They surge and swell with Orpheus' name. His songs still urge the oared vessels on to nameless lands. These nocturnal ships further invite us to embark ourselves upon this uncertain, downward voyage into paint, poetry, matter and death, a descent without clear boundaries, destinations, or goals. The potential *telos* for making this journey is also there, however, on the canvas itself, luminescent blossoms on the far right section of the painting, gloriously bursting explosions of pure color which dissolve and efface themselves on the surface, leaving afterimages of intense, nonverbal and preverbal feelings of euphoria and *jouissance,* 'joy.' "Untitled, Say Goodbye ..." is suffused with light's oblivion, promise, and ecstasy, crowding and jostling memories of civilizations and people long gone, as well as those yet to come. It radiates and streams those vertical moments of time stopped, "*simply being there* in the world in ... 'transversal ecstasis'" (In Merleau-Ponty 1993, p. 51). It harbors the effulgence of the gods' abandonments, the incandescent scatterings of fiery sparks, cast off in their hurried flight, gleaming and scintillating throughout the paint, disseminating illuminations and enlightenings all over the broad reaches of

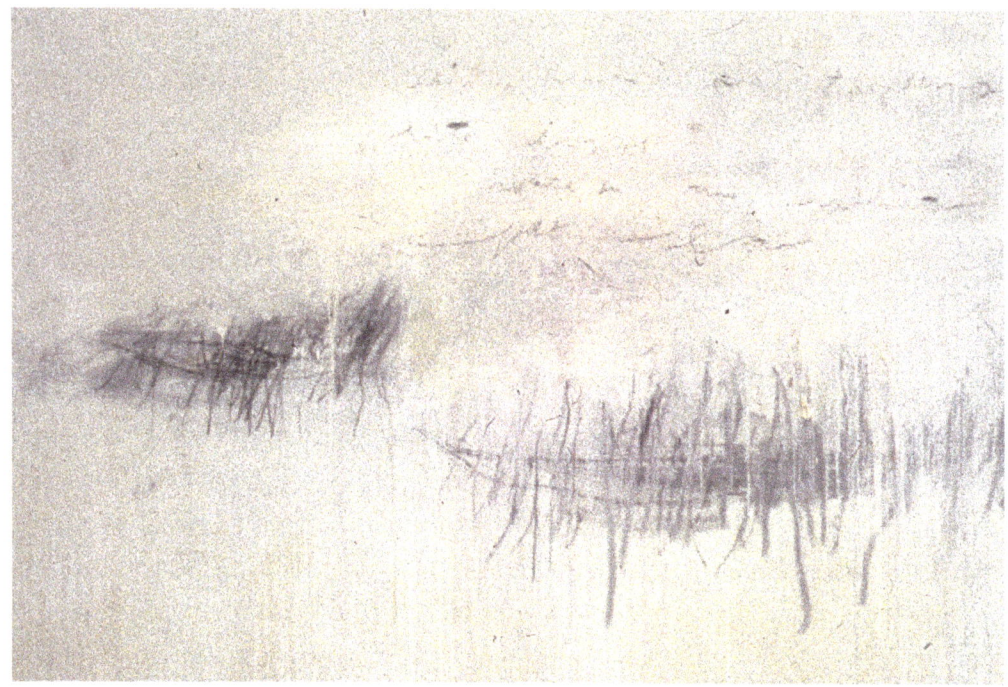

10.   Cy Twombly, *Untitled (Say Goodbye, Catullus, to the Shores of Asia Minor)*, detail, 1994.

the canvas. The poet Patricia Waters could be telling us of this numinously solemn scene of leave-taking when she writes in a passage Twombly actually later used in his own "Coronation of Sesostris" (2000) series: "When the gods leave,.../When they leave/ music is loudest,/sun high, stores fat/with harvest" (Waters 2000, p. 31).

Amidst such lavish and gorgeous painting, the viewer is challenged to pick out and decipher the several texts embedded in different portions of the work, seemingly placed there as much for their poetic, personal, and formal visual counterpoint and stimulation, as for their decodable and intelligibly relevant meanings to the deeper themes of the work. Besides the references to Burton, Keats, and Catullus already touched upon, the painting also bears fragments of poetry from Archilochus and Giorgos Seferis, an ancient and a contemporary Greek poet, both of whom Twombly deeply appreciated and used several times in other works.

Then we come to the quotes from Rilke incorporated into this work, four in all. In reading this magnificent painting, perhaps the single most synthetic and panoramic work of the late 20th century, from left to right—contrary to how Twombly himself suggested reading it, "like a Chinese one, from right to left" (Twombly 2013, p. 28) which we will discuss later—we first come across the longest passage of Rilke's inscribed here. It is written into the glazed white and gray finishes in the lower first quartile of the piece, and nearly dissolves in the surrounding mists, evoking transience, as well as the passages and movements of the soul towards ultimate destinations. Adapted from the ninth of the *Duino Elegies,* the text reads:

> (T)his fleeting world, which in some
> strange way keeps calling to us.
> Us, the most fleeting of all. *Once*
> for each thing. Just once, no more.
> And we too, just once. And never
> again. But to have been this once
> completely, even if only once ...

> (Rilke 1939, p. 73; Leeman 2005, p. 275; Twombly 1994b, p. 21)

He then grafts directly onto this portion of the quoted elegy two additional lines: "highlights how the dizziness, /slipped away like a fish in the sea" (Pincus-Witten 1994, p.21). Onto Rilke's poignant fragment of the world's transformations, its passing from visibility to invisibility *in us,* Twombly thus appends a coda of vertiginous falling, a drowning into depths, a somehow familiar disappearing and sinking into the sea. He records an oneiric lightheadedness, a sudden flash, and then a going-away, as the firm grasp of life relaxes and loosens into the further deep of water.

The second quote of Rilke's which appears in "Untitled, Say Goodbye ..." is just to the right of the painting's central portion and prefaces the most florid and flamboyantly colored passages of the work. It is our old friend, the 'falling' fulcrum of our discussion, the very same stanza from Rilke's tenth and last 'Duino elegy,' which as we know, already takes place in the underworld, among the souls and topography of the deceased: "And we, who have always thought of happiness rising, would feel the emotion that almost overwhelms when happiness falls" (Rilke 1939, p. 85). This motion of falling, a slow, slippery sliding into depths continues.

Moving left to right across the canvas, the force of art's gravity exerts its downwards pull. Much of the painting's action and movement is in descending. The passages of paint come down to meet the viewer. The soul's itinerary and trajectory in this painting, though tinged with melancholy and loss, moves ultimately, however, towards joy, hope, and exultation. In fact, if we adopt Twombly's suggested reading of the painting, from right to left, despite moving *away* from the beautiful explosions and cloudy burstings of pure colors covering nearly the entire right third of the grand canvas, they still, he insists, represent "an ascent" (Twombly 2013, p. 28), and the directional movement of the boats towards the left, the milky light and the mists of a mystical void disappears into the invisibility of origins and beginnings, the formless sources and destinations of painting's process. The right to left pointing and journeying of the boats, also, of course, underlines the actual arc of the poet Catullus' homeward sailing from the Near Eastern Mediterranean shores and plains of Asia Minor back in a westerly direction towards his native Roman homeland. Like Rilke, Twombly whole-heartedly embraces the reality of life's sensuousness and transience, and both poetizes and paints out of the "dual realm," while also portraying the place, space and parallel universes of *non-being*, where "voices become eternal and mild" (Rilke 1942, p. 33), holding the tension between the two worlds that comprise human living. It is only *poiesis* itself, creating, as he performs it in this work, which is capable of holding the tension between our inner human oppositions.

And then, near intense vermillion and brilliant red hues, with even the last word of the quote painted in blotched and blossoming crimson, the third quote from Rilke on this one painting draws from sonnet I:7 to Orpheus: "His mortal heart presses out (a deathless,) inexhaustible wine" (Rilke 1984, p. 235). Using the Mitchell (1984) translation for his more recent work, as he used the Norton translation of the *Sonnets* in his earlier Orphic pieces, the artist deletes 'a deathless' on one side, and then draws out and extends the last word 'WINE' three times along and beneath the quote, the first two times in black crayon and oil pastel, before the third and final blaze of blood and wine-red oil stick, a sacrament staining and illuminating the canvas, the word exultant, declaiming: 'WINE.'

The whole first stanza of this plundered Rilke sonnet to Orpheus deserves to be quoted in full:

> Praising, that's it! One appointed to praising,
> he came like the ore forth from the stone's

silence. His heart, o ephemeral press
of a wine that for men is unending.

(Rilke 1942, p. 29)

Twombly, like Rilke, like Orpheus, is a praise singer (Astrachan 2017), sharing himself out endlessly, each work a song of devotion and dedication to the powers of life *and* death, being *and* non-being. This painting and the multiple verses drawn on it, all honor, embrace and sing this unitary reality of the objective psyche, the *unus mundus*, the imaginal space of the soul wherein all people, times, and places converge and commune in reverent concordance.

The fourth Rilke quote Twombly employs in "Untitled, Say Goodbye..." is again from the *Sonnets,* and is perhaps the most heart-rending cry of them all, to end Part I:26, the death of Orpheus at the hands of the raging Maenads: "*O du verlorener Gott! Du unendliches Spur!*" "O, you lost god! You endless trace!" (Leeman 2005, p. 312). This heart-stopping sonnet itself finishes by bestowing this legacy of the last two lines to Orphic acolytes everywhere, the testament of Orpheus as vouchsafed to Rilke and Twombly both, to continually voice and assume this sacred responsibility and lament: "Only because at last enmity rent and scattered you/are we now the hearers and a mouth of nature" (Rilke 1942, p. 67). The artists provide voice and vehicle to this deep plaint and essential nature of the world which speaks through them, so that they might change this nature and world into poetry, thereby revealing, re-creating and preserving its soul values for those who will follow. Orpheus lends the artist, analyst and alchemist, his voice, lyre and command of language to communicate with and perform the transformations of both the inner and outer worlds, of both inner nature, *psyche*, and outer nature, matter, *physis*, and the body. The many voices and languages of art and analysis perform the revealing and unveiling of what is hidden in nature's own slowly shifting, emergent representations, images, symbols and materials. "Nature loves to hide," ancient Heraclitus tells us (Kahn 1979, p. 33). The Orphic songs of art and analysis aim to penetrate to the wordless core of music, feeling, memory, and rhythm at our centers, *our* most inward nature, that we may once again become one with it. Soul *wants*, yearns, and desires to become language.

The medium of psychoanalysis, the voice, words, and the various languages used in the 'talking cure,' perform their meanings through the resounding effects they have upon us, in their *playing upon* the soul, in their plucking of the resonant strings of *psyche* and producing rhythmical responses. In *doing* both art and analysis, one learns how to *play,* ideally as freely as possible, with words, forms, images, materials, and languages. Twombly calls it the "absolute 'freedom from purpose… the freedom in the painting process that is not bound to any real form'" (Bastian 2018, p. 15). It is an erotic process, relating and desiring. In analysis, a great deal of the so-called 'method,' as well as what could be considered a conceivable 'goal' of the journey, would be developing the capacity for, after all, *free* association, unguided, imaginative reverie, striking up and carrying on an authentic, respectful, creative, playful, and loving relationship with the 'other' in us, with the 'he,' 'she,' or 'it' who has been lost, with the un-conscious, with the deep world of soul at our base.

Twombly's works in particular, in all the mediums he chose to use, reveal more so than any other artist in the modern and postmodern periods an unrestricted and unbridled freedom. He allows for the completely liberated and uncensored rein to his own imaginative, aesthetic, psychic and playful expressiveness, all the while guided by a wise and sure hand steeped in the soulful histories and techniques of his cultural predecessors.

Going even further, one then can perhaps imagine that art, alchemy, and analysis all attempt to erotically re-claim and re-connect not only with the individual soul, the unique soul, but with the soul of the world, the *anima mundi.* One dares, courageously, with art and analysis, to descend to those unspoken, muted depths. One sings and hopefully even finds one's voice there, and returns, uttering things that have perhaps never before been said, or at least not in these differing contexts and necessarily changed ways. This path of *poiesis* leading endlessly downward is the way of individuation.

This tending towards the earth, hiddenness, and invisibility, this movement down and away of a happiness or 'beauty that falls,' finds its last and most recent concrete expressions in a sumptuous series of paintings, also completed in 1994, and exhibited the same year as "Untitled, Say Goodbye…," at the MoMA retrospective. From 1991 to 1995, Twombly worked on two large cycles of paintings on the same theme, starting them in Bassano in Teverina and finishing them in Gaeta, each one composed of four canvases, each measuring approximately 124" x 80." Each cycle is titled "*Quattro Stagioni*," "The Four Seasons," and each "Part I-IV" is titled by its respective season. The themes and arrangements of the works once again echo Keats' poem, "The Human Seasons"

(1818), quoted in "Untitled, Say Goodbye ...," in their quarternary structure and progression. There in his sonnet, Keats, who like Twombly also lived in Rome, writes: "Four seasons fill the measure of the year; There are four seasons in the mind of man" (In Cullinan 2011, p. 155). Twombly, when embarking upon this project was also the same age as the painter, Nicolas Poussin, a very important touchstone and predecessor for him, when that much earlier artist painted his four-part, "The Four Seasons," which he, an expatriate like both Keats and Twombly, also created in Rome as well (1660-4), completing them just before his death in 1665. In Twombly's second cycle dated 1993/1994, now in the Tate Collection in London, "Part I: *Primavera*," "Spring," bears down its entire lower right side, again, this last stanza of Rilke's, though with one word reworked, from the tenth 'Duino elegy': "and you who have/always thought of /happiness flowing/ would feel the/emotion/that almost overwhelms/when/happiness/ falls" (Leeman 2005, p. 312).

The motion of falling is also picked up on two of the other canvases in both of the "Four Seasons" cycles. On "Part II: *Estate*," the "Summer" panel of both series, he writes: "high on light/how the dizziness/slipped away/like a fish in the sea" (Twombly 1995, p. 175, 180). These are almost exactly the same words he added to the excerpt from the ninth 'Duino elegy' in "Untitled, Say Goodbye ..." Another overlap between these major projects, all being worked on in different locations at around the same time, is his inscription of the phrase, "say goodbye Catullus to the shores of Asia Minor," drawn three times, on this final *"Estate,"* "Summer" panel of the Tate series. Both of the "Summer" panels, drenched and dripping in bright acidic yellow, and in the first series, also with bold, red lettering for the title, place, and date, this poetic quote, and two bright red rowing vessels slashed by red oars and obscured by yellow and white paint drippings and streamings, conjoin images of fire and water, the sun, sea, and heat, a sizzling combination and combustion of flames and cool, watery depths.

Images of fire on and in the water, boats, torches, sparks, and blazing barks, are a powerful and recurring theme that became common to Twombly's paintings since the '80s, and became especially gloriously arrayed both in the 10-part "Coronation of Sesostris" series (2000), and particularly in the "Lepanto" series (2001), a 12-part painting and re-visioning of the famous and ghastly naval battle between the Turks of the Ottoman Empire and the combined Spanish, Venetian, and Papal forces that took place off the western coast of Greece on a sunny, October Sunday in 1571. Fire and water are here wedded into alchemy's sublime *aqua permanens*, the improbable conjunction of extreme opposites, which when united, are capable of cracking open all space and time.

The phrase and image of a fish slipping away into the sea repeating three times in the '90s, echoes two other even earlier cycles of paintings which Twombly clearly made with Rilke in mind. The first from 1985, he dedicates, "to Rilke (with obsession)." This inscription appears to the right of an oval waterscape, painted on paper and stapled to its rectangular wooden panel. The painting itself, "Untitled," is brooding and moody, fierce and threatening. A spectrum of greens from very dark to light-filled, a tangle of sea grasses waving in grayish, watery mists, swirling paint and turgid, liquid depths, all reveal a furiously applied acrylic pigment. Beneath the pond image, he alters a fragment quoted from Rilke's poem, "*Fortschritt,*" "Progress," or "Moving Forward," which comes from *The Book of Pictures,* a volume of poetry he wrote specifically about paintings and looking at paintings, a pleasure he enjoyed so frequently and deeply: "and in the ponds/broken off from the sky/my feeling sinks/as if standing on /fishes" (Rilke 1981, p. 100). 'FISHES' is here scrawled hugely in gray paint over a ghost of itself showing through underneath, a palimpsest receding into a milky background. That first painting in the series is followed chronologically by 12 more pieces done seemingly sequentially going into 1986, with three of them on large, shaped canvases. All 12 of which, however, continue the theme of total immersion in cool, green water, light-suffused depths, seascapes or pondscapes, ebbing and flowing, and darkly enmeshing, clinging grasses.

"The fish image," for Robert Bly, himself a poet and a Rilke translator, "is a triumph, an amazing union of senses. It embodies exaltation, humility and danger in a single image" (ibid., p. 68). Here in these 13 paintings and in the next series as well, Twombly goes to the deepest point of a poem, painting an image from a poem about looking at painting, furthering both poetry and painting in the process, allowing himself to sink away, to fall down into the viscous depths of water and painting, clutching only smooth oily liquids, sometimes with his fingers and hands, and seeing where they will lead, pull, and flow.

Three years later in 1988, Twombly conceived his largest 'Rilke' cycle to date: a nine-part painting on wooden panels which was initially shown as a group in a single room at the Venice Biennale that same year. He executed this astonishing ensemble over one furiously continuous forty-eight hour stretch using entirely his own hands. Part I, again a similarly large long rectangle, is inscribed with his initials "CT," the date, "May 88," and then, "(Ponds)/to Rilke." Underneath, written down nearly the entire length of the canvas, is again: "and in the ponds broken off from the sky/my feeling sinks as if standing on Fishes." This time, 'Fishes' is written so largely and wildly that it overlaps on both sides the wooden, white-painted, artist-made frame of the panel itself. Interestingly, the short poem from which these last two lines are taken, also includes the lines: "I can see farther into paintings./I feel closer to what language can't reach" (ibid., p. 100).

A year earlier, in the *Untitled* sculpture done in Rome in 1987, Twombly stapled to the back of the board, centered behind its upright support, a piece of yellowed paper on which he had written in red pencil the same lines from Rilke: "In the pond broken off from the sky my feeling sinks as if standing on fishes" (Nesin 2014, p. 75). The sculpture itself looks like a white-primed and stretched rectangular canvas—it is actually a thin wooden panel board—leaning against an easel or propped on a vertical support for either reflection, inspection, or even further painting, over its 'empty' and plainly layered, creamy white surface.

The installation of the nine panels of "Untitled" (1988) as a whole, again plumbs the watery depths of darkly dangerous grasses and vegetation, massing and curling in indistinct waters. The total loss and lack of all perspective whatsoever, and the overall forcefully flat quality of the painting engulfs the viewer in a powerful experience of pure nature. It tugs us into thick, grasping, painterly clutches of amorphous pond water and grasses. It makes us peer further into these opaque depths of paint which are at times a greenish tint of black.

Despite the hardness and coldness of the dark greens and blacks, all of these aquatic pieces are slightly softened and punctuated as well by powerful bursts of grayish white light. Grasses and shifting reflections, watery depths, and the total submission to the process of painting, though reminiscent of both Turner and Monet, especially the latter's great "Nymphéas" and "Waterlilies" cycles of his old age, which basically ushered in modern and abstract painting in the twentieth century, here, through Twombly's refractions, now reflect something more fragmented, shattered, partial, temporary, and violent.

J.M.W. Turner and Claude Monet also both famously painted Venice's palazzi and canals, trembling and dissolving in the hallucinatory light and watery reflections of that fabled, mysterious and ambiguous city. The application of the quick-drying acrylic paint throughout Twombly's Venetian project is wild and urgent, however, progressing darkly through the series with increasing overpaintings directly smeared and smudged on with fingers, the pulsating forms still swaying with the speed and spontaneity of his rapid execution. The sculpted baroque and rococo lunette frames on two of the pieces, were clearly also designed with Venetian style and architecture in mind, and provide elegant classical foils for these totally contemporary and immediate gasps of sudden painterly process, power, and dynamic forcefulness.

Though Turner, Monet, and Twombly span nearly three and a half centuries between themselves, all three are gripped and fascinated by the very same mysteries of nature's mutability. Philosophers, poets of light, physicists, and alchemists of paint, they each handle the basic materials of their craft remarkably similarly when confronting the elementals of earth, air, fire, and water. Undoubtedly as a result of their obvious thematic and aesthetic painterly sensibilities, styles, and concerns, the three great artists were indeed joined together in a brilliant exhibition of their late work which was organized in Stockholm and travelled to two different European venues in 2011-12 (Twombly 2011b).

With Twombly's 21st century experimenting, however, we see that the embracing arc of their historical contexts has become radically disfigured from Turner's late eighteenth century beginnings. The human figure itself has indeed vanished, and its 'natural' matrix has meanwhile undergone such traumatic and total transformation, that here in "(Ponds)/to Rilke," nature and landscape is now completely wrenched and torn out of its own organic context, altered, psychologically 'other-ed,' and is then reinstated as something slathered, squished, and slashed onto these wooden panels of paintings. Nature, since Turner and Monet, is no longer being happily, or even curiously, represented. We recognize, with apprehension and some dread in these ground-dematerializing works of Twombly's, the fluid pull and tug of a dark nature that falls away to bottomless depths, veers off the edges of painting and actually breaks the bonds of canvas and frame altogether. The boundlessness, autonomy and continuousness of nature here dwarfs and dissolves us, drowns us, and alludes to the conditions, mediums, and tones in which we now live and move, awash and adrift on empty barks sailing vastly luminous spaceless seas, as in "Untitled, Say Goodbye ... ," and here, sinking and falling into a strange time-space, blindly groping, trying to swim and breathe underwater, out of our element, without boundaries or orientation, without any upwards, downwards, or sideways. There is no place to touch down in any of these green paintings from '85-'88. There is no 'there' there. One falls freely through nature's deep watery spaces. Surely no longer a romantic or nostalgic refuge, 'nature' and landscape has by now not only suffered innumerable, dubious and disastrous metamorphoses, but it has also become sinister, uncanny, and menacing, though still alluring for all of that, as it nevertheless continues to hold the 'other' of our selves, the 'otherness' that we seek, our shadow sides, our own darkened, deepening natures, the un-known, the non-human, that which is not yet, and *must become*, both conscious and human.

In these paintings we are being forced to learn how to breathe underwater, how to survive in this contra-natural environment, which we must learn to do, especially since we do not know how long we may be submerged. Pushed down, we try to accept it, to sink into it, to become somewhat familiar in the hostile and even toxic foreign elements that surround us. We have become alienated strangers in a world we continuously contribute to making even stranger. These paintings trace and describe the sensations of our human lives at these endings of a frenzied epoch, during the decline and decay of a socially and environmentally untethered, politically maddened, and culturally chaotic (American) imperium.

In a much more recent series of paintings referencing the Arab world, "III Notes from Salalah" (2007), Twombly has once again used a similarly broad range of aquatic greens as grounds, from intensely dark and nearly black to pale, swirling verdant surface overlays, in order to reflect the bounteously lush seaside oasis of Salalah, in present day Oman, once Zafar, and the source of frankincense and other spices for the nomadic caravans of antiquity. Painted liquidly and running with white wet drippings over the extremely deep green backgrounds, an abstracted Arabic calligraphy dances in swirls and spirals across the multi-panelled canvases, and bridges the profound depths of the '80s 'green paintings' from 1984, 1985, and 1988 (Sylvester 2008), to remind us today of the renewing and refreshing effects of *viriditas*, the alchemical 'greening' of culture which flowed from these Near Eastern, Oriental, and Islamic sources of scholarship and wisdom to inspire originally both Graeco-Roman civilization, as well as to provide the major source materials for the revivifying effects of Renaissance learning and humanism which spread from the erudite Arab diaspora into Spain, Provence, and especially Italy, and thus to the rest of Europe. As against the linear seriality of horizontal temporal references, however, as in the 'green paintings,' in "Salalah" Twombly paints the 'vertical history' of creation, the 'there is' as it arises from the flesh, folds, and especially from the liquid depths of water and the sea world's primordially procreative nature. The format of these paintings echoes tapestries, wall hangings, and Asian scroll paintings.

It would seem that watery depths, Arabic calligraphy and the brilliant whiteness of the sea continued to be profound motifs for Twombly to plumb into his late years, guiding him into the essence of language, writing, and the fluidities of speech, all based upon the movements of the Mediterranean harbor port just outside his Gaeta studio windows. The year after the Salalah 'notes,' he completed a cycle of nine paintings, "Untitled I-IX" (2008), for the opening of the Louvre museum franchise in Abu Dhabi. Four more works in the exact same format followed and extended his probing into the poetics of the deep blue views which had daily dazzled his vision and spoke to him in the bright white flowing lines of the pure painterly song and dance of musical 'otherness' waving across their surfaces. These are his own signatures upon water.

Writing in the early (1905) *Book of Hours* about 'man,' Rilke says: "There is one thing he must again grow capable of: falling, patiently resting in heaviness—he who presumed/to surpass all the birds in flying" (Rilke 1939, p. 117). The falling is for Rilke an embrace of the turgid watery depths, of being itself, the constant magnetism of the earth, complete acceptance of the 'open,' including as many of its shadowy, difficult, and dark sides as possible.

The activity of *poiesis,* the creative making, doing, and fabricating of the artist, in its furthest reaches of activity, is not only always accompanied, as we have seen, by its dusky twin brother, but in its most sublime fulfillment, arrives at its destination and culmination through a turning *into* its *other* side, its (only) *apparent* opposite: not-doing, not-acting, de-creating. Letting go of the attachments to any particular appearances, representations, or any phenomena whatsoever for that matter, allows for the possibility for 'other' appearances to arise, for that which is *not* conscious, not identical, for manifestations of the noumena instead of the phenomena. *Poiesis* in this sense, is thus not only a not-doing, it is rather an active and conscious process of an *un-doing*.

Like *poiesis,* a sublime psycho-analysis, too, effects a de-construction—of everything. In the acceptance and embrace of what *is,* our unavoidable destiny, Nietzsche's *amor fati,* we fall into and open downwards to the earth, to the depths, to matter, and the body, and to the darker sides of our being which hold this numinous and 'wholly other.'

Poiesis appears then, as Heidegger says, as a "preparation of the readiness, of keeping oneself open for the arrival of or absence of the god" (In Wolin 1993, p. 108). Radical transfiguration takes place invisibly, hidden, in the deep. "This is why in the Greek tragedy virtually nothing occurs. It commences with the downgoing" (Heidegger 1996, p. 103). True creation begins with this movement of falling, the sudden halting and reversal of all of our upward strivings.

Returning to Rilke's tenth 'Duino elegy,' the stanza just prior to our continuing refrain of the last stanza, tells of the poet among the 'endlessly dead,' who, in attempting to indicate an image, resemblance, or symbol of this 'downgoing' and 'falling' in us, an image and feeling of a life after this one, our known actual life,

> would point to the catkins, hanging
> from the empty branches of the hazel tree,
> or else they'd be meaning the rain
> that falls on the dark earth in the early Spring.

> (Rilke 1939, p. 85; 1984, p. 211)

And in the poem "Gravitation," "*Schwerkraft,*" he again gestures toward an "invincible centre" in us that tugs us downwards:

> Stander, through whom earth's pull
> Hurtles like drink through thirst.
>
> Sleeper, from whom, as though
> from a crouching cloud, it falls
> in large and liberal rain.

> (In Jacobus 2012, p. 1)

In yet another even earlier profound witnessing to the myth of Orpheus and Eurydice, eighteen years before Rilke transcribed the *Sonnets,* he wrote the poem, "Orpheus. Eurydice. Hermes", in Rome in 1904. There, in the later lines of that masterpiece, inspired by an equally breathtaking Hellenistic bas-relief copy of an original third century B.C. Greek sculpture by Callimachos of the three poignantly-standing figures, when Orpheus attempts to return to the upperworld with Eurydice following behind, she is already so deeply rooted in her new state of non-being, in her enclosed and fulfilling virginity of death, and so distant from earthly life and her previous flesh and blood lover, that, as the poet says,

> She was already loosened like long hair,
> poured out like fallen rain,
> shared like a limitless supply.

(Rilke 1984, p. 53)

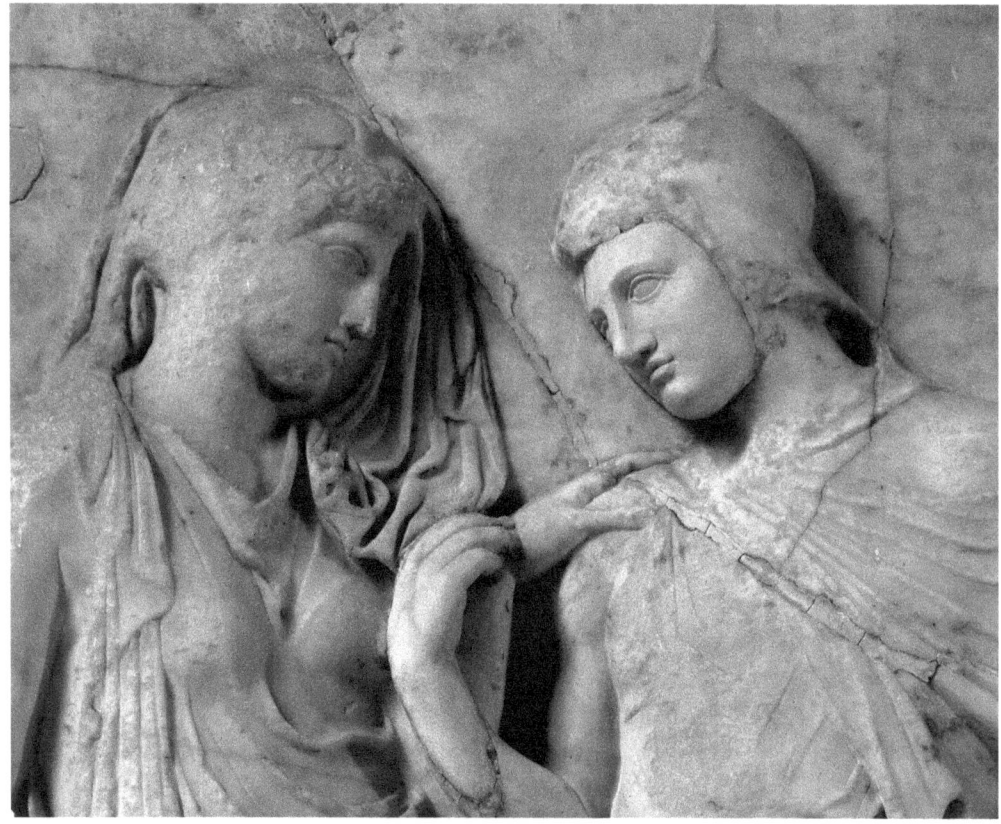

11.   *Orpheus and Eurydice*, detail, Roman copy of 420 B.C. Greek original by Callimachos.

This tending towards the depths, the pull of gravity, loosening, pouring out, raining down, falling and decline, heralds the artist's search for origins and beginnings. It signals a reversion to the originary creative moment, when all the bonds and boundaries fall away into the 'moving void.' To arrive at this beginning point which has no beginning or ending, and is not even a point anywhere in space or time, is to come into nothing, *no thing* at all, nothingness. It is to embark upon a commencement before the beginning, and to engage in a leavetaking "in advance of all parting" (Rilke 1942, p.95). This Orphic "condition of not-being," Rilke says, is "the infinite ground of your deep vibration" (ibid.). It is that *place* that *poiesis* reveals, that *space* of beginnings, that empty void at our center from which all things must emerge.

The works of art produced out of that place, whether poems or paint-ings, sculpture or song, are thus not representations of that space. Rather they are descriptions or traces, or perhaps signs, maps of the process of journeying downwards, of the *katabasis* itself, the descent. These are the songs and the stories, *that there is such a place,* that Orpheus brings with him back from the underworld. The work itself, the prize, the *telos,* the goal, beautiful Eurydice, is not herself revealed or retrieved; *she* is not brought back or finally possessed through this downgoing. The movement of falling instead initiates a process which must always be renewed, and followed down as far into the darkness as one can go. Blanchot writes: "The presence of poetry is still to come: it comes from beyond the future and does not stop coming when it is here" (Blanchot 2003, p. 239). The language of poetry lays bare, he says, not only a different temporal dimension, but the space of its own unfolding. And it comes further-more, with the additionally heightened paradox, that: "Nothing certain seems to appear" (ibid.); yet everything is changed. Everything has a different rhythm. While rhythm as we know, has the obvious capacity to transform time as in music, we can see now that rhythm in the hands of Hölderlin, Rilke, and Twombly, also has the preternatural capacity to totally bend, stretch, and alter space as well.

Sublime works of art are thus not destinations. Rather they are the provisionings of an impetus to engage in a further travelling onwards—and downwards. Like Hölderlin's caesura, *poiesis* first effects halting places, pauses, a metamorphosed space and time that disrupts and interchanges one journey, 'reality,' and itinerary for another. As presentations of loss, lack, and emptiness, these works of art convey a disquieting sense of vertigo, an absence of closure. The "experience of this absence," Heidegger writes, notwithstanding its lack, "is not nothing, but rather a liberation of man from... 'fallenness amidst beings'" (Heidegger in Wolin 1993, p. 108). It is freeing.

This language of the deep, to which we are turned over in the analytical journey and in sublime art, is, by definition, unknown to us; it is un-conscious, foreign, strange, and uncanny. It *is* 'otherness.' We are nevertheless fully responsible for it when it comes.

> We are drawn, by too strong a movement, into a space where truth lacks, where limits have disappeared, where we are delivered to the immeasurable. And yet it is there that we are required to maintain an even step, not to lose a sense of proportion and to seek a true language by going all the way down into the deep of error.
>
> (Blanchot 1982, p. 184)

When we go thus all the way down, we are plunged into Twombly's watery depths, and our feeling sinks with Rilke's, 'as if standing on fishes.' We allow ourselves to be immersed in this strange atmosphere and medium, unimaginably ancient while yet still of this moment, deeply connected, albeit in uncertain ways, with our "invincible centre."

In the space of this work, art moves along a gradient that follows the gravitational pull of nature downwards. Rather than "being the force of the beginning, the work becomes a thing beginning" (ibid., p. 206). It is a

> work where the very experience of a work—art, the communication of the origin as a beginning—is affirmed in a presence which is also a disappearance.
>
> (ibid.)

Into the work which is the expectation of the work, the artist gathers the impersonal attention that has the unique space of language or gesture as its medium, track or path.

> From that deep place where language, at its most basic, continually encounters the question of longing, Twombly produces a text that creates nothing, has no definitive or finished version, and consists only of its own genesis.
>
> (Leeman 2005, p. 163)

All of Twombly's art works could thus appear from this perspective to be drafts for a future project, studies, sketches, or designs for a work yet to come, yet to be birthed. Thinking with his hand and arm, this master of *disegno* creates grand tableaux for the sweeping arcs of history and nature to unfold and become transformed; his pieces are laboratories for *physis* and *psyche*. Risking everything on the materials of his craft, Twombly forges on ever deeper into matter, into history and into nature, letting Orpheus sing and speak in paint. His art seeks to explore, probe, and continue the patterns and designs of nature *herself*, by descending to the level of nature and natural bodies. Twombly's art performs the subject matters of his soul as they are executed by his body.

Rilke, in his touching poem, "To Hölderlin" (1914), once again describes the creative journey as a descent:

> We are not permitted to linger, even with what is most
> intimate. From images that are full, the spirit
> plunges on to others that suddenly must be filled;
> there are no lakes till eternity. Here,
> falling is best. To fall from the mastered emotion
> into the guessed-at, and onward.
>
> (Rilke 1984, p. 141)

For Rilke, Hölderlin and Twombly, this 'onward' is finally not about the artist, his life or concerns; it is not personal; it is a movement and thrust *outward*, into nature, into matter, and into the world that stands outside the creative process. "Seeing...is the means given me for being absent from myself, for being present from within at the fission of Being" (Merleau-Ponty 1993, p. 146). One abandons one's self in order to become immersed in the pure play of the deep. Heidegger writes that:

> When Hölderlin poetizes the essence of the poet, he poetizes relations that do not have their ground in the "subjectivity" of human beings. These relations have their own essential prevailing and flowing.
>
> (Heidegger 1996, p. 165)

The artist, Blanchot says,

> the "poet," concerned for his art and in search of its origins—is he
> for whom there exists not even one world. For there exists for him
> only the outside, the glistening flow of the eternal outside.
>
> (Blanchot 1982, p. 83)

As we come now finally to this subject matter of art, we also arrive at our heart of the matter, this matter of space, the true matter, material and 'materia' of the subject, our *alma mater*: the soul. The singular American artist, Joseph Cornell, in a collaged work of his from 1963, quotes Hölderlin: "Home, poor heart, you cannot rediscover if the dream alone does not suffice." We are indeed such stuff as dreams are made of. How to put down roots into this soul ground, the oneiric world, our support, our earth, the alchemists' *terra nostra*, to establish it as the sole/soul reality, the space where soul lives? This soul which we have always imagined to be inside of us, in us, however, is in fact, outside of us, in the world, in the world around us, bristling and sparkling with soul, dripping, filthy, muddy, luminescent, and breathing with soul. It *is* in all of nature. When we fall back into this ordinary, amazingly transfigured world with Orpheus, we see that the loss and disappearance of his belovéd is as much a part of *poiesis* and the working process, as it is the inevitable end of the art work itself. It is of the essence of the work that Orpheus sees Eurydice's 'otherness,' her death, that she is of the 'other world'; she is not of his world, and that there *is* only this world, this reality, not different worlds, the 'not even one world' as Blanchot says. There is just this space where soul and matter are continuously interpenetrating each other.

Appearing as he does in the artwork of Cy Twombly, Orpheus as the figure of the artist, the art form itself, whether painting, poetry, song, or sculpture, and the artistic product, performs his own appearances and disappearances. As Rilke says: "He comes and goes" (Rilke 1942, p.25). Through the metonymic power of his name alone, just the name ORPHEUS itself, he enters the world, through its enunciation. He appears *in* and through the word. He is the bringer of the word, the *logos*, the language, poetry and rhythms of life. He *is* song as the bridge flung out to other worlds. As the angel announces the appearance and conception of the divine child in the Annunciation of the Virgin Mary, Orpheus himself is allowed to manifest through the speaking of Twombly's fragmentary Thracian artworks and their specific plastic forms and arcane languages. The words, language itself, is procreative, seminal, inseminating. The Holy Ghost manifests and impregnates through *logos*, the Word, and performs the epiphany of 'speaking in tongues,' all language blazing with meaning. As we write, utter and portray his name, he is reborn anew, in this thing and in that. And he inevitably gets torn apart as well, destroyed, time and again, his body rent, pulverized, crucified and scattered. So, *we* have to get it right this time, that he is also *not* this and *not* that. He knew that this would happen, from his own beginnings. He came into the world to sing for a time, and then he is dismembered, dissolved, disintegrated, perhaps, according to Orphic doctrine at least, so that he might come yet again, at another time, although some part of him always stays and remains with us, resonating, singing here still. It is "only song over the land/(that) hallows and celebrates" (ibid., p. 53).

Besides appearing as his name, through his attributes, stories, and images, he also appears in the subject matter, mood, and tone of his materials, of his songs, paintings, poems, and languages. His appearances and disappearances, losses, absences, transience, melancholy, joys, and delights, all become manifest in Twombly's *way* of working, his actual methods and means of applying paint, pencil, brushes, fingers and materials to surfaces and forms. His way of handling paint is alternately elegiac, wistful, lyrical, dreamy, ruminative, and meditative, and fierce, furious, angry, violent, forceful, and destructive. A nominalist at heart, Twombly allows Orpheus to appear *in* the paint, to sing with desire in the erotic strokes, spiritual slashes, and sexually swooping folds of furling color. Eurydice too beseeches us through the splendid swirls and whorls of heart-rendingly beautiful blushes and shades, diaphanous mists, streakings, striations, and tender gradations limned out by the artist's deeply soulful feelings of brush, arms and hands—his whole body rhythmically swaying in tune with the materials—to acknowledge and embrace her infinite and unknowable depths.

His *way* of working thus expresses itself in *what* is presented, and appears, always there, on the surface. His method and materials *are* the message, and they sing the same song. His oneness with both methods and materials becomes, and *is*, the meaning of his work. It is that part of his art which lingers on, in, and around us, and continues to vibrate in the soul and to *sound*. In a wonderful photograph of Twombly taken in his Rome studio in 1953 by Robert Rauschenberg, the artist sits by the open window, meditatively plucking on an archaic, obviously hand-crafted, ancient-looking tortoise shell-like lyre instrument, the figure of Orpheus himself, musing on an open-ended present and a futurity yet to come (Twombly 2000, p. 165). Blanchot's title for a collection of his essays echoes this thought of Twombly's expression and the Orphic 'long view': *The Book To Come* (1959/2003). The art work of Orpheus in whatever form it appears is yet to come. And once it arrives, it does not stop coming.

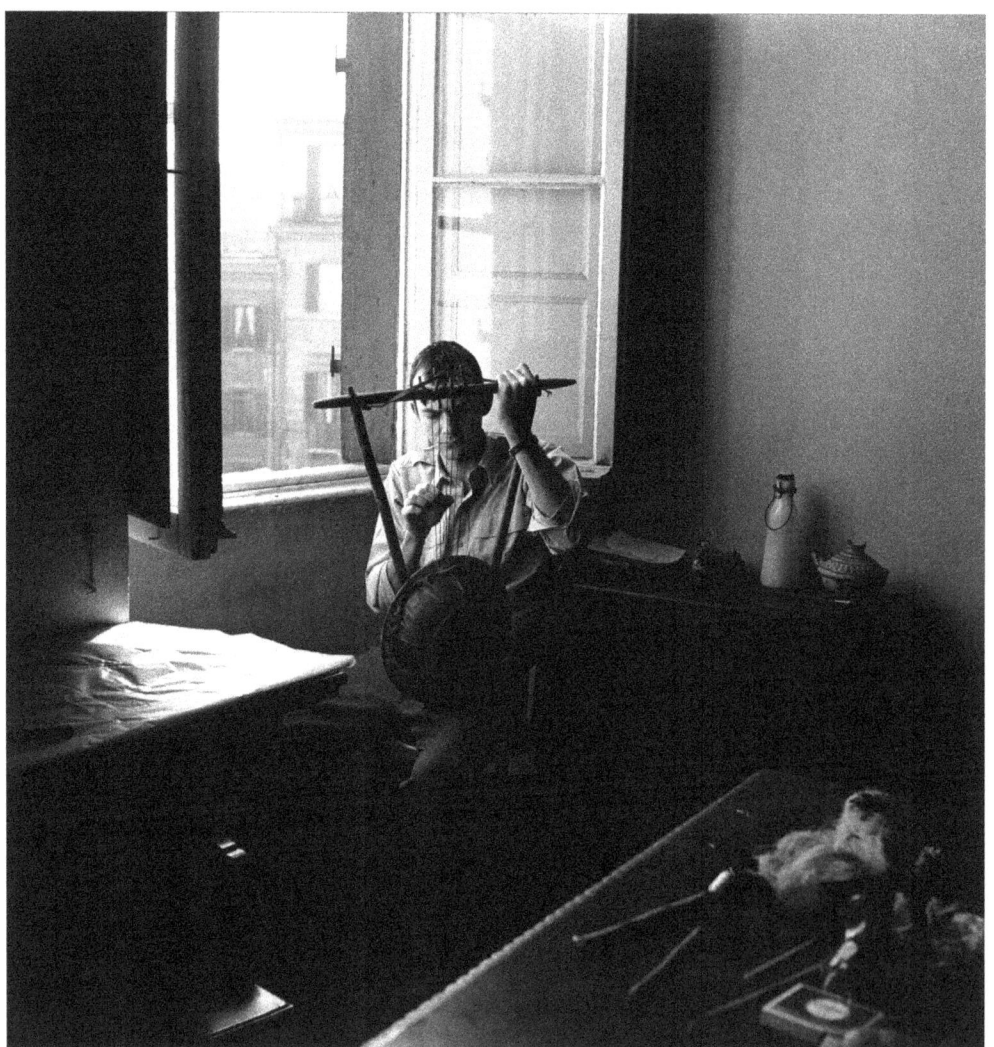

12.   Robert Rauschenberg
Untitled [Cy with Musical Instrument, Rome], 1953
Contact print
2 ¼ x 2 ¼ inches (5.7 x 5.7 cm)
©Robert Rauschenberg Foundation

The ultimate emptiness of Twombly's canvases reveals a hand that does not cling or grasp. His artist's palms at the end are upturned, giving away whatever they held, disseminating the art work. He lets his markings go freely forth into the open: hearts, buttocks and breasts, dots, crosses and Roman numerals, and they arrange and array themselves on the surfaces and supports of his canvases. Orpheus supplies the music, rhythm, poetry, and song. Twombly stops working and finishes a piece when it seems that the work is 'enough.'

Lastly, in this ongoing rush and body of *poiesis*, Orpheus the artist appears as the praise singer, the one who plays and sings to the birds, trees and stones, lions and stars, to the clouds, rocks, hills and fishes. He moves them all with his song. He knows their stories, speech and inner rhythms. He penetrates to the center of nature's most ancient memories. Through his mother, Kalliope, the Muse of music, one of the nine daughters born to the great goddess Mnemosyne, Mother Memory herself, he recalls only the most primal tunes and melodies of this earth, this world we are generously granted to share, in all its particulars, particles, and broken pieces. Yet he always sings the whole of it, not the parts. He re-members all of the scattered fragments with his song. The seven strings of his lyre correspond to the seven notes of the musical scale, the seven colors of the rainbow, and to the seven heavenly spheres, and his music hymns the movements of the planets and facilitates their orbits. He gives voice to all the correspondences and connections, to the *invisible* rhythmical bonds and threads, to the ratios, harmonies and intervals, to the silences and empty between-spaces that link it all together, indivisibly relating the moons, minerals, and mosses, to the bodies, muscles, and blood running, flowing and streaming through us.

Through the lyre, Orpheus both explores and hymns mother nature, lyrically spinning and weaving, rearranging, and furthering *her* elements, reconfiguring *her* guises. He operates, plays and performs her meanings in song. His voice reaches out as a vibration audible to *psyche,* to the soul, to this soul which is everywhere, in each and every thing, waiting, desiring to be caressed, aroused, and wakened into the crashing of sunlight, into the over-whelming and clarifying din of the cosmos, to come in glory into the clanging roar of silence, language, and rhythm which reverberates in harmony with the earth's deep mystery and molten core.

IV

Leaving Traces and Making Marks

As we further explore Cy Twombly's art work into the depths of soul, we now arrive at the one major figure guiding, directing, and organizing the propulsive creative output of his lengthy career—the powerful presence and overriding eminence of Orpheus as we have just seen him notwithstanding—and that is, the ancient Greek god of wine, madness, and ecstasy, Dionysos, or as the artist often prefers to call him, Bacchus. Dionysos, Bacchus, the venerable benefactor of alterity, intoxication and procreative passion has appeared to consistently inform the thematic, stylistic, and energetic sensibilities of Twombly's most basic mark-making impulses since his very beginnings.

Even in his earliest works, Twombly has clearly evinced an urge to return to the fundamentals of his own physical and bodily experience. His art has always been seamlessly driven by a fierce desire to get back to basics, to elementals, to origins and beginnings. We can discern in the sheer intensity of his lines and marks themselves, in how they are applied, a burning need to uncover a primal and originary layer of experience, first and foremost *within himself*, through however, and fortunately for us, the events and processes of *poiesis,* a creative, externalizing process. The line, he himself says, "is an involvement in essence (no matter how private) into a synthesis of feeling, intellect, etc., occurring without separation in the impulse of action" (Twombly 2013a, p. 113). His art 'work,' his production, is in a sense, the residue or remains of his research into the innermost nature of experiencing, thinking, and seeing. It is also the medium he uses to explore 'other' realities within himself, to journey to altered realms. Time and again we discern in the work how he is urged toward more and more primitive levels of expression, only in order to lay bare in as unmediated way as possible his own directly intuited instinctual sources. The art work itself reflects a compulsive drive towards self-transformation, overcoming, and transcendence. Art-making is the chosen medium, practice, and process for Twombly's own psychic renewal and rejuvenation.

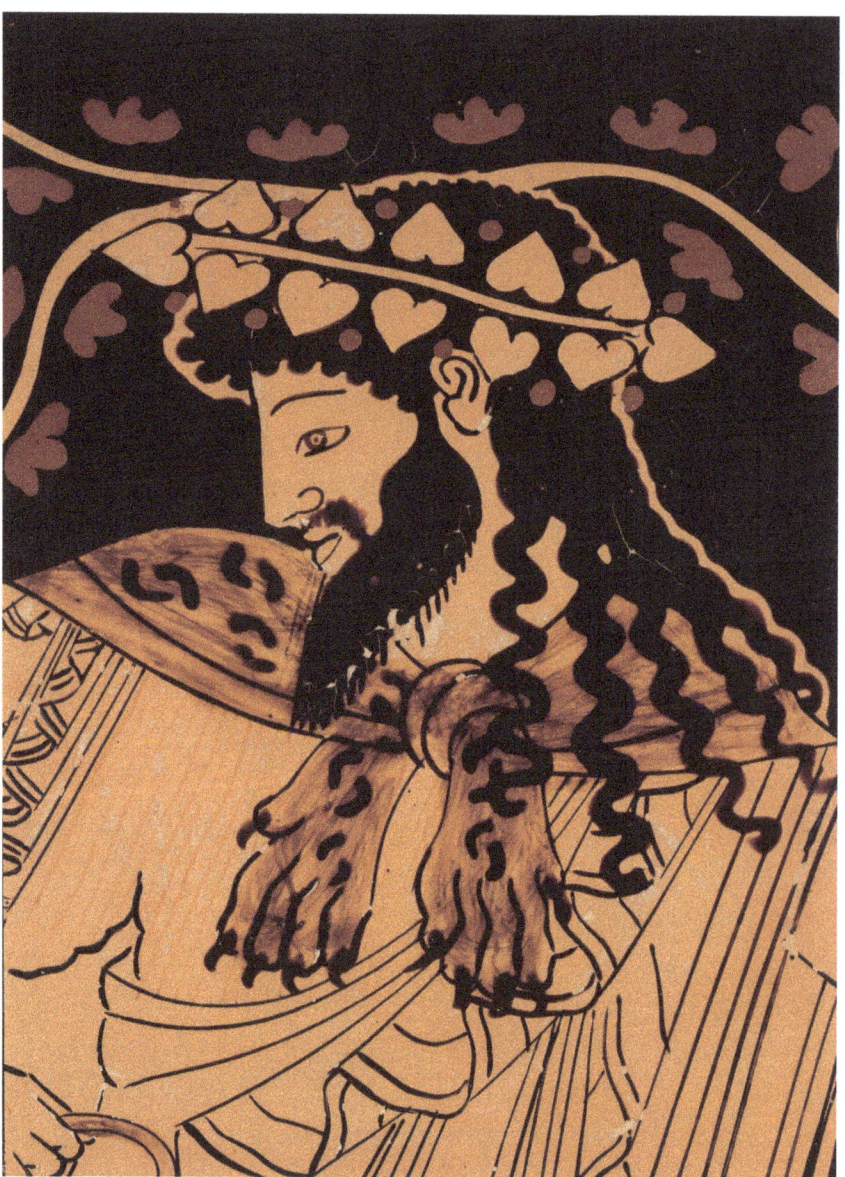

13. *Dionysos in Ecstasy*, detail, c. 490 B.C., Kleophrades.

The impetus for his mark-making has always seemed to further derive from his efforts to evade and avoid the snares and traps of his ordinary conscious mind, with its intellect, thoughts, and ideas, in order the better to allow more urgent bodily responses to counsel, and perhaps more wisely, lead his head, heart, and hand. Fascinated and impelled by essentials, essences and the bare bones of things, his own aesthetic drive aims at uncovering, excavating, un-working and revealing further layers of the unknown, penetrating more and more deeply into the realms of the 'other.' His journey is one of constant and unremitting discovering and a re-membering of distant origins. Mark-making is his epistemological method.

In a magnificently meandering monograph on the god Dionysos, the classical mythologist Karl Kerenyi begins his lengthy tome by circumambulating the one particular aspect or epithet of this god that gives his study its subtitle: 'archetypal image of indestructible life' (Kerenyi 1976). Dionysos *Zöe*, the god of 'infinite life,' in Kerenyi's view, contains just within his name alone, an entire way of living, and a way of looking at the world that the Greeks cultivated for the discovery of truths that were previously unknown to them. In the preface, he carefully distinguishes between the Greek word *bios*, as particular, individual, characterized life, which has a finite end, and the more universal *zöe*, the primal energetic force which throbs and pulses in every living thing and courses throughout all of nature and phenomenal existence.

This suprasensible life which we only dimly and occasionally apprehend at particularly enhanced moments of experience, lies at the root of Twombly's artistic impulse. The unquenchable vitality of Dionysos *Zöe* resounds and manifests itself in the forceful dynamisms and rhythms of his painterly gestures and distinctly manual moves. Twombly enacts the spontaneous portrayal of bodily experience on the surfaces of his works. As viewers, we can recapitulate his corporeal activities within our own bodies, re-staging his performative processes within ourselves. Twombly's work embodies the multilayered histories and tracings of its own mark-making processes. His canvases contain a pictorial space, a record and a site for the strewn markings and residues of his own drifting corporeal passages through time. He approaches his canvases as sites for acting, not representing. The works themselves, literally and visually, often drift towards the right and upwards, that is, towards consciousness and the corner of the canvas that through a 'classical' Jungian interpretive perspective symbolizes 'the father,' the masculine; and the multitude of marks, incidents and accidents they carry along and bear are transcriptions of a temporality and transcience, passing us by as we gaze. His entire *oeuvre* can be read in this sense, as a *memento mori*, reminding us that we too are in transit, and that we ultimately *are* and endure only as our actions.

When we view his work, we must typically stand outside of our usual lives in order to at least temporarily inhabit a differently constellated kind of psychic space created by these unique configurations of markings, colors, and forms. First of all, they are unusual, often difficult to initially enter into, fragmented and disconcerting, jarring, sometimes even almost overwrought in a way. The presentness of his work, especially the Dionysian pieces, however, engages us in a direct bodily process of identifying with the *dromenon*, the physical movements and behaviors, or the particular tragic dramatic actions on display right there before us, that is, the entire spectacle being played and *acted* out on the canvas, but, and this is the catch, only so that this sensate viewing may completely rupture and disconnect us from the multiply accumulating acts of perceiving, thinking, and experiencing we may be ordinarily having, or, that the artist himself was possibly having *before* and *while* he was creating these pieces. The works are thoughts and feelings transformed, by, in, and during *poiesis*. This dis-play of artistic impulse is not there to be imitated or mimicked, or conceptually understood, explained, or even interpreted, for that matter. At their best, his work, like tragic drama itself, acts *upon* us, and transports us to a totally *other* place, a space of experiencing which is impersonal, unique, and transcendent. "Art," Artaud says, "is not the imitation of life, but life is the imitation of a transcendental principle which art puts us into communication with once again" (In Derrida 1978, p. 234).

Or, perhaps these tremors and shocks of discontinuity emanating from Twombly's pieces of art may be unintended by the artist. These extreme disjunctions from the everyday, whatever their source, seem nevertheless to frequently be the net cumulative effect of deeply looking at, and seeing the many built-up layers and innumerable incidents of his mark-making processes. His pieces thus activate an actual deconstruction of us, his viewers, along with our expectations and assumptions—about 'art' in general, as well as about looking, perceiving, feeling, and experiencing. His work prompts a heightened germinative reverie which flings us into the openness of *other* worlds. It reveals a kind of pre-thinking, the thinking of matter and 'things,' as well as a fantasizing and a revealing of alternative modalities of being-in-the-world, and being-with-the-world.

The contemporary artist Per Kirkeby writes: "The world is material. Material thinks in material" (Kirkeby 2012, p. 10). Twombly's works *act* upon us and can literally make us *substantially* different, and change our minds, impinging upon the very materiality of the embodied soul itself.

Like many artists of his age and generation, Twombly, at the beginnings of his creative career felt the need to engage in this search for the 'other' far from the familiar comforts of 'home' and his native American shores. Pursuing this desire for the alien, foreign, and strange, however *he* then conceived of his urge to travel, already having travelled in the American south and to Cuba, he set out in 1952 with his friend Robert Rauschenberg on their first trip abroad together, to Europe and North Africa. Debarking in Palermo, Sicily, and then journeying around Italy, they eventually left Rome for North Africa and spent the winter of 1952-3 in Morocco. Upon their return to Europe, they had a joint art exhibit in Florence where Twombly showed a group of wall hangings and tapestries whose designs and patterns were clearly influenced by the archaic folk art he had seen during his explorations in Morocco and Tangier. Later that same year and once back in the United States, Twombly and Rauschenberg were invited to have yet another joint show in New York. On this occasion, Twombly exhibited paintings based upon sketches which he had drawn at the ethnographic museum in Rome, titling many of the pieces after North African villages he had actually seen, like "Volubilis" (1953), "Quarzazat" (1953) and "Tiznit" (1953). He was also simultaneously pursuing and exhibiting his interests and budding collection of Central African art, masks, ritual objects, and artifacts, some of which were shown in these early exhibits along with his own work.

These still stark and strong pictographs from the early '50s indelibly highlight his precocious fascination with what he himself called even back then, "primordial motifs," or "the primitive, the ritual and fetish elements" which were emotionally gripping him (Leeman 2005, pp. 14-15); and they clearly delineate the formative power of his first major encounter with ancient, pre-literate, and indigenous tribal cultures. During this period, he filled notebooks with pencil drawings. One also sees and senses the marks made by his own hands at that time as if he had scratched into, bit, and gouged the surfaces, interacting with and imbuing the works with his own physical powers or 'mana.' The strongly drawn forms, etched and incised lines and loose calligraphic scrawls, combining with bold symbolist glyphs, all done in earthy tones of black, white, brown, and yellowish house paints, all together definitely present an aura of a ritualistic or fetishistic sign system of indecipherable though portentous meanings. Repetitive, often symmetrical patterns of totemic forms move rhythmically across the bounded surfaces of the paintings, like segments of an ongoing, pictorially-represented shamanic tribal discourse-in-progress. The rough-hewn intensities of the images already reveal him grappling with the deeper symbolic currents of non-Western visual languages, as well as with the purely human impulse to make marks. Fascinated by the magical, sexual, and mysterious powers of art to conjure up alternative visceral and spiritual realities, Twombly intuited that these archaic and animistic tendencies found in most pre-industrialized cultures allowed for a communion with the soul values inherently residing in nature itself, in materials, in things, in places, and in the world at large. And these numinous signs inhabiting exteriority from early on, seemed already to be speaking, sometimes cryptically though often eloquently, directly and encouragingly, to him.

As Walter Benjamin saw in the prose writings and poetry of Charles Baudelaire the 'shock of intimacy' evoked in and by the 'auratic gaze,' so Twombly was already viewing the world as a co-respondent: that is, as looking back at him. From the first, it seems to have been a reciprocal gaze. In the sonnet, *Correspondances*, Baudelaire writes:

> Nature is a temple of living pillars
> where often words emerge, confused and dim;
> and man goes through this forest, with familiar
> eyes of symbols always watching him.

> (In Santner 1990, p. 123)

The rapprochement the young artist felt from the beginning with these ancient, pre-literate cultures, was the deep experience of the blood and soul that he immediately sensed saturated, imbued, and permeated these people, places, artifacts, and objects of past civilizations. Always implicated bodily as a *partici-pant* in the visible world of his residences and travels, he accurately intuited that the multilayered textures and *topoi*, the very spaces of Europe and North Africa opened him up to a reciprocal rapture and 'delirium' of both pure seeing, and in turn, being seen, lain exposed to the genesis and miracle of vision itself. Seeing became his foundation and platform, the originary, quintessential creative act, a genesis. Through vision he was becoming born, re-born, and turned inside out.

Twombly was now fully embarked upon his journey, both within and without, to the roots of human nature. Experiences of 'otherness,' geographical distances, the many ancient and disappearing worlds of the Mediterranean, and his passion for travelling in general, were to remain for him throughout his life veritable techniques of anamnesis, a re-collecting of origins that was at once intensely "intimate and personal as much as historical and collective" (Michaud 2004, p. 35).

What Twombly also appears to have had deeply inscribed within himself during these earliest forays abroad, where he could freely breathe and imbibe the sights, sounds, and smells of long-historied societies and wholly pantheistic civilizations, was the irreducible force and primordial significance of *the line*, the singular, discrete gestural mark, erupting from within and made simply by the instinctual burst and sudden stroke and sweep of hand and arm. The graphic impulse to describe sensation, intensity, and feeling through one unique movement, became the foundation and building block for the entire evolution of his complex scriptural language, which from the beginning, developed and came to include its own original vocabulary, logic, grammar, phonetics, and syntax of painterly signs. Like poetry, lines for him became a dance of both semiotics and semantics, sense and sound converging through movement.

Drawn for over half a century to the use of simple lead pencils, graffiti-like scrawls, scribbles, squiggles, and doodles, often dug into paint, Twombly has always historicized his lines. He writes in his own "Untitled" article originally published in the Italian journal, *L'Esperienza moderna*, in 1957: "Each line is now the actual experience with its own innate history" (In Leeman 2005, p. 54). The line "does not illustrate," he says further, "it is the sensation of its own realization" (Twombly 2013a, p. 113). Harald Szeemann wrote in 1987, that "for Twombly the first thing is the line" (In Twombly 2014, p. 246). Twombly describes his paintings also, as something "instinctive." "Not as if," he says, you were painting an object or special things, but it's like coming through the nervous system. It's like a nervous system. It's not described, it's happening. The feeling is going on with the task... It's more like I'm having an experience than making a picture... it's the instinct and the motion and the whole all together.

(In Sylvester 2001, pp. 179-180)

Simon Schama writes that "Twombly's energies are all about local animation; the unpredictability of the wayward line" (Schama in Twombly 2014d, p. 12).

Twombly told David Sylvester in 2000:

The line is the feeling, from a soft thing, a dreamy thing, to something hard, something arid, something lonely, something ending, something beginning. It's like I'm experiencing something frightening. I'm experiencing the thing and I have to be at that state because I'm also going.

(In Sylvester 2001, p. 179)

By way of contrasting inspirations of 'otherness,' it is interesting to note that another much earlier, twentieth century master and pioneer of abstraction was also formatively and irrevocably influenced by a youthful trip to North Africa. Although what he primarily brought back to his native Europe from his exotic travels in Tunisia, turned out to be vastly different from what Twombly, nearly a half century later, derived from his confrontation with these similarly antique, alien and non-Christian worlds. In 1914, the Swiss artist, Paul Klee, transcribed in his diary the singular experience that became absolutely primary to him for the rest of his life: the shocking awareness of pure color.

Color possesses me. I don't have to pursue it. It will possess me always, I know it. That is the meaning of this happy hour: Color and I are one. I am a painter.

(Klee 1964, p. 297)

This exultant revelation transformed his perceptual world and lasted for another 35 incredibly productive years, until he applied his last daub of magically scintillating paint just before his untimely death on June 29, 1940.

From Klee's experiences of the festivities and sheer foreignness of Tunisia came the awareness of color itself, its irreducible and super-natural reality. For Twombly, also travelling in North Africa, came, however, first the line, then the light, and then white itself, the absence or rather, presence, of all color. In his parallel though altogether differently mined vein, Twombly writes of his own earth-shattering and revelatory encounters with the Arab world while journeying in North Africa, by underscoring in his sketch book: "CHALK WHITE" (Twombly 2008, p. 59).

Even before North Africa, in 1951, Charles Olson, the poet and dean of Black Mountain College where Twombly attended, wrote of him: "There came a man who dealt with whiteness. And with space. He was an American" (Olson in Del Roscio 2002, p. 9). By then Twombly had already at that point been making sculptures for three years which he was covering exclusively with white house paint, which he called his 'marble.'

White, the primal color of both life and death, Twombly grasped from early on, contains within itself an inherent dichotomy, a doubleness, like the psyche, both a conscious and an un-conscious aspect. It is split, as our psychology casts its own shadow, broken off from itself, as we *are* and enact the images projected by our deeper selves. "The reality of whiteness," Twombly begins his "Untitled" piece by writing, "may exist in the duality of sensation (as the multiple anxiety of desire and fear)" (Twombly 2013a, p. 112).

We may wish to sully or deface the white surfaces, the page or paper, to add something to it, an impurity, a mark, a thought, and we are also at the same time afraid and inhibited to do so, to act, to put our selves 'out there,' into and onto that blank void. "One must desire the ultimate essence even if it is 'contaminated'", he says (ibid.). The desire to penetrate to the essences of things overrides the artist's fears. He takes the plunge; he is always risking and putting everything on *the line*. And for Twombly, lines do trace the *essences* of things. They are the invisible linings that are *within* the visible. To violate the pristine surface and support of the canvas with a line, not only "sets in motion a certain disequilibrium within the space of a surface," but it also traces "a metaphysics of space" (Johnson in Merleau-Ponty 1993, p. 41).

"Whiteness," Twombly says, "can be the classic state of the intellect, or a neo-romantic area of remembrance—or as the symbolic whiteness of Mallarmé" (Twombly 2013a, p. 112). Whether to fill the emptiness or not, nevertheless remains for Twombly a fundamental and creative ambivalence, and yet the whiteness itself always persists, as he admits, "as the landscape of my actions" (ibid.). Whiteness and silence are never ending. The finite line is imposed upon the infinite whiteness of space. It is the stab into the *tabula rasa*. It is the heroic human stain upon 'being' itself.

While on his journey in Morocco, Twombly also participated in his first archaeological dig at a Roman bath near Tangier which clearly brought home to him the multi-levelled and stratified nature of civilization, and perhaps of the human psyche itself, as well as of what was to be his own working creative process. He seemed to immediately grasp in an existential sense, the experientially layering effects of time and duration, as well as the artistic expression of it through necessarily overlapping material applications, and in multiple mediums and in impasto which was to become an integral aspect of his own unique art-making style, repeatedly cycling through creating and destroying, making and un-making.

"In ancient Egypt," which also later became very important for Twombly as he visited the revered Pharaonic sites numerous times, "white was considered sacred due to its lack of color, and symbolized omnipotence and purity. The name of the holy city of Memphis means 'white walls'" (Saville 2014, p. 63).

The shock of whiteness, ancient fading plaster surfaces, the expanses of desert, the unrelenting African sun, all seemingly combine to sear his consciousness back into the primal whiteness of birth and death, experiences at the limits, the first blinding light of an infant's life, the nurturing breast milk, and the mute pallor of a marble tomb. In Twombly's endless succession of white canvases, the bright whiteness of the linen supports become like surfaces of skin, funereal shrouds, and cinema screens, boundaries, limits to be transgressed. This bright whiteness becomes the cinematically empty surface and blank depth out of which Twombly's works emerge, and into which he pours his marks and records intensities of feeling. Like the movie 'screen' itself, or the background psychical screen upon which our dreams, our inner nocturnal movies are projected, Twombly sees the milky white profundity as an ever-replenishing support and surface to both destroy *and* feed upon. He defaces, erases, gouges and scratches that all-accepting whiteness. He also symbolically defecates and ejaculates upon it. Those celluloid, psychic and virginal surfaces are for him in their emptiness, the foundational milky whiteness of a pure, fecund and fertile void, a mystical and possibly maternal nothingness/fullness which both accepts everything he has to offer, and gives birth itself out of its own boundless and nurturing depths to his visionary patterns. It is as if the images arise, at least at first, *out* of the supports, emerging out of the emptiness. Twombly would sometimes just sit and stare, looking at a canvas for hours, days or weeks, before, in a mad fury, he would begin making his marks. His supports become a veritable womb, an incubating source and matrix of an ever-replenishing creativity, the pure white surface already containing everything, and yet at the same time, soliciting his contemplative desire.

After this formative time in North Africa, Twombly's palette for many decades to come was quite dramatically to evoke "the brightness of Mediterranean sun through echoes of crumbling chalk, bleached bone, and eroded lime" (Varnedoe in Twombly 1994c, p. 19). "The Mediterranean," Twombly says, "is always just white, white, white" (Twombly 2008, p. 71; Sylvester 2001, p. 175). In his very first, great, long, actual series of paintings, which was to become a prototypical way for him to work, "Poems to the Sea," 24 small pieces on paper made in Sperlonga in July of 1959, he used whitish and beige house paints, pencil and wax crayon in an evocative meditational and tonal ode upon a mind's wandering and thinking over an undulating white sea, a Tyrrhenian sea gently washed over with creamy white paint, numerals, and gently rolling waves of scribbles.

His work becomes in the ensuing years essentially an ongoing dialogue and relational discourse with the basic materiality of the white surfaces upon which he lays his grounds and then makes his marks. It is a continuous conversation, a tête-á-tête, and sometimes dispute, between lovers. The white and off-white grounds of the canvas or paper become for him the expansive empyrean fields out of which arise and are birthed the marks, slashes, lacerations, and scars which will score his surfaces for the next 60 years of his career. Spreading across all of his works for decades to come, the many gradations and shades of whiteness appear as the grounds of non-being onto which he will array the bright colors and indelible sensations of the life of nature and the world. Like the natural oscillation of sounds and silence, Twombly's palette provides the music and melody that elicits and seduces rhythmical performances and presences out of a yawning emptiness and stillness. He "adheres to the principle of *white*," Tacita Dean writes:

in order that his painting can reside in a warmer place, where the
white is the white of a gleaming Acropolis in the midday sun and
of a long bleached past so palpably beyond our collective reach
that it makes us desire it more.

(Dean in Twombly 2008, p. 40)

His works ache towards whiteness.

Collaborating as a friend, fellow student, and colleague with Twombly
both at Black Mountain College in North Carolina and then later in New
York City during these same 1950s, John Cage wrote: "For it is the space and
emptiness that is finally urgently necessary at this point of the history" (In
Twombly 2009a, p. 31). Twombly, like Cage and others of his generation,
with this need for 'space and emptiness,' was responding to an historical
imperative, the 'angel' of his time, and the need to return to elementals and
origins. After the horrors of World War II, they were also reacting to the
endgame of European technology and science, and seeking older, earthier,
and more rooted, primordial modes of relating to self, society, and nature.
Between Auschwitz and Hiroshima, the humanistic vision, and with it the
image of the human figure itself, had become irrevocably distorted, tortured,
and destroyed beyond recognition, so that Twombly and many of his peers
sought out a more universally valid ground for establishing and laying a
renewed foundation for art-making, beginning with the beginnings. It was to
become a new language, both acknowledging and liberating itself from the
strictures of the past. Modernism for these avant-garde artists had already
run its course, crumbled, and lay in ruins. Out of Europe's smoldering ashes
were slowly emerging the bolder, more violently original forays of quintessentially expressive and experimental paths of painting, led by the more
famous, heroically American brand of abstract expressionism of DeKooning,
Pollack, Kline, Mitchell, and numerous others, as well as the more idiosyncratic
directions of Twombly, Rauschenberg, Johns, Motherwell, Rothko, Louis,
Newman, and Still.

Referring to Twombly's wildly gestural and abstract chalkboard 'panoramas'
of the early and mid-'50s, one critic notes that they present a

"narration of indeterminacy," in which the simultaneity of competing
views is raised to the status of a principle of formation. The white

amounts to the matrix on which the process of signification both arises and collapses.

(Hochdörfer 2009, p. 31)

From the time of the pictographs on, the single constant in Twombly's two-dimensional work and also on most of his sculptures, is that the blank grounds of his surfaces, whether in all conceivable shades of white, beige, gray, or even black, or as in much later years, yellow, and toward the end of his life, green, all become for him a primal screen, an oneiric plane, which acts as a field, site and witness, testifying to the appearances in a multitude of forms of the god Dionysos. Dionysos *dunamis* is the god, as we shall see in detail, of palpitating heart, boiling blood, frothing wine, shooting semen, and erectile phallus, who presents and enacts himself on the rolling fields of the artist's canvases as the autonomous, independent mark, a spontaneous upsurge of primitive gestural intensity. This autochthonous vitality, *dunamis*, which Aristotle describes as "the capacity that one possesses in oneself" (In Detienne 1989, p. 61), is the potency and potentiality which springs from the primal humors and living saps of the human body, its original and enlivening fluids. Aristotle in his *Metaphysics*, calls *dunamis* a "vital liquid," both humor and sap, and "a source of movement and change" (ibid.). It arises unbidden from the most basic and instinctual layers of our body's liquidities. Aristotle, in discussing this fundamental physical law and primary impetus of development, compares the human embryo growing in the womb to the similar way that all plants emerge from the fluid, germinating powers within the earth. This humid principle, he says, which is responsible for increase in growth in humans, animals, plants, and in all of nature, when heated by the sun, exuberantly springs up and bursts forth.

These are the same archetypal dynamisms and features behind Twombly's lines, gestures, scratches, squiggles, smears, scrawls, and slashes. The motive and motion of mark-making is for him its own end. It forcefully asserts pure existence and presence. The lines and marks declaim: 'I am here.' *Some thing* exists. Some *thing* appears, out of nothing, *ex nihilo*. It is the same basic urge and drive that Twombly saw in the earliest cave dwellers of Lascaux, Montignac, and Rouffignac, emblazoning their palm prints, shaggy bison, antlered reindeer and lions upon these rough, inaccessible stone walls deep in the earth. Representing and testifying to the mysteries of life and non-life, these archaic images still bear witness to the powers of art's endurance beyond death. The 35,000-year-old images *remain*. They still exist. From the dawnings of prehistory onward, 'art' becomes *the* creative response to the shocking discovery of mortality and the irreversible material reality of death; the attempt to differentiate between organic and inorganic life. Making art is both the spontaneous *and* ritualized response to the experiences of living and dying. Representation itself institutes and affirms a deep magical bond with the world of nature, a unifying and participatory mystical identification with modalities of presenting and enacting existence both before and beyond life.

Besides frequently expressing his deep appreciation for prehistoric cave art, Twombly also borrowed numerous motifs he found there, and further, he saw in those darkened recesses and grottoes that in those places, some *thing* comes into being, some thing appears and emerges into presence, and presentness, and basically that: *some thing happens*. Through drawing these lines and making these strenuous efforts to present sheer manifest existence, *some thing will have happened*. Some *one* was here as witness, leaving a mark and asserting an ineffable, fleeting and incommensurable presence and affirmative testament to life's will in the face and facticity of our unthinkable non-being. This is the pure, basic, creative *act*.

From very early on in his work, from the "Panorama" series of 1955, white chalk scrawled freely over black grounds, we can see

> a form that paradigmatically inheres across the oeuvre and that is present discursively: the dissolution of semantics and everything conceptual. Metabolically recurring, the absoluteness of the action was the basic element of the entire work.
>
> (Bastian in Twombly 2014b, p. 27)

Twombly was indeed always returning to the primordial roots of creation in the ensouled material body in action, in making things.

"One is a reflection of meaning," Twombly writes. "So that the action must continually bear out the realization of existence. Therefore, the act is the primary sensation." He continues:

In painting it is the forming of the image; the compulsive action of becoming; the direct and indirect pressures brought to a climax in the acute act of forming.

(Twombly 2013a, p. 113)

In the very first images he ever created specifically referring to this god of dynamisms and assertive movements, Dionysos/Bacchus, lord of urgent epiphanies, Twombly did a series of drawings at the end of 1963, all of which contain the name 'Dionysos', either as their actual title, or written onto the paper as a kind of label. Arriving as the emblematic culmination of perhaps between 30 to 60 drawings of spurting, leaping, flying, slashing phallic ejaculations, gesturally and wildly swiped with pencil or crayon from the lower left to the upper right hand corner of the horizontally formatted sheets, the first mention of the name 'Dionysus' appears in the drawing, "Untitled (Study of Painting)", Rome 1963, which is a virtual diagrammatic blueprint for several series' of paintings which he went on to do later that year, including "Venere Franchetti" (1963) and the very important series, "Discourse on Commodus" (1963). Besides bringing the name 'Dionysus' in this piece together with the name 'Actaeon,' the god's own first cousin and alter ego who suffers dismemberment and death at the jaws and teeth of his own hunting dogs for having inadvertently looked at Artemis (Diana) when she is bathing, he also includes the name of the goddess 'Venus' on the sheet as a summation of the dozens of paintings and drawings he was also doing of images of her, the love goddess, her birth out of the sea from a severed phallus, her numerous copulations, and both her nurturing *and* potentially destructive and erotically passionate desires. Twombly views and images her activating Venusian libido analogously to the impulsive dynamics of Dionysos, as also self-generated, spontaneous, volcanically powerful and instinctually autonomous, overcoming everything in its path, terrifying, amazing, and wonderful.

Steeped in Ovid's *Metamorphoses* at this time, and portraying and titling works as what he called, 'deeds, death and deification,' as well as the 'lives and deeds of the gods' (Twombly 2013b), Twombly was constantly mixing, matching, and oscillating between images of the feminine watery birth of a centralized voluptuous Venusian form, and the forward thrusting, multiply polyvalent movements of propulsively directional Dionysiac energies. Finally, in the five "Dionysos" drawings ending 1963, he appears to reconcile the polarized masculine and feminine forms of a rectangular, monumental containment in black and gray pencil, with the red and black crayon-scribbled globular eruptions and phallically shooting penile forms which both unite and surmount the exploding, holding, and grounded 'female' figure. Containment and bursting, geometrical stasis and total loss of control, bounded form and the freedom of overwhelming disseminative release, reflect the twinned modulations, rhythms and movements of pulsatingly creative Dionysiac energies animating his work all through the '60s.

Dionysos, this god in the blood, is behind the movement which suddenly erupts, jumps and bolts into activity and actuality. He *is* the creative impetus, *poiesis* personified, the force behind the form. He spontaneously arises to fill the void. Dionysos *dunamis*, heated by the body's fluids, spurts, shoots, starts, leaps, bounds, and boils. Seemingly self-generated, his hierophanies and parousias are startling, immediate, and sudden. The god appears in a swelling and bursting. He manifests in a powerful and profuse springing up out of the earth and body, a riotous overflowing and overrunning of all usual limits, inhibitions, borders, and boundaries. God of orchards, wild vines, the shooting sprout and staining blossom, effervescent bubbling wine, Dionysos jumps, swells up and bursts into being. Dionysos' polyvalent modes of action in blood, wine, rage, fire, sex, sap, and semen, all "flow together", Marcel Detienne writes, to form a common principle: "the 'power' of a vital humor that draws from itself and by itself its capacity to liberate its energy, suddenly, with volcanic violence" (Detienne 1989, p. 64).

V

DIONYSOS: PERFORMING MADNESS AND ECSTASY

The first explicit references and depictions of Dionysos, the Graeco-Roman wine god of antiquity, linking him to Orpheus, appear in Twombly's work amongst a series of 21 pieces on paper, all completed in Naples in January and February of 1975. It just so happens that Naples and its environs are an area of Magna Graecia that is particularly sacred to the god, and is the scene of several of his major mythical hierophanies; and furthermore, that the mid-winter period of Twombly's residence there was also coincidentally the same time of year that the main festivals held in honor of Dionysos-Bacchus, the Anthesteria and the urban Dionysia, actually used to take place in ancient Greece and in its 'Italian' colonies. A number of the pieces from this drawing series are also inscribed with the name of the 'Hotel Excelsior' where he was staying at the time and was using as his temporary studio.

The first item of the series, and the one with which we now begin our own chronological Twomblyan Dionysia, is a kind of cover page for the whole suite and it comprises a single sheet of paper with the names of the principal subjects written on it in crayon: 'Orpheus/Dionysus/Narcissus/Allusions/(Bay of Naples),' and it is signed and dated, 'C.T. Jan. 75,' with the words listed vertically down the paper, iterated like a program or an announcement. This initial piece is the project for an unrealized poster for the exhibit of the whole 21-part drawing collection which was indeed held at a gallery in Naples in that same year, 1975. So here in this first concrete conjunction of the names 'Orpheus' and 'Dionysus,' we can see in his work the specific harbinger of their entwining mythemes which are to come for the next thirty-five years; the one, Orpheus, a tragic, poetic, and fraternal alter ego of the other, an all-powerful god of transformative energies, Dionysos.

The first part of this 21-drawing suite consisting of a set of five collaged works on paper all referring to and honoring Orpheus and containing excerpts from Rilke's *Sonnets to Orpheus*, was discussed previously in the chapter on Orpheus. The second part now at hand, however, consists of seven designs, all prominently bearing the name 'DIONYSUS,' scrawled in oil stick, oil paint,

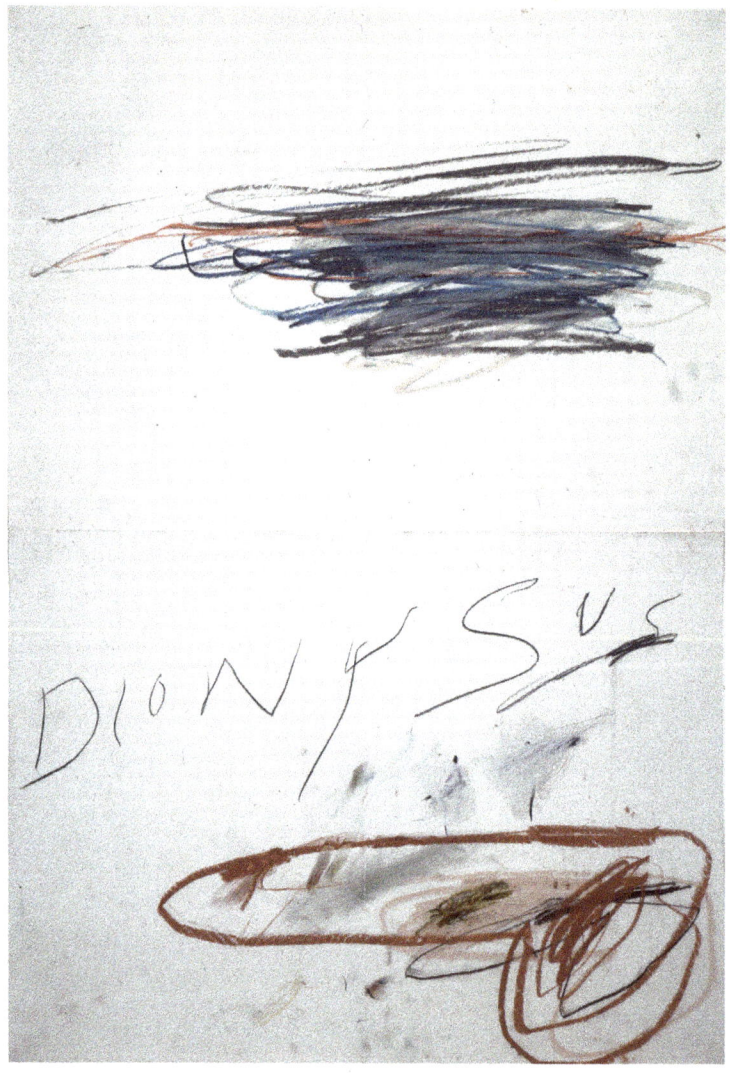

14.   Cy Twombly, *Dionysus*, 1975.

or crayon near the central portion of the sheet, and portray as well, and most formidably, the blackened or colored outline of an outsize, crudely-drawn penis and scrotal sac. The phalli in all of these works point from right to left and are mounted on 100 x 70 cm. pieces of paper. All seven of these phallus works on paper are collaged drawings, with two smaller juxtaposed pieces of paper collaged onto the larger third sheet. Most of them also contain some colorful scribbles and smears of wildly drawn oil stick on paper collaged either above or below the phallus. The jumble and swirl of primary colors in these sections, though frantic, is bounded, and appears like a very loose bundle of beautifully pigmented thick strands of yarn. It contrasts quite strongly in its abstracted formlessness *and* bold colors with both the blackened graffito concreteness of the name 'DIONYSUS', as well as, and especially with, the darkly outlined phallus. The overall effect is that there are at least three visually separate things going on on each of the sheets. And besides and in addition to those three discrete standout pictorial events, the background surfaces on all seven sheets are suggestively smudged and blurred with tinted pale colors and off-white grounds, providing impressionistic stagings for the foregrounded formal elements. Clearly drawings, they bear all the signs nevertheless of lush painterly pleasures created and enjoyed in an abstracted and voluptuous state of erotic dreaminess.

The only pieces to really differ in their formal arrangement are the last phallus in the series which clearly points upwards, tilting to the top left corner, and the first, which is surmounted by the word 'wing,' prefiguring by exactly three decades Twombly's 2005 show of 'Bacchus,' which has as part of its subtitle, the Greek word 'Psilax,' 'wing,' an uncommon descriptive epithet of Dionysos, the 'winged' god. The last phallus which culminates this celebration of the male member also looks like a huge dirigible rising slightly into the air, airborne, with its nose pointed towards the left, the side of the unconscious, sniffing out the times, remembering the actual Graf Zeppelin, the record covers of the rock band Led Zeppelin's first two LP record albums, and the historically phallic aircraft's repeated figurings also on the group's later recordings released during the same decade of the '70s. Twombly's anthemic 'penis rising' is jubilantly unencumbered, however, by the disastrous overtones of either the real Graf Zeppelin, the passenger airship 'Hindenburg,' which catastrophically burst into flames and exploded when it caught fire at the air station in Lakehurst, New Jersey, on May 6, 1937, killing 36 of its passengers and presaging aerial warfare with Nazi Germany, or the actual zeppelins the Germans used to bomb France and England during the first world war. The inflated phallic flights of a solar Apollonian masculinity doomed to failure as imaged by Icarus is notably absent as a motif in Twombly's own mythologically based works, which would further support the notion of his own phallic sexuality as being rooted in earthier Dionysiac sources, and perhaps also, more introverted.

The lightness and winged mobility of Twombly's Dionysian phalli also rise up over the leaden heaviness of the times when they were created, the mid-'70s, and rock 'n' roll music's shadowy slide into the backlash of heavy metal, punk, violence, AIDS, and addiction. As in all of Twombly's art, he inescapably alludes to the *Zeitgeist*, the times, events and atmosphere in which he lives and works, while also rigorously sublimating its contextual density, first by intuitively grasping its archetypal emotional core through his individual artistic lens, and then by rising above it symbolically, taking it to an actually sublime and sublimated impersonal plane of creative presentation through the use of various aesthetic personae.

From some perspectives, this attitude, as well as Twombly's art production during this period, was seen as aloof, overly refined and the result of his European distance, *hauteur* and aesthetic isolation. While in fact, his literal remove from the noise, distractions and diversions of the United States and the New York art scene undoubtedly provided him with the necessary freedom, psychological space and emotional clarity to return and remain faithful to his own deeper sources, as well as to the roots of our cultural heritage, and allowed him to grapple with the basic and fundamentally recurring classical concerns of what it is to be a human being in our own time, and in our always turbulent epochal crises of the moment. He was able to continue the probing archaeological inquires he was discovering and digging out of himself, both individually and collectively. Europe and his long-time residence with family and studios in Italy, and the mobility of his peripatetic lifestyle, seemed, in fact, to suit Twombly and his authentic artistic production extremely well.

In journeying from Twombly's sheets of paper depicting the phallus, into the specifically mythical topography of the god Dionysos/Bacchus, we find at the beginning of our route, already way back in the sixth century B.C.E., along the Ionian coast of contemporary Turkey, the pre-Socratic philosopher, Heraclitus of Ephesos, writing:

> If it were not in honor of Dionysus that they conducted the pro-
> cession and sang the hymns to the male organ (the phallus), their
> activity would be completely shameless.
>
> (In Hillman 1979, p. 44)

It was well known throughout the ancient world that the rites and celebrations of Dionysos held in Ephesos, as well as in many of the other islands
and towns of mainland Greece, Italy and Asia Minor, had as a central part
of their festivities, a parade bearing and honoring a carved, usually fig-wood
phallus as an image of the god. The god for his worshippers in this case *is* the
phallus; he is identified with the phallus, *pars pro toto*. Twombly exemplifies
this nominalistic tendency throughout his artistic practice, and especially in
all of the seven phallus drawings where 'DIONYSUS' is literally written over,
under, or inside the phallus, naming it. *Nomen est numen*. There, in this space
of naming, not only the phallus, but as we shall see, a huge variety of natural
objects, of an animal, anatomical, vegetable, mineral, astronomical and cosmic
nature, though especially in this case, figs and the fig tree, were also sacred to
the god and become him, *are* him. Dionysos was called, *Sykites*, 'the fig-god.'
These energetically-invested objects, fruit, plants and trees, *become* him through
a variety of performative ritual activities that stem from his etiological myths
and appearances. They *are* the god. As true symbols, they are also revelations
of the god's munificence. The lush ripened fruit of the split-opened fig speaks
to the vulnerability of a fleshy sexuality, as well as to its many seeds, *Samen*, in
German, representing the inseminating and fertilizing potency of the Dionysiac
phallus, and the semen itself.

The gods, as Twombly well knew, are both named and present themselves
through their names and images, and furthermore, they come to be known
through their manifesting of the specific signs and aspects with which they
are generally identified. The images of gods, and with them, art itself, thus
becomes a totally 'other,' autonomous, non-discursive language of performative
representation. The gods speak to *us* through their images and appearances,
that is, via their *personae*, or 'masks.' This mode of representing the gods, their
sacred stories, images and rituals becomes of course, all the more predominant
in pre-literate cultures. Art and image, in fact, *is* the language of the 'other' with
which *we* may talk to and with the god(s). Art is the language and vehicle of
communication with their transpersonal realm. Twombly becomes here, early
on in his career, the artist who *names* things, people, places, and especially

the gods. He establishes himself as the *naming* artist *par excellence*. He is the artist who names things in order that they may *exist*. His unremitting efforts in naming through *poiesis* bring these things into presence, and into our *present*, into our lived world-space and existence.

Speaking of Friedrich Hölderlin, Lacoue-Labarthe could just as well be talking about Twombly when he writes:

> The voice of Hölderlin is that prophetic or angelic voice which announces the God who is to come and prepares his coming, or in other words, which 'discovers,' by naming, the 'space-time' of the sacred.
>
> (Lacoue-Labarthe 1990, pg. 56)

The viewers, ourselves, are left, of course, to learn how to decipher the signs, the images and fragments which the artist spreads and strews across his canvases. This is how we as observers must come to 'know' anything, by interpreting, understanding, deciphering, and deepening the signs, and/or, by making and naming things ourselves, becoming creators and furthering the images. Heraclitus again, in one of his fragments, writes: "The Lord whose is the oracle in Delphi neither speaks out nor conceals, but gives a sign" (In Hillman 1979, p. 131). It was left to the Delphic priests to analyze, interpret, and provide the meanings of the oracle to the questioning supplicants, since only they were trained in reading and understanding the secrets, prophecies and messages hidden in the 'signs,' thus engaging in a proto-psychoanalytic hermeneutic.

Regarding this kind of 'narrative knowledge' (Lyotard) in relation to signs, symbols, and the gods, the anthropologist James Fernandez observes that:

> "to know" is to have the capacity to read signs or marks which appear spontaneously or in uncertain circumstances. Knowing is being able to find a path by reading available signs where no path exists.
>
> (In Gilmour 1990, p. 114)

In thinking about the significance of the 'power of naming,' and concerning Twombly's own nominalistic tendencies, we read Lacoue-Labarthe:

> The faculty of language, the ability to name, is in reality intimacy itself, the intimate differentiation of the being. Through this differentiation, man, beyond what he is, corresponds to a being (*l'être*) by naming what is, by naming himself, by naming who he is not (God). For this reason language is not, in its essence, purely and simply being (étant)...Language is the other in man; it constitutes him as man *himself.*

> (Lacoue-Labarthe 1999, pp. 95-6)

Twombly makes manifest these basic and primitive identifications with the god while simultaneously apotheosizing the images in all of their fullness, roughness and even crudity. Does he de-mythologize or re-mythologize? What is the nature of his artistic project in naming the gods? He clearly makes the god, in this case Dionysos, and the rich cultural tradition of feelings, images emotions, places and symbol complexes associated with him, his 'own.' It is a private ritual, though one obviously not lacking in portentous auratic meaning for us as viewers. He appears to be offering us through his images an approach to the numinous. Myth, and perhaps an entire mythology, is presented through his painted poetry and language of signs. Art, in his hands, becomes at these times a devotional activity; it is sacred, though not at all as much 'religious' or pious, as imbued rather with erotic and bristling creative energies—and still decidedly spiritual and aspirational. And all the while he is exploring and discovering these new aesthetic terrains, he is also simultaneously acknowledging their incredibly deep roots in the soil of the soul's history. Twombly himself was enthused to literally walk the grounds of all the ancient Mediterranean lands of which he had long dreamed, and to immerse himself in the people and places he found there. Travelling in the classical world appears to have been his great ongoing adventure. "For myself," he said, "the past is the source (for all art is vitally contemporary)" (In Twombly 1994c, p. 56). In his 1955 application for a fellowship to the Virginia Museum of Fine Arts for a return trip to Italy, Twombly writes:

> I want very much to finish my study of the Mediterranean, the areas I didn't get to; the great Greek isles; the fantastic Istanbul, and then to Percepulis (sic) and to Egypt with Karnak, Luxor and Thebes. I have infinite longing to see and feel these ancient wonders (my work thirsts for their contact). Before I covered almost inch by inch the rest of the land bordering this ancient Sea (which holds every form that has ever existed to the history of Western man). The opportunity to continue my search will be of the most profound importance to my work.
>
> (In Twombly 2008, p. 59)

The awesomeness of his artistic project lies in the breadth *and* depth conveyed through an economy of means in images which have the power to inspire wonder, to conjure up these 'other,' bigger, more spacious and imaginary worlds, and to bring them back intact and resonant in absolutely contemporary terms—into the present, re-newed.

Another singular feature of Twombly's art is that it is also geographically rooted. It is an art of a particular place; it remains specific to the contours of unique locales. He often literally writes the studio's place name or his current location at the time of making art on the surfaces of his works. He presents a mythography. The symbolic richness of these soul-drenched *topoi* become the actual material for his lifelong career in re-creation. In the delimited case of these 21 drawings, the area around Naples (*Napoli*), Pompeii, ancient Baia, Cumae and the Sibyl herself, are still speaking, whispering in the sibilant slurrings of speech in these very *topoi* transported by Twombly onto paper of the long-gone peoples who lived there, in Southern Italy, around the Bay of Naples, Etruscans, Greeks and Romans, slaves, workers, householders, poets, and emperors. The places themselves, the locations, artifacts and atmospheres, somehow also symbolically re-appear in his work as gritty, actual patches of earth and light, rocky terrains, a field of olive trees, strewn pieces of pottery, still palpably there waiting to be discovered. He is known to have actually put local dirt, clay and dust into his white paints to give them a worn tactile patina, and a tangible locus of feeling for the place itself and its sedimented history.

Perhaps Twombly's project is then one of first de-mythologizing, deconstructing, and *then* re-mythologizing images, a re-investing of meaning, potency and value into places, people, periods and objects that have over the long course of centuries been trampled, stripped, defaced, and obscured by the tides of time. He re-finds and re-creates a poetics of place. He re-sacralizes images, materials and gestures which have been shattered and buried by the more immediate, secular needs and inclinations of various cultures, by so-called "progress." Creating his own personal and private mythologies, he honors and redeems the numinous soul energies of gods who have themselves had to hide, flee, and disappear into exile, and have been consequently disguised and camouflaged since they were no longer being acknowledged or re-membered. His is an art of re-calling and re-collecting these arcane powers from their occlusion, from their scattered and fragmented pieces, out of the shards and chunks, columns and statuary, which have been smashed and lay about in ruin, and whose sparks he would occasionally see glinting throughout the worlds of his travels. He calls them out of hiddenness, and once again names them into existence through *poiesis*. He shores these scratched, jittery, and spontaneously-marked works on frail paper sheets as a transient creative bulwark against the abandoned wreckage and ravaged debris of time, history, and the onslaught of events, and as a kind of resistance to sprawling growth, modern development, technology, war, strife, and decay, posing his own substantial mythopoetics against all the other many would-be destroyers of meaning.

In an incredible inversion of psycho-logical thematics, this same region around Naples is also the site of Lake Avernus (*Averno*), one of the rare entrances to the underworld and to the nether regions in both Greek and Roman mythology. Actually, Orpheus too was said by some to have mourned his belovéd Eurydice by the side of Lake Avernus for seven whole years and to have raised a marble tomb to her there. In one ancient tale, in order to retrieve his mother, Semele, from the realm of death, Dionysos has to himself submit to the phallus at the edge of that deep, dark lake. That is, he must become like a woman and subject himself to anal penetration by Hades, the lord of death, in order that he may go down to the underworld and search for his own mortal mother. He thus, with this adventure, earns the epithet *Gynis*, 'woman,' or 'womanly,' and thereby reveals his own feminine receptive attributes in being penetrated by the phallus. Dionysos is often represented as highly androgynous, especially in the Hellenistic period, and Apollodoros tells us "that Zeus instructed Ino to raise (him) as a girl, and that Mise seems to be interpreted as Dionysos in his feminine manifestation" (Athanassakis and Wolkow 2013, p. 126). In another variation of this story at Avernus, in order to fetch his mother, Semele, back from the underworld, and needing a guide and pathfinder, he promises complete female surrender to a fig-wood phallus which he himself creates, erects and autoerotically uses on the spot. The pathfinder for this task of redemption, the cult-object itself, the venerated phallus, was called *Prosymnos*, or *Polyhymnos*, 'the much sung-of' (Kerenyi 1951, p. 259). Lastly, Avernus also becomes the ghastly entrance to the underworld for Rome's mythical founder, Aeneas. After the long voyage from Troy and via Carthage, making landfall with his men near Naples and Cumae, Virgil tells us that Aeneas descended to Hades with the Sibyl herself as his guide in order to find and converse with his father, Anchises, there in the dark and gloomy halls and lands of the deceased.

Despite the prominence of the male phallus in the mythologies of Dionysos, he is always and everywhere, and more typically, also polymorphously perverse, pan-sexual, ambiguously gendered, polyandrous, and polyamorous. The Homeric Greek heroes castigated him for his effeminacy, his sensual, 'eastern,' Asian/oriental origins and dress, as well as for his subversive, transgressive gender boundary crossings. He was seen as a threat to the manly warrior ideal. Though decidedly masculine in appearance and manifestation, especially throughout the archaic and classical epochs, the god remains indissolubly attached, attracted and attractive to women and to the feminine in general. He is at bottom as we shall see, an avatar of the Great Mother.

Throughout his mythologem, Dionysos is also a figure of luxuriant fluidities. Known most famously for his appearance in the intoxicating powers of wine, the ritual cultic vehicle of his devotees' transports, the revivifying effects of wine and its consciousness-altering properties additionally stand in for the actual life-blood of the god, and his literal incorporation by those who worship him. Once again, they *become* him in the partaking of wine during the primal totemic feast.

Blood, wine, semen, and sap, the thick oozing stickiness of pine resin and all evergreen trees and plants which throb with life and vitality throughout the winter, all belong to him as well. Dionysos *endendros*, *dendritos*, *dendrites*, is the ivy-clad god 'of plants, trees, green-growing shoots.' Besides being 'the power in the tree,' the fecundity of his earthy nature is evident in his other nurturing botanical and arboreal epithets, like *Anthios*, 'the blossom bringer,' *Karpios*, 'the fruit bringer,' and *Phleus*, 'teeming with abundance.'

The pinecone, which surmounts the *thyrsus*, the fennel stalk wand entwined with ivy or grape leaves often wielded and waved by himself and his accompanying followers, the Maenads, echoes the pineal gland buried deep in the brain at the very top of the spinal column, the elongated stalk supporting the human skeleton and nervous system upright. The pineal gland is, in fact, the activated part of the brain precisely in these specific states of ecstasy and enthusiasm that are the particularly civilizing gifts which Dionysos ushers into Greek culture, and thereby into Western civilization, as well as facilitates during his rites. Through his mythical appearances, the very possibility of experiencing ecstasy or enthusiasm becomes socially and collectively available to human beings for the first time. These are the true sacramental experiences of what founds, constitutes and originates authentic 'human being,' which he both reveals and personifies. Ecstasy is an epiphany of this god. The *thyrsus* and its coned tip, as his transformative scepter, is an atavistic emblematic image that the ancient Greeks intuited and ritually externalized of an actual neuro-physiological event and anatomical structure and feature of the human brain, skeleton and nervous system, as well as of the functioning sacralized body.

Garlands of ivy are also seen curled around the *thyrsoi* as his revelers dance and wend their ringing way round the many thousands of surviving ceramic jars, vases, pitchers, plates, and the drinking vessels which once contained his sanctified substance, the wine of the god. This age-old drinking rite, of course, finds its natural evolutionary channels flowing into the transubstantiation portion of the Catholic mass, the transformation of wine into blood in the communion service of the Eucharist, the initiate's participation *in* the god, as the god enters *into* the participant. The bread as the body of the goddess, Demeter/Ceres ('cereal,' grain), together with the dynamic Dionysiac wine/blood of spirit, thus ritually taken in, has the power to effect a total change of state and substance in the 'Christian' congregation's communing members (Detienne 1979).

The phallic symbol of male creative power, so sorely absent from later Christian imagery, symbolism, or liturgy, is also quite healthily evidenced by the first century A.D. historian and poet Plutarch in his description of the original simplicity of the Dionysiac celebrations:

> In ancient days, our fathers used to keep the feast of Dionysos in homely, jovial fashion. There was a procession, a jar of wine and a vine branch; then some one dragged in a goat, another followed bringing a wicker basket of figs, and, to crown all, the phallos.

> (Harrison 1913, pp. 150-1)

In the panhellenic rituals of Delos, too, a large wooden phallus was carried in the processions of the Dionysia. Moreover, "each Greek colony sent a phallus regularly to the Athenian Dionysia" (Otto 1965, p. 164), which was the largest of the sacred festivals held in his honor.

The image of the phallus in all of its splendor, rising, leaping, spurting, ejaculating, thrusting, flying, and penetrating, had already long been a staple feature of Twombly's artistic iconography since well before the '75 'Dionysus' drawings, however. The bountiful multiplicity of the phallus as a joyful sign reached perhaps its grandest profusion and gloriously baroque epiphanies already in the "Ferragosto" paintings of 1961.

In these five relatively large canvases, all painted in the hot Roman summer of 1961, during the time of the 'Feriae Augusti,' the ancient pagan festival period, aesthetically-speaking, nearly anything and everything goes. Twombly opens the wild and rip-roaring '60s all by himself and lifts the lid right off of the id, with his uncensored, uninhibited artistic gestures and abstractly expressionistic wildness. "Painting" and "paint," he says, particularly about this series, is "in a sense a certain infantile thing. I mean in the handling" (Twombly 2002, p. 72; Sylvester 2001, p. 178). And in fact, this was one of the first times that Twombly began really using his hands spontaneously and immediately, building up these large canvases with smears, squeezing globs of paint directly onto the surfaces, pushing them around tactilely into excremental piles, breasts, penises, buttocks, and ejaculations, juices streaked by fingers filled with viscous paint, a riotous and at times child-like orgy of bodily pigments, opening viewers up to their own earliest sensations of playing, mark-making and physically 'producing' out of one's own self, the inside coming outside. Bodily creation runs triumphantly rampant in these orgiastic explosions of scatological and libidinal energy as they perform a complete releasing and liberation of immediate impulse and desire. Everything gets realized in paint. And during this period, mainly in Rome, Twombly was indeed incredibly prolific, producing literally hundreds of paintings and drawings in an outpouring of phallic abandon and abundance.

The predominance of the phallus also recurs powerfully, though much less playfully or sensuously, in the awesomely intense world rendered by Twombly of Homer's masculine warriors of *The Iliad*. There, in fact, the phallus poses as the exact opposite of the erotic, honoring not Eros, Aphrodite, love, or even sexuality, but instead appearing as Thanatos, death, and death-dealing masculine warfare. Standing in for the valor and brutal violence of Greece's greatest heroes, Twombly lays bare the destructively pure male force of unleashed murderous aggression. The sheer madness and unappeasable furor of hand-to-hand combat spreads across the ten huge canvases of his monumental, "Fifty Days at Iliam." Installed for decades in the gigantic mausoleum-like space, now renovated, of the Philadelphia Museum of Art, this shrine and valedictory ode to the single-pointed intensity and ravaging waste of the hateful male violence deeply inscribed in our animal impulses, genes and DNA, is filled to bursting with images of the destructively masculine phallus, and its ultimate consequence, total holocaust. There the phalli are massed in ranks like a phalanx of soldiers, or they point dumbly and blindly erect, solitary and isolated on broad martial fields of paint like the heroes whose names are written over their jagged directionalities. Ajax, Agamemnon, the Greeks, 'Achaeans in Battle,' proud Achilles and Odysseus, are all fated to jab and thrust their way home, ultimately to death and toward immortality, determined and fierce, their code of war unbending and inviolable. Faced off against the Greeks on the opposite wall of the cavernous museum room is the equally gigantic painting, 300 x 380 cm., of the Trojan warriors, the soldiers and citizens of ancient Ilium, all of them also depicted as aggressively pointing triangles and weaponized phalluses, marching left to right, armed and grimly advancing, powerful Hector, Troilus, and Aeneas, Politis, Priares, handsome Paris and their leader and general, Priam.

In a virtual study of the phallus in detail, Twombly had also earlier done a series of collages in 1968 based upon Leonardo's anatomical drawings, bringing the penis into visual counterpoint with images and sensations of generativity, temporality, and movement. He thereby prefigured and laid the ground for his later iconic use of the phallic imagery as denoting either the 'lover', or the 'warrior.'

Twombly's honoring and aesthetic valuing of the phallus, whether in love or war, whether under the spell of Eros or Thanatos, raises the anatomical image and its function to the level of a cosmic principle. Like Parmenides of Elea, himself from an ancient town visited often by Twombly since it was close to one of his own homes and studios in Gaeta, between Naples and Rome, and yet another pre-Socratic philosopher from whose Italian soil came at least indirect inspiration for the artist's numerous large works dedicated to both the clashes and concords of those two Titanic powers, and even more like Empedocles of Akragas (in Sicily), who so influenced Freud in his polarizing 'life versus death' dualisms, Twombly often portrayed the symbolic confrontations between Eros and Thanatos, Aphrodite and Ares,

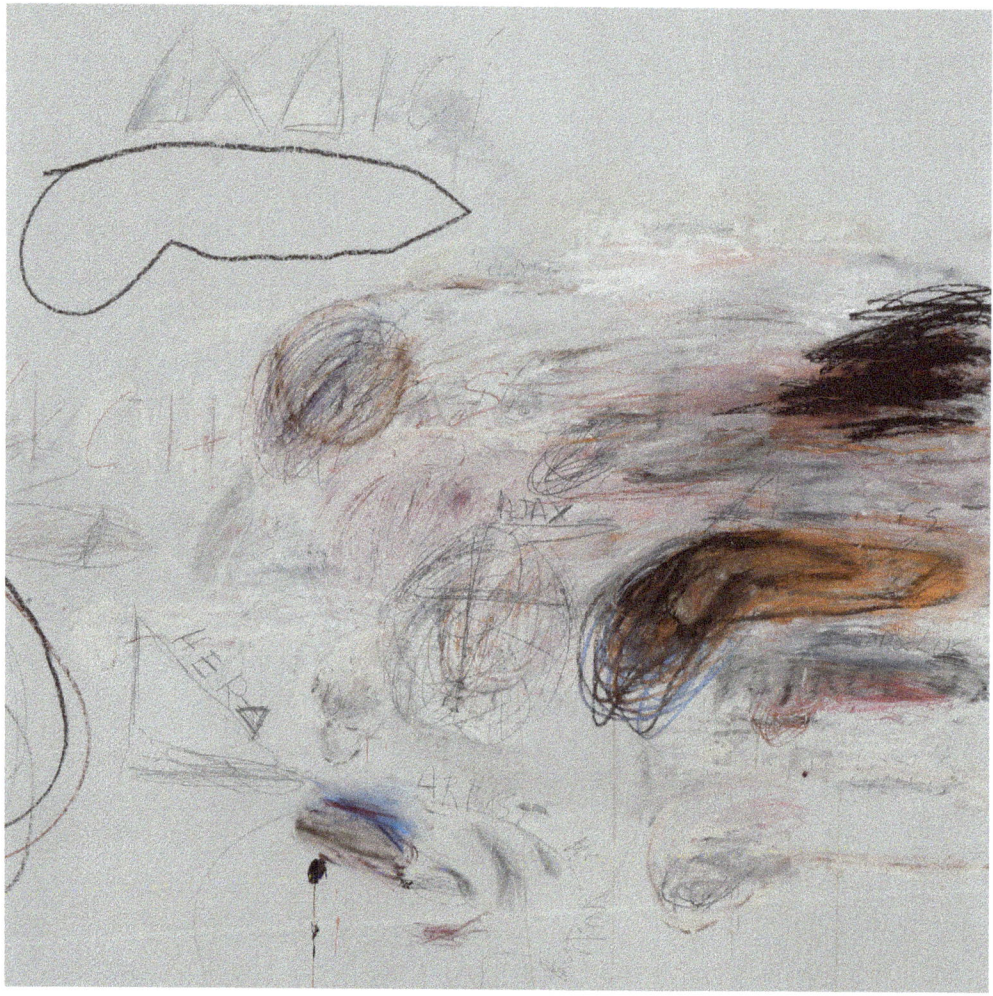

15. Cy Twombly, *Fifty Days at Iliam, Part IV: Achaeans in Battle*, detail, 1978.

Venus and Mars, Love and War, Love and Death, the feminine and masculine principles par excellence, in multitudinously various configurations throughout his career. Also earlier, throughout 1962, he worked on a series of drawings specifically entitled "Venus and Mars" (Twombly 2013a).

　　For the closest cross-cultural analogies to Twombly's relation to phallic power as the definitive male procreative symbol and cipher, as in the seven drawings of part two, "Dionysus" (1975), we would have to look at the Hindu, Buddhist, and Tantric imagery of the *lingam* to appreciate the veneration accorded to the phallus as the quintessential symbol of masculine spirituality. The Hindu creator god Shiva is most frequently imaged as a phallus all over India, and his holy conjunctions with his female consort, Shakti, represented by the *yoni*, or the vulva, is portrayed in images ranging from the intersection of two conjoined triangles in the six-pointed star, or, seal of Solomon, to the figurative embraces of Shiva and Shakti in intercourse on scrolls, wall-hangings, and banners, and festooning the pillars, walls, panels, and pediments of temples throughout the subcontinent of Asia, from Turkey and Afghanistan to Tibet, Cambodia, and China.

Returning now to the 21-drawing Naples suite, the third part basically concerns the mythological figure of Narcissus, and his mythopoetic connections and associations to both Orpheus and Dionysos. As a text for these works, Twombly uses fragments of lines and phrases from Rilke's poem, "Narcissus," as well as allusions to the sculptor Auguste Rodin's poem on 'Narcissus,' written while Rilke was working for him as an assistant in his studio. Rilke went on later in 1903 and 1907 to write an entire two-part book about Rodin whom he greatly admired. During this same period, Rodin also sculpted a marvelously touching and poignant scene of Eurydice as she vanishes away into the underworld from Orpheus' outstretched arms, desperately reaching and straining for his lover, all in exquisite bas relief, the figures just barely emerging from the hard stone.

The fourth part of the Naples cycle returns specifically to the implicit and subterranean bonds which exist between Orpheus and Dionysos. The format of these drawings is completely different from what preceded them. These last five of the 21-drawings are wide rectangular pieces, 70 x 200 cm., and are each composed of two smaller pieces collaged onto a third larger sheet. Titled "Allusion Bay of Napoli Part II," they are drawn using similar multi-medium materials like the others, and each piece contains the same line written on one side: 'Orpheus (brings order and beauty) to Dionysus.' The name 'Dionysus' itself is repeated on some of them, and one piece has the additional text: 'all my boundaries are in a hurry, plunge out of me and are already yonder,' from Rilke's 'second' 'Narcissus' poem (Rilke 1942, p. 153).

Into the actually widespread pan-Mediterranean religion and practices of Orphism, Twombly has concisely inscribed with his brief text what had literally and historically occurred there, ritualistically and symbolically as well, in a cultural evolution that spanned several centuries both before and after the time of Christ. That is, the mythical figure of Orpheus, with his own rites and mystical beliefs and practices of rebirth, essentially tamed and domesticated the wilder orgiastic rites of an archaic Dionysos, traceable back to Greece's proto-historical period and Linear B clay tablets from around 2000 B.C., which had persisted full-blown at least well into the classical age (fourth century B.C.E.), and by most accounts, also far into the imperial Roman times and into the early Christian era before the god was finally forced into hiding—subject to repression. Dionysos, of course, never totally disappears, but only goes undercover, into a kind of exile, into the un-conscious, and then, only for a short while. This god of primitive life impulse so integral to human consciousness, is not about to be suppressed by collective codes of beliefs, changeable moralistic trends, or rigidly prescribed behaviors.

Twombly's work itself encapsulates and traces the gradual assimilation of the underground, mystical, and unconventional rites of a phallic and erotically intoxicated Dionysos who had thus been around for centuries, and who eventually became relegated to the margins of actual Greek cultural life, into the Orphic eschatological promises of an afterlife for those initiates who were able and willing to redirect and channel the orgiastic and concretely sexual impulses into 'purer' and more spiritually focused and harmonious beliefs and behaviors congruent with the larger mystical and religious counterculture to which they belonged. This should begin to sound familiar in its obvious foreshadowings of Christianity. Orpheus/Dionysos, in bringing 'harmony and beauty to Dionysus,' as Twombly writes, actually made it possible within socially mainstream Greek religion and spirituality for the first time in Western civilization, to have a direct and immediate experiential encounter with a god-figure, without hierarchical priestly intermediaries, and within an organized communal religious context. Dionysos *Demotikos* was, and remains, after all, the god 'of the people.' As Nietzsche writes in his early, groundbreaking *Birth of Tragedy*:

> Now, with the gospel of universal harmony, each one feels himself not only united, reconciled and fused with his neighbor, but as one with him, as if the veil of *māyā* had been torn aside and were now merely fluttering in tatters before the mysterious primordial unity.
>
> (Nietzsche 1967, p. 37)

Dionysos breaks down social, ethnic, racial, caste, class, and gender barriers. All of this direct, unmediated, pagan spiritual experience came clearly from the Dionysiac cults, and then added to it through the figure and rites of Orpheus, the magical musician, the new elements: the promise and reward of an afterlife for its adherents, and an escape from the endless cycle of reincarnations. On the thin gold tablets buried with Orphic initiates throughout southern Italy, we find symbolically imagistic lines like: "I have flown out of the sorrowful weary Wheel" (Harrison 1980, p. 585); "Happy and Blessed one, thou shalt be God instead of mortal" (ibid., p. 588); "I have passed with eager feet from the Circle desired" (ibid., p. 592); and, "A kid I have fallen into milk" (ibid., p. 594). These manifold prayers and practices of the Orphic religion and beliefs in reincarnation, metempsychosis, or the transmigration of souls, especially popular in the newer colonies of Magna Graecia, were the last gasp of a vigorous, organized, specifically Greek mystical experience which lasted for several hundred years before the Orphic faithful themselves began to abjure sexuality altogether, and therefore eventually and literally died out as sustainable religious communities. Secondly, the Orphic belief systems and rituals were at this same time gradually becoming subsumed by the new religion of yet another Mediterranean, Near Eastern, young, son-lover, male god of fertility, who like Orpheus and Dionysos before him, undergoes a divine or miraculous birth, then suffering and persecution, and finally death and eventual rebirth; that is, of course, Jesus Christ, who additionally brought with him the new gospel of Christianity. Orpheus was in fact the bridge, link and direct predecessor from the ancient world's polytheistic paganism to Christianity. In the centuries around the time of Christ, it is actually sometimes quite difficult to iconographically differentiate between images of Orpheus and Christ, both portrayed as musical shepherd, priest, teacher, preacher, and tamer of wild nature, complete with congregation, albeit often one of animals, trees, and rocks. And, as in the relationship of Orpheus as prophet, sacrificial victim and incarnated symbol of the actually presiding god figure of the cult, namely Dionysos, in giving his name to the religion of 'Orphism,' so too as we can see, does Christ the son, analogically provide his name in 'Christianity,' to the belief system and theology of resurrection stemming from the overarching, omnipotent God and Father figure of the Old and New Testaments, the patriarchally supreme, 'He who rules and resides in heaven.' Thus, Orpheus is in relationship to Dionysos, as Christ is to 'God.' Christ and Dionysos are also, of course, both born to mortal mothers and supremely omnipotent, sky-god fathers, the recurring pattern of the divine child mythologem.

The very next year after completing the 21-piece Naples suite, in August of 1976, Twombly chronologically continued his Dionysiac evolution with a series of three collages, all entitled "Dithyrambus." This word is written in large letters on the top of the first sheet of the three separate pieces. Underneath on all three is written 'Dionysus,' and under that, '(of the double door).' They are then signed as usual, 'C.T.,' and dated. Executed very simply, softly and subtly, the first made in shades of yellow, tan and brown, and on the third set of the series, done in a green wash of oil paint, with Twombly smudging and rubbing the letters of 'Dithyrambus' to a ghostly haze, they radiate an eerie and strangely beautiful charm. The plant-like forms of almost-waving underwater stalks are themselves also bathed in an aquatic blurry green.

'Dithyrambus,' *Dithyrambos* in Greek, the uncanny epithet adhering to Dionysos, derives from his tragically conceived birth story. Ripped out of the womb of his mortal mother, Semele, one of the three maiden daughters of King Cadmus of Thebes, by Zeus, his father, just prior to his mother's immolation at the hands of her lordly lover, the neonate Dionysos is then placed into his father's own thigh and closed up there with clasps of gold. Once Zeus himself thus brings the child to full term, the infant god is then born for a second time out of his father's male thigh. Dionysos, 'the twice-born,' is the god thus resurrected from both, first, his mortal mother and blasting fire, and then, the divine flesh of his procreator's thigh. Rescued from the lightning's fiery death bolts that claimed his mother, and then fathered in Zeus' masculine womb, he arises reborn from Zeus' thunderous loins to earn his epithet, *Dithyrambos*, 'he of the double door.'

Euripides tells the tale in his tragic play, *The Bacchae*, in just a few words:

> For Zeus the father snatched his son from deathless flame, crying:
> *Dithyrambus, come!*
> *Enter my male womb.*
> *I name you Bacchus and to Thebes*
> *proclaim you by that name.*
>
> (Grene and Lattimore 1960, p. 216)

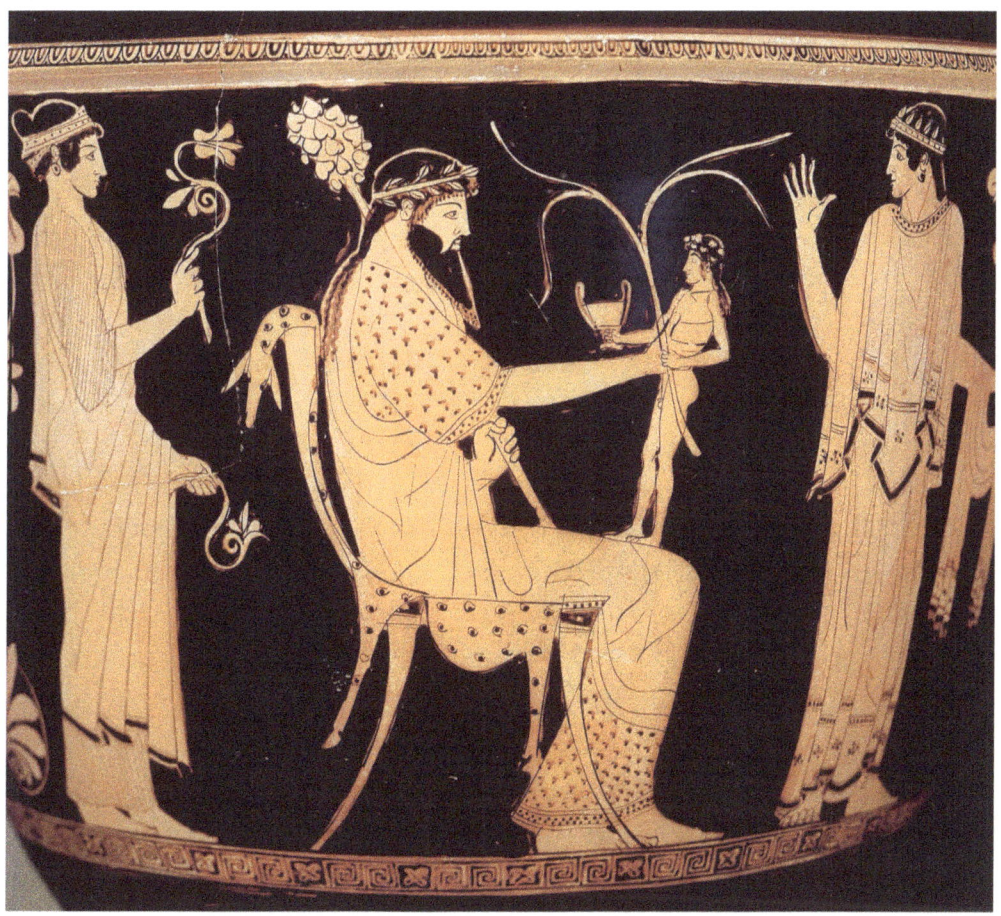

16. *Zeus and Dionysos*, detail, c. 460 B.C., Altamura Painter.

This named doubleness, duality and twinned circuitry of being and non-being, is, as we shall see, absolutely intrinsic to his nature. His comings and goings, ascents and descents, presencing and sudden absences, are all a part of his immediacy and always startling epiphanies and vanishings. Especially in the Orphic, underground and alternative version of his birth story and early life and times, he is there dismembered and devoured by the barbaric Titans, acting at jealous Hera's implacably vengeful bidding. In that story, Dionysos, also called *Zagreus, Brimos* or *Iakkhos*, the 'horned' child god of Hades and Persephone in this variation, is eaten by his murderers, except for one limb or organ overlooked at his bloody demise and gruesome fate. In some versions of the tale, it is his heart that is found by an unnoticed god or goddess who was lingering around the obscene feast. And in yet other mythical variants, it was his phallus that was discovered, overlooked by the

Titans in their cannibalistic frenzy. Obvious traces of actual human sacrifice and omophagic practices pervade this birth story originating in proto-historical times. In either case, whether of internal organ or phallic member, this body part was then given by the witnessing divine rescuer to Rhea, the grandmother of all the gods, who then bore the fragment or bodily piece in a basket, a *cista*, which she placed upon her head for a full nine months, or until the child god is then reborn anew, whole once again. Dionysos is then through this myth, actually, thrice-born, trinitarian, '*Trieterikos*,' and triennially celebrated. Again, the recurring motif of death and rebirth, whether from womb, thigh, heart, or phallus, signals the god's dark origins in blood, violence, jealousy, murderous feeling and primitive emotionality. From the beginning, his mythologem is indelibly stamped with passionate love, envy, sexuality, and destructive death. The genesis, birth and/or rebirth of the god remains due in every case and throughout the many thematic variations of his stories, however, to the facilitating efforts of his actual or foster mothers. Throughout his myths, Dionysos is invariably supported and backed by women, the nurturing great earth mothers of life to whom he is always and everywhere indivisibly linked.

The *dithyrambos* itself is also a Dionysian song of triumph, and as a poetic, oral and literary form, was actually ceremoniously employed on ritual occasions throughout antiquity and beyond, both musically and poetically to this day. The Dionysiac heart and phallic dithyramb still continues to pound in the more contemporary rituals and loud anthems to the altered states of sexualities, drugs, and rock 'n'roll, heard and celebrated in our own culture, especially since the 1960s until today. The dithyramb was said by Plutarch to be characterized as "full of passion and change, of confusion and swaying" (Kerenyi 1976, p. 215). It was the name given specifically to the type of choral ode or song whose original theme was the long and difficult childbirth of the god. Its literal sound and swinging rhythm, again, performatively conveys the wrenching experiences of passion, suffering, and transcendence which permeate his myth. Kerenyi writes:

> Archilochos, the earliest known composer of dithyrambs, confessed that he knew how to sing the dithyramb as soon as the wine shook his mind with its lightning, a clear allusion to the lightning that struck Semele and ushered in the birth of her son.
>
> (ibid., pp. 305-6)

The fiery fluidity of wine jolting and altering consciousness is already integral to the god's capacity to unite the opposites in one shuddering experience. He conjoins fire and water and himself arises as spirit, the spirit in the wine and blood, just as he is snatched from the amniotic fluid of his mother, Semele, immediately prior to her destruction by fire at the hands of Zeus' lightning bolts.

This same Archilochos, the soldier, lover and great rough-edged poet of the archaic age, enjoyed and aesthetically favored by Twombly in his works, writing around 650 B.C.E., himself sings:

> And I know how to lead off
> The sprightly dance
> Of the Lord Dionysos,
>   the dithyramb.
> I do it thunderstruck
> With wine.
>
> (In Davenport 1980, p. 69)

The dance, the choral ode, the song sung wildly, violently even, is ignited by the fire of the vine's squeezed fruits. Torn, dismembered grapes, crushed, and trampled upon, the vinous juice running out, pours forth an ecstatic spirit.

Jelaluddin Rumi, the thirteenth century Sufi mystical poet, also clearly appreciated and celebrated in various art works by Twombly, writes:

> The grapes of my body can only become wine
> After the winemaker tramples me.
> I surrender my spirit like grapes to his trampling
> So my inmost heart can blaze and dance with joy.
>
> (Wroe 2011, p. 41)

The story of the first making of wine, its mythical creation, and the first vintner, legendary Ikarios, and his daughter hanging herself from the vine stock, the tragic Erigone, is a sad series of tales told about wine's origin and related marvelously in detail with their numerous variations by Kerenyi (1976). Dionysos though, the god himself, is reborn from his near-death by fire, and he forever after exults his overcoming of fearful obstacles and existence-endanger-ing threats through the glories of life's many transformative intoxications.

The sublimity *and* horror associated with this threatened, threatening, and unsettling god was captured by Rilke in his very first Duino elegy: "For beauty is nothing/ but the beginning of terror, which we still are just able to endure,/ and we are so awed because it serenely disdains/ to annihilate us" (Rilke 1989, p. 151).

Scanning one of Twombly's later sculptures, we find this quoted gloss from the Portuguese novelist Fernando Pessoa referring to this particular qualitative consciousness of Twombly's, as well as to that of his ancient and mind-altered Dionysian Greek predecessors:

> To feel everything in every way,
> To live everything from all sides,
> To be the same thing in all ways
> Possible at the same time,
> To realize in oneself all humanity at all moments
> In one scattered, extravagant, complete, and aloof moment.
>
> (In Twombly 2006, pp. 100-1)

This same key quote appears on later important paintings as well as this sculpture, underlining its meaningfulness for the artist.

The very next year after "Dithyrambus," Twombly embarked on the series of four large collages entitled "Bacchanalia." The first, "Bacchanalia Fall (5 days in October)," is written, drawn and painted in earthy autumnal colors, all under a postcard-sized reproduction collaged on to the picture plane of Poussin's drawing, "*Renaud et Armide*," "Armida Bearing the Sleeping Rinaldo" (1637), from the book, *L' Univers de Poussin*. The Poussin reproduc-tion is scotch-taped to the paper and partially effaced by Twombly's dark scrawlings and scribbles of oil stick. On the reverse of the piece, there is a photocopied idiosyncratic translation in English from the Greek pastoral poet, Theocritus, "Thyrsis, a lament for Daphnis":

> Sweeten your mouth with honey Thyrsis with honey comb. Eat
> your full of Aegilus' finest figs, for your voice outsings the circuits.

> Here is the cup. Smell, find its sharp freshness. You would think it
> had been tripped and bathed in the holy well of Hora.
>
> (In Cullinan 2011, p. 144)

The second piece in the "Bacchanalia" series, "5 days in Nov," has Poussin's drawing, "*La Fête de Pan*," "The Triumph of Pan" (1636), collaged to the surface and sheathed in a sheet of graph paper. Poussin's great painting, "The Triumph of Pan," also from 1636, is a virtual encyclopedia of wild Dionysiac revelry, replete with goats, nymphs and satyrs dancing orgiastically around a red-faced herm to Pan. Engorged with blood and/or wine, Pan's entire head echoes Virgil's *Eclogues*, where he has "cheeks incarnadined with blood of elderberries and vermillion dye" (ibid., p. 134). In 1635-6 Poussin also painted a fantastic "Triumph of Bacchus," which though relying heavily on Titian's earlier version, has its own unique force and riotous power as the Bacchic cortège advances with wild music and dance across the canvas. The next in the "Bacchanalia" series, "5 days in Jan.," has the drawing, "*Venus à la Fontaine*," "Venus at the Fountain" (1657), with an ithyphallic herm directly behind the goddess, affixed to its surface. The fourth, "Bacchanalia," "5 days in Feb.," bears a closely-cropped copy of Poussin's drawing, "*L' Extreme Onction*," "Extreme Unction" (1644). All four of these pieces are made out of the earthy brownish colors of autumn turning to winter's black, both the actual time of the year of their making, as well as of the late fall harvest and wine festivals.

Twombly as we know, admired the artist Nicolas Poussin a great deal and said as much on several occasions, even stating once he would have "liked to have been Poussin" (ibid., p. 73). They both came to Rome at the same time of their mid-lives, and Twombly painted many of the very same mythological motifs as his illustrious predecessor. Poussin himself also painted several scenes either entitled "Bacchanalia," and referring explicitly to the festivals and orgiastic celebrations of the god Bacchus, or a variation thereupon, alluding to a similar, classically-based theme of unbridled abandon and sexual and/or aggressive license, taking place in a naturalistically-rendered, idyllic, 'ancient world' mythological setting.

In 1636, Poussin actually painted four "Bacchanals" for his patron, Cardinal Richelieu, depicting the 'Triumphs' of Neptune, Silenus, Bacchus, and Pan. Steeped in classical literature, Poussin was also undoubtedly aware that in ancient Greece there really were four Dionysian festivals which punctuated the year in sacred succession and provided discretely separate occasions for ritualistically honoring different aspects of the one god: the Anthesteria in January and February, the Lenaia, December to January, the rural Dionysia in November and December, and the urban Dionysia, in February and March. It was at this latter festival that all the great dramatic plays, the tragedies of Sophocles, Aeschylus, Euripides, and many others, numbering nearly a thousand lost manuscripts perhaps, mostly unknown to us today, were staged as the high point of the holy Dionysian celebrations in the still-extant theatre of Dionysos just below the Acropolis in Athens.

Another major influence that Twombly shared with Poussin was their affinity for the notion, experience and image of Arcadia, the edenic, rustic, bucolic, and pastoral life of the earth and its consequent closeness to nature. Twombly created his own 'Bacchanalia' suite at the time of the autumn wine festival being held where he then had his studio in Bassano in Teverina. He was also reading deeply among the classical authors on rural life who were attentive to the calendrical changing of the seasons in agriculture and in ritual agrarian practices, including Hesiod, Theocritus, Bion of Smyrna, and especially Virgil, whose *Eclogues*, *Georgics* and *Bucolics* he admired. Virgil also lived and did much of his important writing in Formia, close to where Twombly had his own house and studio in nearby Gaeta. Twombly also named a series of drawings as well, after Edmund Spenser's allegorical poem, "The Shepheardes Calender" (1579), and additionally created paintings after Andrew Marvell's pastoral poetry. His deep love for landscape after Poussin is reflected in many of his own painted tributes to the landscape traditions of the Renaissance, from Giorgione through Poussin and beyond, to the Romantics and Impressionists, all done, however, in his own inimitably contemporary and unique style, where 'landscape' describes a psychic terrain even more than it does a naturalistic one.

The name 'Bacchanalia' which both Poussin and Twombly used for their works, itself derives from the Roman period and the rites of Bacchus which were held in Rome all through the Imperial dynasties and well into the Christian era. The mysteries of Dionysos/Bacchus were prohibited for a while in 186 B.C., due to some improprieties allegedly taking place during the performances of some of its secret cults. The initiation rituals nevertheless continued to take place throughout the Graeco-Roman world, albeit sometimes in a relatively clandestine fashion, until Julius Caesar explicitly lifted the prohibition against them himself (Kerenyi 1976, p. 363).

From about 1975 till at least 1981, Twombly seems to have been completely immersed as we have seen in classical themes and antique culture, both literary and visual, although he was always involved in the classics at some level throughout his whole life. After completing four large, multi-sectioned works on Plato and his three dialogues, the *Phaedrus*, *Republic*, and *Symposium*, and numerous drawings working with the same themes, he made one very interesting smaller drawing with oil and crayon on paper, entitled "Lysis" (1977). This work consists simply of the word 'Lysis' written across the sheet of paper. *Lysis*, which means in Greek, 'loosening,' 'dissolving' and 'releasing,' is cognate both with the remarkably evocative epithet of Dionysos, *Lysios*, the 'liberator,' 'deliverer,' or 'the untier of knots and bonds,' as well as it is with the word, 'analysis,' ana-lysis. Another closely related attribute and nickname of the god is *Lyaios*, 'the unbinder.' Dionysos as the 'liberator' and 'releaser,' besides his obvious loosening effects through wine, is the role played by the god as 'the loosener of the soul,' as this function was developed in the practices of the eschatological rites which were sacred to him. Cultic aspects of these attributes were played out throughout the Mediterranean basin in the Orphic communities, particularly in Asia Minor, on many of the islands, especially Crete, and most abundantly, in central and southern Italy and Sicily where Orphic towns and entire city-states of believers flourished for centuries. It is highly likely that Plato himself was an avowed adherent of Orphism, and was known to have actually made two trips to Sicily, visiting the Orphic communities there, conceivably with a view towards literally establishing the ideal city state ruled by the philosopher-king about which he wrote at great length and spelled out in detail in his dialogue, the *Republic*. Plato often prefaces many of his own teachings in the *Dialogues* with, 'as Orpheus says,' paraphrasing him as a venerable master of initiation, and he was also said to have himself "kept hold of an Orpheus-scrap...and used it like a mantra, repeating it often to bring to mind that One in which all become the same":

> fire and water,
> Earth and Aether,
> night and day.

(Wroe 2011, p. 55)

More popularly, in ancient times, 'analysis' came to be subsumed as the originally philosophical practice of the early Greek metaphysicians, physicists and thinkers, to describe an emerging modality of cognition. The word was applied to the specific strategies of allowing 'things,' whether materials or thoughts, beliefs or ideas, to unfold, come apart, or dis-solve into their basic, elemental component parts or constituents. Subjected then to the scrutiny of the emerging rational thought of the time, these aspects of either the internal or external worlds were considered to have been examined, investigated, catalogued, or 'analyzed.'

Aristotle further used the word *lysis* in his *Poetics*, his structural analysis of Greek tragic theatre practice, to refer to the end or final scene or act of tragic drama itself, the *dénouement*, or the 'untying of the knot,' the finale. Well over two thousand years later, it was also used by C.G. Jung in the explicitly dramaturgical model he employed to delineate the very structure of dreams and oneiric activity in general. He adapted his own theory regarding the dramatic narrative structure of dreams wholeheartedly from Aristotle's discussion of ritual spectacle theatre and tragedy, as well as via his own teacher and mentor, Sigmund Freud, and his already substantial analytical work on dreams. Following Aristotle's fourfold outline of classic tragedy performance, Jung says that dreams begin with an "exposition", statements of time, place, and protagonists, the initial scene and basic situation. The second structural phase is the "development of the plot", bringing complications to the dream and an increase of tension. "The third phase brings the culmination or *peripeteia*", a decisive happening or a complete change of events. To denote the fourth and last phase of the actual dream itself, its finale, what he referred to as "the final situation", result, or "solution 'sought' by the dreamer", Jung uses the very term *lysis* (Jung 1969, pp. 294-5). Thus, for Jung, dreams, when they do have an ending, unlike anxiety dreams or nightmares which terminate in waking, conclude with a *lysis*, an appearance of the god, Dionysos *Lysios*, and psychologically, produce a dis-solution of the tension created by the fear, anxiety, and panic of the dream. Dreams in this sense, are then successfully disentangled, re-solved or dis-solved, and are thus able to maintain and prolong the biologically necessary state and duration of sleep, *through* their *lysis*.

The releasing powers of *Lysios*, the 'loosening god,' are perhaps nowhere more markedly manifest, however, than in the one uniquely participatory form of communally ritualized religious celebration which Dionysos founds, is identified with, and is performatively re-enacted exclusively in his honor: tragic theatre. Tragedy, drama, *dromena*, 'things actually done,' *dromenon*, 'enactment,' as a form and modality of religious ritual behavior and activity, from its earliest inception in the Attic countryside in proto-historical times, *is* the story of the birth, suffering, death by dismemberment, and re-birth of this one, young, dying, son-lover god (Harrison 1962, p. 42). Dionysos himself, historically and archetypally, arises out of a *mêlée* of male Mediterranean fertility figures, all of whom are closely allied with the great goddess. Though they are all called somewhat interchangeably by a variety of names: Osiris, Attis, Adonis, Tammuz, Sabazios, Zalmoxis, Iakchos, Brimos, or even Orpheus or Zagreus, Dionysos/Bacchus is the only one among them whose cultic re-creation birthed a new form of numinous dramatic spectacle which has endured and flourished until this day.

In the archaic period, before the development of classical tragic theatre with its particular individual actors, characters and differentiated story lines concerning specific mythological motifs, like 'Oedipus,' 'Medea,' or the 'Bacchae,' the *tragoidia* was the 'goat-song chorus' sung by a group of male performers dressed collectively in goat skins. During these very early sacred rituals, the young 'goat' or baby goat, the 'kid,' the *tragos*, perhaps the most common theriomorphic representation or form of the child god Dionysos himself, was sacrificed as the 'scape-goat,' dismembered, and eaten raw by the devotees, the actors *and* the spectator/participants, performatively sharing in the totemic feast. There was originally in this first form of cultic 'theatre' complete communion between actors and audience. "The theater," Artaud writes, "like dreams, is bloody and inhuman" (In Twombly 2014a, p. 17). This merging and collapse between spectacle and spectator was also re-awakened during the theatrically experimental 1960s in numerous ritually staged performances by many different acting troupes, including The Living Theatre, and Richard Schechner and The Performance Group's "Dionysus in '69."

This god Dionysos whose story lies at the heart of the first ritual dramatic narrative spectacle performed for the communal transformation of the entire assembled *polis*, essentially then gives birth, out of his own body, as it were, to this profoundly participatory art form of ritual theatre. Theatre, and tragic drama in particular, is founded in order to perform a spiritual, socio-political, and psychologically religious renewal of the entire collective community. Tragedy, as the dramatization of the life, suffering, death, and rebirth of the god, enables the participant/spectator the opportunity to identify with and re-enact in themself, *his* destiny, surmount *his* direful fate, and to make *real* in themself, that is, *real-ize*, their own immortality, god-likeness, or oneness with the resurrected god.

The collective renewal and rejuvenation of the entire *polis*, seen to be effected through the performance of tragedy, occurs via what Aristotle tells us in his *Poetics*, is the overarching and specific function of tragic drama: the production of a *katharsis*—the cleansing, purification and purgation of the emotions, especially those, he says, of pity and fear (Aristotle 1958). Tragedy is thus ritually dramatized for the participatory benefit of the entire congregated *polis*, precisely in order for it to perform its prescribed socio-political and psychological functions of purifying, revivifying and cohering the entire community fabric through a collectively shared and emotionally experienced *mythos*.

The true avatars of Dionysos in the early modern period, Hölderlin, Erwin Rohde, and especially Nietzsche, provided the intellectual and cultural background for both Freud and Jung to develop their specifically psychological theories and practices within the new emerging theoretical framework of psycho-analysis, psycho-ana-*lysis*, literally, the 'liberation, release, and dissolution of souls'; and in its practical form, the 'talking cure' of psycho-therapy, the 'caring for', *therapeia*, of the 'soul', the *psyche*. Within the confines of the consulting room, the practices of psychoanalysis were seen to allow for the individual's re-creation of an entire dramatic, narrative, tragic spectacle *within* the psyche, 'inside,' internally, symbolically, which also facilitates the renovation and rebirth of the analysand, that is essentially and optimally, the birthing and creation of a new personality and a renovated center of self. This analytical transformation is not enacted, however, as Freud initially believed, solely through a dramatic discharge, catharsis, or abreaction of the unconscious pent-up memories, traumas, experiences, and emotions, but through a much more gradual, deeper, and radical change in a sense of foundational personal identity, one apart from the ego or conscious mind, as well as a 're-working through' of the older physical, psychological and behavioral states and modes of being and acting which no longer adaptively fit the 'new' personality style, energetics or renovated character structure. This shift in perspective from the personalistic ego or 'I,' Freud's *Ich*, to the embodied Dionysiac core self as the archetypal and impersonal inner center of personality is psychologically analogous to the Copernican revolution, the Polish astronomer's heretical observation that the earth actually rotates around the sun rather than vice versa. The individual personality or 'I,' one's individual 'identity,' thus needs to be brought into relationship via analysis or *poiesis,* with this greater or deeper 'Self,' the matrix and nucleus of human consciousness, what Jung described as "the totality of the whole psyche" (von Franz 1964, p. 161), its hidden directing tendency, "regulating and organizing center," and "inner guiding factor" (ibid., p. 162).

On an even more interior, microcosmic level, intrapsychically, within the inner theatre of our 'mind' and dreams, and thus multiple times every night of our lives, we also replay these cosmic, dramatic narrative spectacles within dreaming (REM) sleep itself, ultimately, so that we may also be 'reborn,' re-oriented, and/or just as simply, awake refreshed, rejuvenated and ready to face a new day. Dreaming thus provides us on the deepest psychophysiological levels with an evolutionarily inherited aspect of human being which allows for our continuous physical and psychological survival through the basic and primary, organismically integrative processes of dreaming. Dreaming, in addition to its individually purposive meaningfulness deriving from the organizing center of the deep self, is thus an essential and integral part of human life in general, and ensures for the continuing survival, evolution and psychological health of the human species. Every night we participate in this tragic Dionysian drama of dreams, as author/dramatist, director, performer, actors, and even settings and surroundings, and assuredly, as spectator/ audience.

In 1979 in Bassano in Teverina, a studio location he found conducive and seemed to favor for many of his mythological pieces, Twombly made a singular drawing with the name 'Dionysus' on it, followed by a series of the god's epithets. On this relatively large piece on paper (194.2 x 150.5 cm.), he crossed out the word 'artists' written at the very top in small letters, and then wrote, 'Thyrsus/and grapes,' and underneath that in large letters: 'DIONYSUS.' Beneath the name of the god, he lists a series of Greek words, most of them Bacchic epithets: 'Lenaeus,' 'Mitrophorous,' 'Bromios,' 'Pynigenias,' 'Thriambus,' and 'Lydeus.' Of these revelatory naming words evoking Dionysos, it is especially 'Bromios' which resounds loudest and clearest as a favored epithet of the god. Dionysos *Bromios* is the 'roarer,' 'bellower,' 'noise maker,' 'shaker,' and 'shrieker,' alluding to the exultant or frightening din and tumult which presages and heralds his appearance out of the 'beyond' of woods, mountains, and the natural wilderness of his homelands, along with his strange retinue of revelers. The wild rout of the god frequently portrayed on vases shows his followers playing a wide variety of booming percussion instruments and drums, tympani, krotala, and castanets, as well as for the exciting higher ranges, pipes, flutes, whistles, whirring drones, and clashing bells. Euripides in the *Bacchae* writes at length about the uncanny sounds of Dionysiac music which unnerves and entrances all who hear it. It is also an infectious sound and induces a kind of rhythmical trance which is possessive, contagious and epidemic, luring people out of their comfort zones and homes to join in the abandoned revel of the dance. From the middle ages through the seventeenth century, it was known that periodic dancing epidemics sometimes overcame whole villages and towns throughout central and southern Europe, providing people with a ritual outlet in a kind of collective hysteria or Dionysian mania (Dodds 1951, 1960).

Later in that same year, Twombly created two collages dedicated to the Maenads, the favored Dionysian familiars, those beautiful women devotees most frequenting the god's celebrations. The word 'MAENADS' is scrawled across the top part of the sheets on both images. Underneath this designation, there is a wildly scribbled and slashed passage of color in crayon and oil stick collaged onto the supporting paper. Beneath that middle swirl and swipe of red, yellow, blue, and green, there is again the image of the phallus, once again roughly outlined and pointing from right to left. In the earlier of the two pieces, the name 'Dionysus' is written under the phallus and takes up the bottom third of the sheet. In the second, 'Dionysus' is written in small letters above the phallus, and the very large, again dirigible-like penis shape, swollen and inflated, points to the top left corner and takes up a full half of the sheet.

In these two works from 1979, both titled "Dionysus," Twombly again features the phallus, though now conjoined with the word 'Maenads.' *Maenad* means literally, 'mad women' in Greek, from *mania*, 'madness,' and refers to the ecstatic women followers of Dionysos. Also called the 'Bacchantes,' 'the initiated ones,' as in the title of Euripides' play, *Bacchae*, the women as we see them in ancient art, are usually raving, spasmodic, and imbued with magical powers, heads flung back back or down in ecstatic trance and possessed by the spirit of the god. They are in love with him, 'filled' by him, *en theos*, 'full of god,' enthusiastic. They follow in his train, heads and bodies sexually and physically swung by him, intoxicated and worshipful; and, as they are under his spell, they also do his bidding.

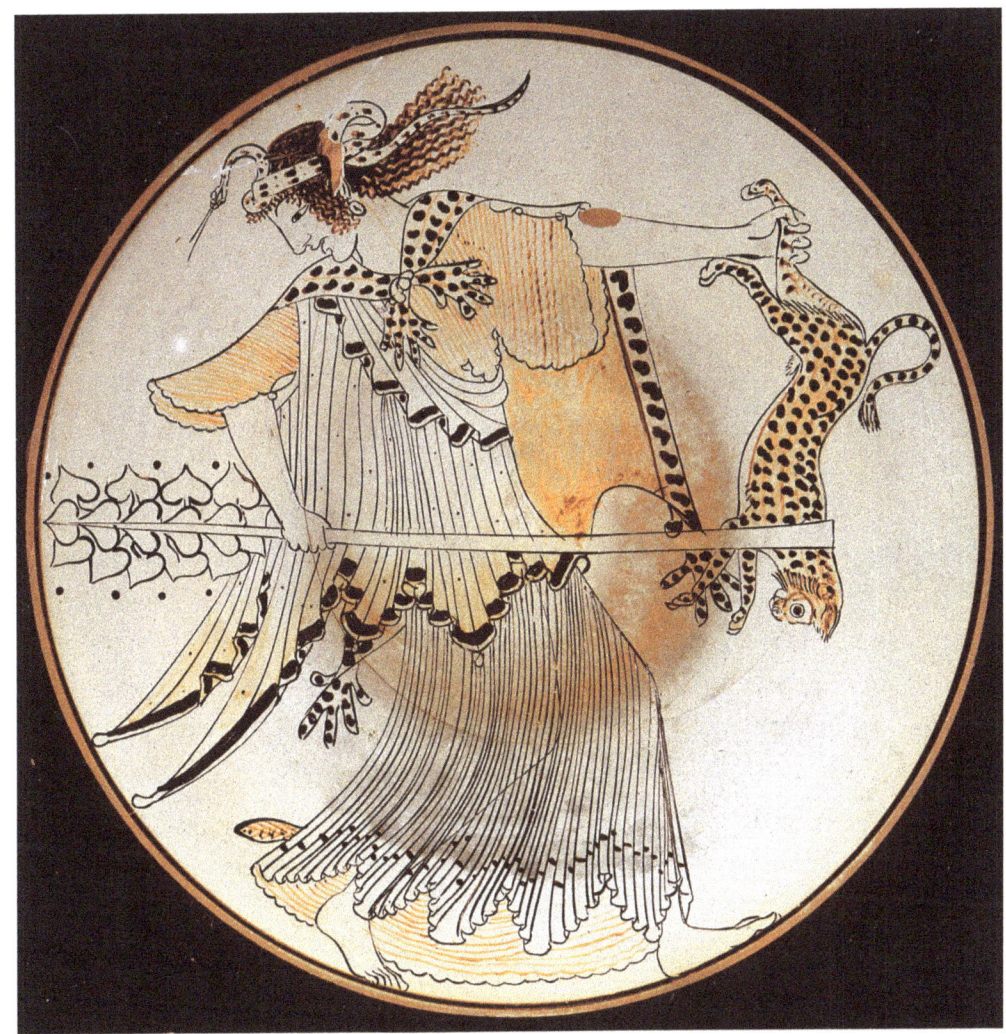

17. *Raving Maenad with Panther and Snake in Hair,* detail, c.490-80 B.C., Brygos Painter.

Since his earliest days, Dionysos was raised, nurtured, protected and loved by women. The cult of Dionysos *is* primarily a 'band,' a *thiasos* or *komos,* of women. Taken shortly after his birth from his mother's Semele's fiery womb and then Zeus' thigh, and entrusted to Hermes, the faithful servant, guide and messenger, to protect him from his persecutory stepmother, Hera, the ancient tales relate that the infant god is then whisked away across the Aegean Sea to the mythical land of Nysos or Nysa, a fabled female region populated solely by women. 'Dio-nysos' is the 'god from Nysos.' Many beautiful depictions in all media from the classical period onwards, show winged Hermes (Mercury) bringing the infant god to his nourishing Maenadic caretakers; and sometimes the women are also presided over by Papposilenus, the mentor and teacher of Dionysos, and the child is being presented to him. These female nursemaids and devotees, sometimes called the *Thyiades*, from *thiasos*, 'group' or 'cortège,' or *Liknites*, when they carry the divine infant in the *liknon*, or 'winnowing basket' used as a cradle or crib, are also his mothers, sisters, and lovers.

Because of these manifold associations with women and his legendary connections with the eastern Mediterranean lands—Nysos was popularly reported to be in Asia Minor, in Lydia or Phrygia—as well as the fact that he himself often wears the long flowing feminine gown of that region, his hair carefully coiffed with long ringlets, made-up, and perfumed, Dionysos invariably arouses the maddened ire and rancor of the typical Homeric, heroic, masculine warrior-type who disdains effeminacy and softness in any form. Dionysos, as an image of the Self, wholeness, purity and innocence, in fact, like many heroes and religious god-figures throughout the ages, constellates a murderous rage in the masculine ego. Over the course of his long, winding mythologem, the god, especially as a divine child or youthful adolescent, is often pursued, hunted, raped, and attacked by affronted 'macho' men, controlling kings, powerful rulers, chiefs or kidnappers, who do not recognize or acknowledge his divinity; in fact they see him as a threat, and he is often forced to seek refuge, relief, and shelter with women or with one of his several foster mothers. In one ancient story, when Dionysos and his nursing Maenads are being hunted down by a murderous king of Thrace, Lykourgos, 'the Wolf-Man,' and slaughtered as if they are cows or livestock, the terror-stricken young god leaps into the sea, where Thetis, the great goddess and mother of Achilles, takes him in her lap for nine months. He then remains with Thetis in her watery womb until it is safe for him to resurface. Lykourgos for his part, "was punished with madness, and, believing himself to be exterminating his vines, he killed his own son and hacked off his limbs" (Kerenyi 1951, p. 262). Again, we hear of the implacable reprisals of this god not-to-be-spurned.

The darker side of the divine madness of Dionysos, the shadow of *Mainemenos*, the positive, blissfully 'raving one,' the crazed *mania* of homicidal impulses and super-human strength possessing his female followers, is reserved only for those who neglect, deny or dishonor him. Like his foolish young first cousin, king of the god's native Thebes, Pentheus, 'the man of sorrows,' and tragic figure of Euripides' testament to Dionysiac religion, the *Bacchae;* or Orpheus, the lyre player, who after losing Eurydice, renounces women altogether, ushers homoerotic love into Greece, and thereby scorns the female, the goddess, as well as her companions, consorts, and heralds—for both of them—their fate becomes brutal dismemberment. They are torn apart, mercilessly rent asunder in both body and soul, by women. Psychically then, those individual men who would reject their own *inner* feminine or loosened, emotional feeling side, risk provoking the terrible wrath and revenge of Dionysos, the god who 'splits apart' the soul, who precipitates 'schizo-phrenia', and brings ravaging psychosis. Dionysos himself images, and *is*, the 'return of the repressed.' He *is* the force of repressed unconscious contents, particularly sexual and aggressive impulses, and when ignored, can embody the dark shadow side of personal or collective consciousness. He bears the rotted fruits of what has been dissociated, psychically cut off, split off from awareness and avoided, and when unrecognized, he brings it back with a vengeance. When not welcomed into the front door of one's psychic house and treated respectfully as an enlivening guest and an honored god, either individually or collectively, he is bound to come roaring and crashing in through the back or side doors, destructively turning everything topsy-turvy, helter skelter, and crazed. At his darkest, he personifies unleashed and murderous madness.

Now, continuing to chronologically follow the Dionysiac theme into the 1980s, as the tenth in a 14-piece suite of collaged drawings, entitled, "V Day Wait at Jiayaguan," Twombly heads the sheet-lettered 'J' with the inscription, 'Wine Taking,' followed by a series of paired, circularly flurried scribbles. Underneath, he pursues the Dionysian motif by writing Bacchically: 'one more cup/of wine for our/remaining happiness.'

In September of 1980, Twombly travelled extensively in Greece. And the suite of three "Bacchus" paintings he made in 1981 remains one of the most purely gorgeous evocations of the god that he or anyone else has ever done. Though created in a variety of mediums on paper, the artist himself classified them as paintings, "since the paint is a considerable part of the entire composition" (Bastian in Twombly 1995, p. 94). All three pieces have as their central image a heart-shaped or triangularly-shaped form denoting a cluster of grapes, as well as a human heart, and/or an ivy or vine leaf. All three additionally have 'BACCHUS' shakily scrawled under and to the right of this main figure. Parts II and III also each have a much smaller piece appended to them. The first of these in Part II, is a reproduced wax photocopied photograph of an acanthus leaf drawn on with wax crayon. The third, Part III, includes a print of a dangling bunch of grapes surmounted naturalistically by two grape leaves and is reproduced in color from a horticultural magazine. Both the acanthus leaf and bunch of grapes reproductions, however, exactly mimic in form and shape all three of the large central heart/grape cluster/leaf images comprising the essential Bacchic thrust of the works. These collaged addendums reinforce and underline the central thematic image from different vantage points and bring in different sets of visual information, mediums, and botanic/scientific/historical contexts to bear on the purely unfettered, loosened art of Dionysiac wine madness and the dashing, raving wildness at the emotional center of the pieces. As with most of his multi-medium collages, he sets up a definite contrapuntal and polyphonic rhythm amongst the different media elements. There is just enough meaningfulness and spontaneous, intuitively-right intentionality in his juxtapositions, that the collages avoid a surrealistic or more random, personal or chance configuration of aesthetic elements. They work as totally coherent wholes, and they additionally convey the very presence of Bacchus in their execution, each medium in turn reinforcing the others.

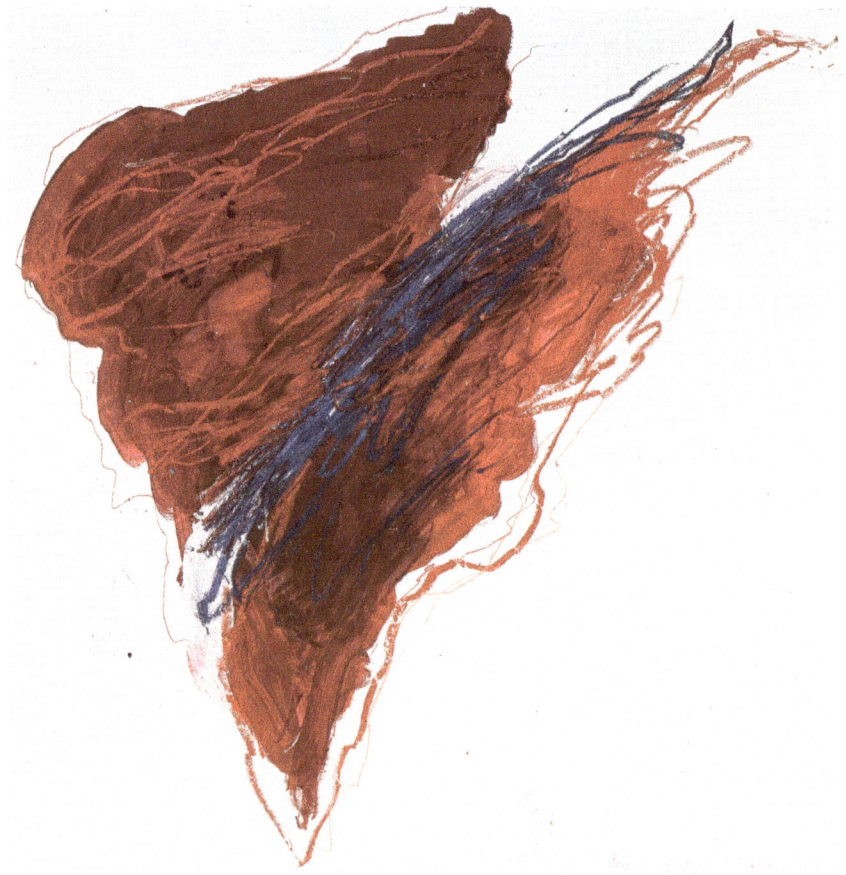

18.   Cy Twombly, *Bacchus*, Part II, detail, 1981.

The whole work, three drawings with paint and the two appended parts, is called 'a painting in five parts' and is dated, 'Nov. 18, 81.' They all come from the same day in Rome, with their intense pinks, purples, and brilliant, flaming reds. The pendulous cluster of grapes, the blood-red heart, the downward pointing triangular energies of Shiva, and the pubic patch of scrabbled lines *and* color, in all the three pieces, *come down*. That is, all three pieces hang heavily downwards. Heavy with fruit, they appear about to burst. Though in fact they are suspended in air on their whitish backgrounds, all the forms seek the earth and pointedly wish to phallically penetrate and touch down on the fertile psychic ground that is within the viewer. Streaks of jagged red crayon are jittery, frenzied and electric. The main heart-shaped forms themselves barely hold their edges as boundaries fly off with highly charged and fiercely applied oil stick and paint, emitting flashes of passion, intoxication, anger, and barely controlled emotional impulsivity.

In "Bacchus I," the leaf-heart form is painted in a "living," fleshly palpitating pink over blue undertones, and in all three parts, the "colours, freed from the objects" (Schmidt in Cullinan 2011, p. 79), seem to be "attacking the roughly sketched outlines, to the point of obscuring them" (ibid.). The ivy-leaf/grape cluster/heart in Part II, "glows in a luminous blood-red that threatens to tear apart" (ibid.) the black and purplish central vein or stalk. They all three conjure pulsating blood, delirious wine and the throbbing veinous capillary action of the artist's racing hand and mind caught up in a heightened feeling state, as if possessed by the spirit of the wine god.

Twombly has described how sometimes he would sit, stare and think for hours or even days before a painting, and then in a sudden and inspired rush of "excitable" activity (In Sylvester 2001, p. 180), would work nonstop to complete the piece. Arriving at these altered states through "long periods of observation and absorption," he would then eruptively burst into a "lucid frenzy" of creativity. Working in a kind of ecstatic "trance," he said he would finish a number of these "extreme paintings" in this heightened state, including whole series of paintings, like the extended 'Sesostris' and 'Lepanto,' cycles, considering some of them to be among his very best works done during these episodes of transport (Larratt-Smith 2014, p. 29).

Already in the early 1957 essay, he wrote presciently describing and predicting this aspect of his practice to come:

To paint involves a certain crisis, or at least a crucial moment of sensation or release; and by crisis it should by no means be limited to a morbid state, but could just as well be one ecstatic impulse.

(Twombly 2013a, p. 112)

Then, in the same year, following the three 'Bacchus' pieces, in an interlude prior to a bigger work, and as the first of a title page, nine-part series of drawings dated 'Gaeta, September 1981' and referred to as the 'Gaeta Set (For the love of fire and water),' Twombly repeats the well-know *coniunctio* of fire and water on each of the sheets. The alchemical *aqua permanens* here becomes a metaphor for the healing elixir of igneous wine. As an evocative and madly done ode to Bacchus, and as the accompaniment to eight poems by Octavio Paz, with whom he collaborated, he writes on the colorful first sheet: 'for the love of fire and water/water.' Many of the sheets in this project have wildly drawn red scribbles and slashes, and many also bear aquaeous blue hazes and pooling azures denoting this marriage of crimson fire and the emotional depths of water, corresponding to Paz's poetic imagery. The drawings and small book of poems were later published in 1993 as a set of ten offset lithographs.

In 1982, the two large drawing sequences of triptychs entitled "Naxos" were first exhibited in Rome and later that same year in New York. The three pieces in both series have an erupting, red-petalled, sharply-pointed flower in their center. 'NAXOS' is written across the top of both very large center panels, and underneath in much smaller script, he scribbled '(blooming).' At the same time, he also completed several accompanying drawings repeating the spiky floral motifs.

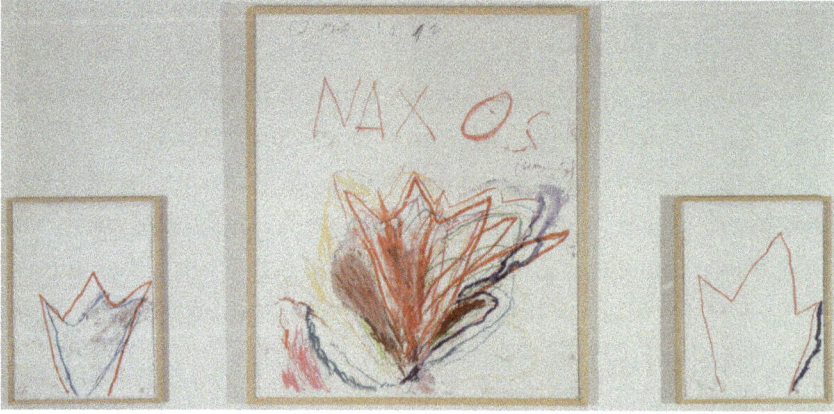

19.   Cy Twombly, *Naxos*, 1982.

Like the 'Bacchus' series of the previous year, the skittishly, crayon-drawn outlines of the flowers cannot begin to contain the throbbing, jagged, pulsating energies erupting manically from their centers and colorfully bursting the bounds of stem, leaf and plant. Outlined, diagrammatic, and basically trinitarian in structure, the flowers and spiky upwardly pushing points necessarily remind the viewer in this context of the riotous plant life on that most lush and green of Greek islands so particular to Dionysos, the island of Naxos. Of all the Greek islands, Naxos, the largest, richest and most fertile of the Cyclades, is the one that stands out as undoubtedly the most sacred site of this god, perhaps in all of Greece. It is there in his mythologem that he meets his one and only truly belovéd, Ariadne, after she has been abandoned by the Athenian hero Theseus, who took her from her homeland on Crete. In some of the more ancient tales, she has neither been cast off and abandoned by Theseus as tradition usually tells it, nor is she legendarily asleep when Dionysos finds her on the beach, but is instead already waiting there as a full-fledged goddess in her own right. Sitting calmly by the sea with her female companions, she greets Dionysos with a bowl of wine, and thus reversing the traditional roles, *she* introduces *him* to his epiphany.

In any event, Ariadne, from *Aridela*, 'the shining one,' 'utterly clear,' was in her own right, a moon goddess and a 'mistress of the labyrinth.' She helped Theseus defeat the Minotaur and with her guiding thread, find his way out of the deadly maze. Nietzsche addressed several poems to her as muse, mistress, and psychopomp. In one of Titian's most famous paintings, and perhaps the most illustrious representation of the Dionysiac retinue from the entire Renaissance period in general, the god is shown in his chariot leading his wild, wine-spreading rout when he comes across the sleeping, sorrowful Ariadne. Rousing her, he presents her with her marriage crown, the sign of their sacred nuptials which resides in the heavens till this day as the constellation, 'corona borealis.'

In the Titian painting, the crown as her actual tiara and the astral corona are depicted by the same ring of stars in the sky over her head. Like a movie montage, this one very strong and exuberantly dynamic painting encapsulates and portrays a whole series of events and characters from past, present, and future in the mythically conjoined lives of Dionysos and Ariadne, all compressed simultaneously into one gorgeously narrative and bountiful image. Contemporaneous, overdetermined, highly condensed, and polyvalent visual story-telling through imaging is a lesson Twombly also learned well from his early artistic forebears. As we know, he can also bring this style to an

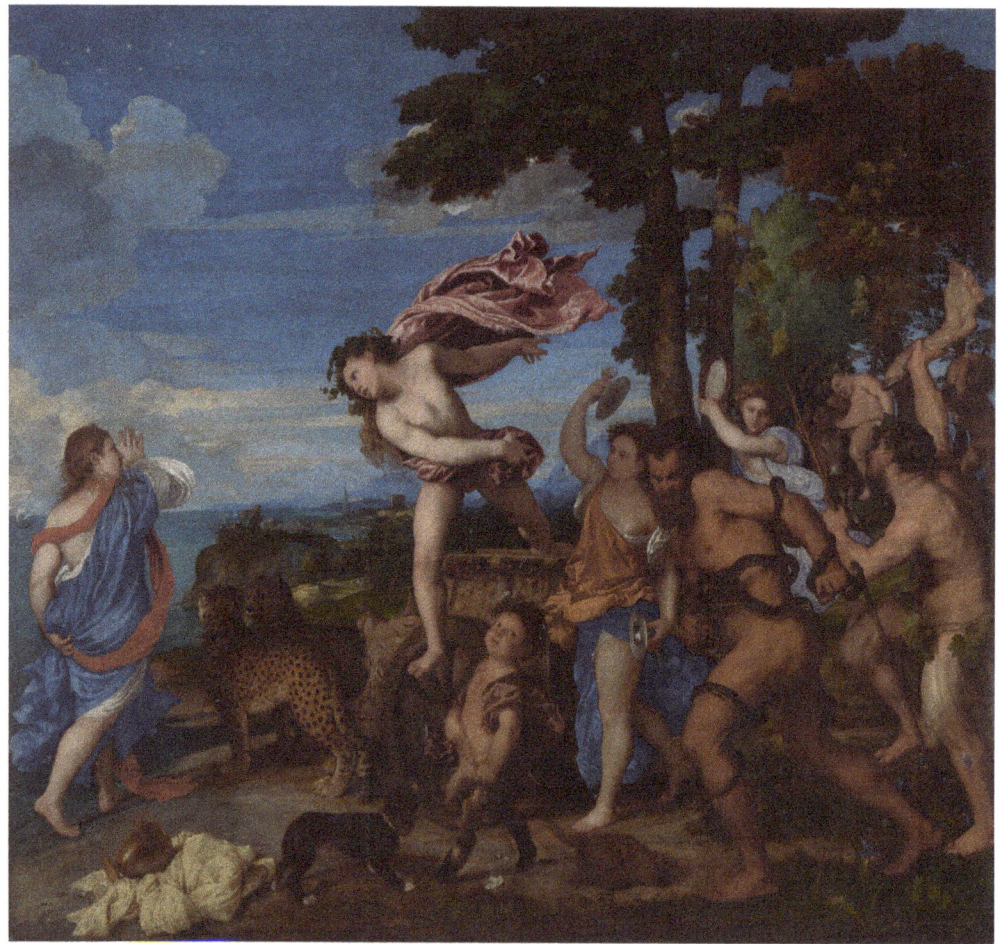

20.   Tiziano Vecellio, called Titian, *Bacchus and Ariadne*, c. 1520-23.

intensely concentrated degree of streamlined reduction. And in his own work from this period, he applies it through the newer knowledge and available techniques of not only painting, drawing, printing, and photography, but of cinema. A lot of information is packed and poured into the essentially one montaged image of these two trinitarian works, or as we have seen before in other pieces, even into one word or name, like the crazily painted, vibrating letters spelling out 'Naxos.' These works, of course, do not depict or portray the island of Naxos any more than 'Naxos' titles, labels or describes the images that appear on the sheets. Rather the two interacting and reciprocally deconstructive pictorial modes of writing and lettering, and expressive, gesturally abstract painting which Twombly employs, "are constantly interrogating each other about the constitution of their identities" (Greub 2014d, p. 231). Freed from the semiotic burden of meaning, both words and image are allowed to take flight. Belying the apparent simplicity of means once again, a wealth of psychological and cultural associations nevertheless brim over and stream out of the images Twombly presents, so that they become in effect, moving images, pictures that set up an indefinably rhythmical movement that ripples throughout the three parts of these two particular triptychs. Though seemingly quite simple, minimal, and direct in their starkly expressed formal content, they pack a powerful punch of rich symbolical material entirely through their psychologically associative networks, and through their contemporaneously novel formats of presentation as well, that is, as three separately framed and differently sized works on paper, nevertheless conceptually conceived, connected, and exhibited as one whole piece.

During the latter part of the 1970s and into the '80s, Twombly created numerous multi-part paintings, using different formats, sizes, mediums, and imagery for the different sections of a single piece of work. In nearly every instance, these polyptychs convey mythological, poetic and/or historical events and stories which have to develop and be 'read' over time and through real space, and are presented in a separated, disjunctive, though continuingly idiosyncratic *series* of frames. Many of his most wonderfully lyrical themes are contained in these multi-part and multi-medium formats with their unconscious symbolic 'narratives' stretching out over several pieces conceptually strung together and unified by cinematically flowing rhythms linking the separated frames into one integral experience. Moving back and forth, one's entire body is engaged in grappling with an encompassing mythopoetic thought form.

Besides being celebrated throughout the history of painting and visual art from ancient Greek vases to contemporary works, the meeting of Bacchus and Ariadne has also been re-imagined by playwrights and poets from Catullus and Ovid, and from one of the first operas ever written, Monteverdi's "*Arianna*" in 1608, through Montéclair's French baroque cantata, to the opera "*Ariadne auf Naxos*" by Richard Strauss, with the libretto written by Hugo von Hofmannsthal in 1916, to later operatic versions by Bohuslav Martinu in 1958 and Alexander Goehr in 1995.

In fact, the first four letters, three syllables, of Ariadne's name, a-ri-a, provide the essential central feature of all opera as a theatrical-musical form since the time of Monteverdi's first forays into lyrical dramatic spectacle, as the *aria*, the nuclear element of the voice, song and lament of a woman abandoned. This image of the feminine, the anima, left or inadvertently wronged by her lover, as seen through the eyes and imagination of predominantly male composers, is the historic heart of the operatic tradition. "Opera's DNA, the aria," is, "that extraordinary musical window into a soul and its passions" (Padel 2006). Ariadne on Naxos, an island, *isola* in Italian, the country where opera was born, is herself an image of the whole *abandonnata* tradition in music, conceived by men and the male psyche, the passive woman iso-la-ted and needing to be rescued by the more mobile, wandering, active masculine hero (ibid.).

In all of these literary, musical, and visual variations throughout the centuries, Ariadne remains the one individual female figure with whom Dionysos has been repeatedly portrayed. Together, they as a dyad comprise an elevated '*coniunctio*' and union of opposites. Quite apart from the polymorphous dallying of the god with his more anonymous manifold of female devotees, when seen with Ariadne, as on the Apulian wine-mixing bowl from around 340 B.C., the Derveni bronze krater, or on numerous later Hellenistic sarcophagi, the couple exhibit a rare tenderness and poignant loving affection not otherwise seen in the ancient arts pertaining to the mythology of Dionysos. Dionysos and Ariadne are, as these images of the illustrious sacred couple display, actually involved in an individual love relationship, and as seen together, are some of the first representations of personalized romantic love in the Western tradition. A proliferation of variations on the motifs and themes of their particular, idealized, erotic/spiritual relationship reached possibly an all-time high with innumerable paintings created by French artists during the baroque era for the enjoyment and entertainment of the courtly aristocracy (Bailey 1992).

Through his own original and oblique working style and modes of presentation, however, Twombly continues and revitalizes the age-old theme and mythology of this pair for the twentieth century in both of these Naxos triptychs which are very large, and are painted, drawn, and exhibited on three separately framed sheets of paper. As a trinity of images, they nevertheless leave an aftereffect of one unified whole. The three essentially become one, as the pair, Dionysos and Ariadne also become united. (Together the three parts are each 338.5 x 268.5 cm., and were completed in Bassano in 1982.)

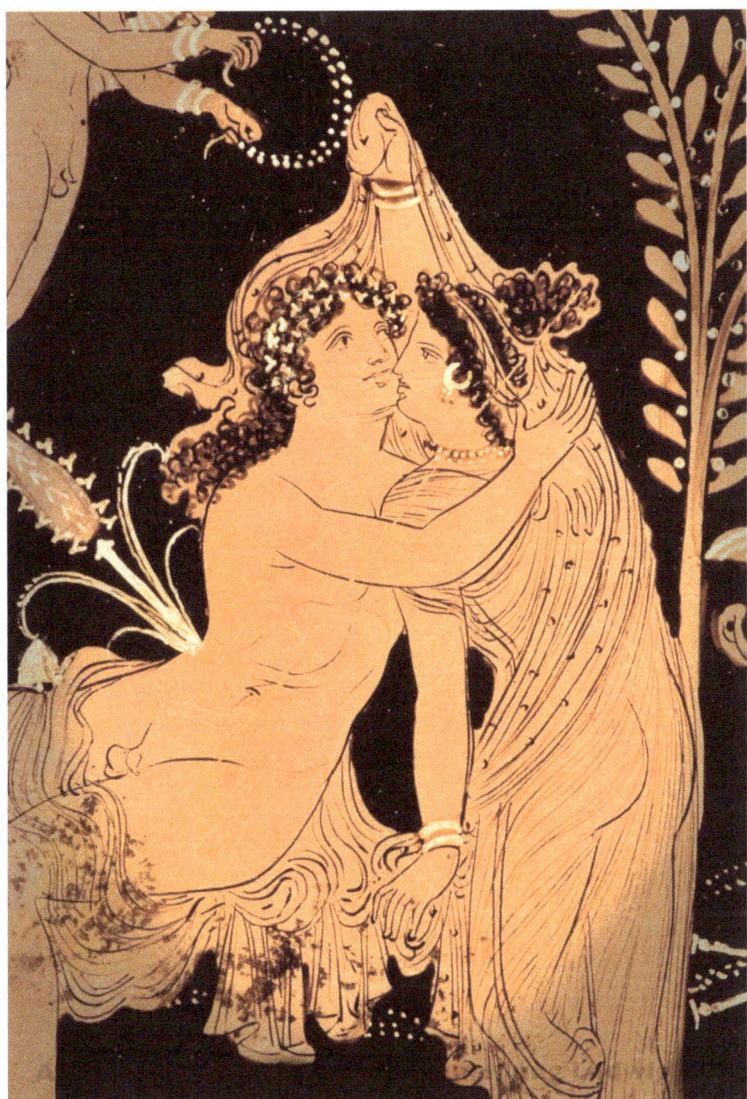

21. *Dionysos and Ariadne*, detail, c. 340 B.C.

In August of that same summer, also in that roomy, elegantly rambling house overlooking Bassano and the Tiber Valley, Twombly did a large drawing titled and written on: "Libation of Priapus." Priapus, one of the phallic gods par excellence, sometimes even bordering on the grotesque, was also a teacher and mentor figure for Dionysos, and was said to have also taught Ares how to dance before instructing him in the martial arts. In art, sculpture and mythology, he often resides in gardens, parks, farms, or in the wild, and is said to foster the fertility of the soil and the luxuriance of plant growth. In other tales, Priapus is actually the offspring of Dionysos and Aphrodite, but due to his overtly obscene and obtrusively phallic nature, is rejected on purely aesthetic grounds by his mother Aphrodite, goddess of love, beauty and physical perfection. The "Libation of Priapus" restores this figure of sexuality and fertility to his paternity, and the ritual gift or offering of wine inscribed on the sheet in its title, figures as part of the image, again in this context, as a devotional, consecrating sacrament, redeeming and reinstating the sexual *as* sacred. Priapus clearly belongs in this *komos*, or 'grouping' of personages who cluster and surround the archetypal ensemble relating to Dionysos.

A wild ball of twirling colors, entangled, moving, darting and circularly winding, takes up most of the sheet of paper under the title and is presented as the earth's generative and creative forces to the viewer, as the bold scribbles spring out of the sheet's lower half and whitish matrix. This painting on paper, coming as it does so immediately on the heels of the two "Naxos" series, seems additionally to suggest that Priapus and his bountifully procreative gifts may be the direct result of the imaginal coupling of Dionysos with his most belovéd Ariadne that takes place on Naxos. For as Twombly writes on several of his late, explicitly Greek mythological paintings, Naxos, like Paphos, birthplace of Aphrodite, is 'ringed by waves,' and is an island that births divinity. He thus artistically confabulates both Ariadne and Aphrodite as lovers of the god, which they both actually were, mythologically. Alkman, a poet of the late Greek Bronze Age, writes in celebration of Aphrodite's sea-borne sensuality: "Leaving Kypros the lovely/And Paphos ringed with waves" (In Davenport 1980, p. 153), which later becomes the motto and title for several series of Twombly's paintings with specifically Aphroditean mythological, nautical and aquatic themes. In particular, the images from the exhibit, "Leaving Paphos Ringed With Waves," which inaugurated the opening of the Gagosian Gallery in Athens in 2009, all bear red ships sailing on deeply aquamarine blue seas amidst splayed fragments of archaic Greek poetry suggestively emblazoned in orange script across their surfaces.

Moving closer towards the present, in 1984 Twombly created one of his most perplexing and puzzlingly abstract Dionysian images to date, and that, despite the fact that it is a photograph of a detail of classical sculpture. "Dionysus" is a single photograph he took in Rome in 1984 of a second century A.D. Roman copy of an originally Greek head of the god. The prints were made by the Fresson family in France from the Polaroid original during 1990 and 1991. It was printed in an edition of 12 as a single photograph, boxed portfolio.

Unlike most of his other printed photographs spanning his entire career and ranging over a wide variety of subject matters, places and styles, including many other explicitly sculptural details, this strangely baroque 'Dionysus' has always remained impossible to decipher or to bring into sharper focus. One cannot determine which portion of the physiognomy is being represented, as its 'true' subject matter is completely elusive, fleeting and infuriatingly unclear. The 'head' appears to be mostly a mass of marble curlicues, perhaps ringlets of hair, many of which compose dark orifices of emptiness wherein vision completely disappears. These pinholes of shadow recede against the yellowish brown and white planes and waving profusions of glistening ancient stone reflecting from the photo's surface. In fact, it is difficult to even definitively say whether the image is indeed in black and white, or has been tinted, taken or made with color film. This image has been lying dormant for years, resting, waiting like a Rorschach blot in its box or frame to click into place, to come into focus and reveal itself, clarified, to finally attain its proper gestalt, its truthfulness, a sudden shift and there it is, or would be. But it never does. It resists and refuses both mind and eye. It pushes back in its lapidary hardness. It is patient, and has already, quietly persisted for two millennia as a sculpture located in Rome, and it has survived very well in relative obscurity. The photographic image on paper does the same. It remains obdurate in all of *its* flat 'thereness,' just seeing out in its two-dimensionality.

The hazy forms of classically sculpted marble never congeal into shape to reveal their secret, the inner life of the head from which the image springs. It remains a mass of maddeningly blurred and abstracted planes, opaque surfaces and globular orbs which form, re-form, disappear and slide away once again into patches of marbleized light and shadow, challenging and obstinate in its abstraction.

Just below the central point of the photo and slightly to the right, there does appear to be an ear, a rather disproportionately large and misplaced human ear with a black cave-like center and a long, extended lobe. It is, however, not connected to other recognizable or discernible facial or cranial structures.

A possible key to the image may be in Syracuse, Sicily, however, at a site Twombly must have surely visited and seen. There, close by the Ionian Sea, is a naturally carved-out limestone quarry and man-made, water-storing cave in Syracuse, called 'the Ear of Dionysius.' It is said to have been created by Dionysius I, the fifth century B.C.E. tyrant of that powerful Greek city-state who legendarily used the acoustically formidable, ear-shaped cave-grotto as a prison. It was supposedly only named by the artist Caravaggio, however, in 1586. Dionysus—Dionysius? Caravaggio himself died under mysterious circumstances in Syracuse in 1609. It remains one of Twombly's most enigmatically shrouded impressions. In this one photograph, 'Dionysus' manages to retain his ambiguities, his silence and deeply occluded identity. Score one for the unusually secretive god.

Less disconcertingly abstracted, is the photograph of 'Grapes' Twombly shot in Gaeta in 1997 and had printed in 2008. They, like the head, are over-exposed, whitened out to points of invisibility, blotches of no particular form or shape, as other grapes group and re-group around the whiteness of a vanishing plate. These grapes are clearly reminiscent of Caravaggio's 'sick' Bacchus portrait (1593-4), who, in stark contrast to his seductively flushed-cheek, wine-drinking Bacchus (1595), as a young man with pallid lips and gray skin, clenches grapes which appear on the verge of being putrid and rotten. These are the rancid fruits of a darkly decaying Bacchus, depraved, perhaps syphilitic, and dying.

Also from 1997, a set of three studies of "Grapes, Gaeta, 1997," are purplish tints of black and white clusters lying flat on a striated base which progressively takes up more and more of the photographic space until the succulently glinting grapes are confined to the top third of the flat-planed image by the third print of the series. The lines running across the face of the surface resemble the time lines of earlier works from the late '60s in their straight-ruled, geometric, conceptual and hard-edged contrasts with the naturally rounded, fleshy, and organically bunched fruit on top.

Decidedly different and in contrast to these more subtle and shadowy reflections of the Bacchus mythologem, in one of his most amazing and nearly overwhelming masses of flowing colors created in a healthily robust Dionysiac vein, Twombly dedicated an absolutely eye-popping drawing/painting to the archaic Greek poet Archilochos in 1989. It is a flailing mountainous burst of purples, cascading rivulets and squiggles of wine-colored paint, poured and pushed in huge grapey clusters of mad finger, hand, and brush pulls and sweeps, cascading down and covering nearly the entire large sheet of paper. The piece vibrates and bursts with lively movement. The paint is palpable and pulsates off the surface, drenching the viewer with barely contained emotions. The whole surface shamelessly confronts one and conveys the feeling of grapes being trampled, smeared and squashed underfoot, so that the piece gurgles and gushes paint forth in thick liquid tresses and juicy clots. Fragments of a poem, '[a thin ribbon of/ paper],' and single words: 'WINE/CONCERNS/WEEPS/INCLINES/CRASH,' are jotted vertically down the top left-hand side in Twombly's usual jittery script. It is a monolithic piece, reminiscent in its craggy, built-up flowing piles and dynamically activated blocks of directly applied color, of an abstracted Chinese mountain landscape, made here however, of running rivers of grapey purple pigments. Passages of paint appear nearly surrealistic in their hyper-defined knots and tubular streamings.

Hung offhandedly once on a back staircase wall at the Gagosian Gallery on Madison Avenue, suspended there all by itself, it loomed and glowered darkly and powerfully, until it exploded the confines of paper, frame, glass, white walls, and rectangular spaces, flooding the entire upscale gallery building, offices, stairwells, and lobby, all awash and pouring with roiling torrents of inundating wine. Even off and away in a back room, in a stairwell and in hidden spaces, Dionysos joyously uncontained, overflowingly enacts his private hierophanies.

'*Et in Arcadia ego*,' Twombly writes twice across his 'Autumn' panel of the majestic 'Four Seasons' (1993/4) series, "*Quattro Stagioni*," once above the mid-point of the canvas and once quite near the bottom. 'Even in Arcadia there am I,' the subject of two famous paintings by Poussin (1628-9, 1637-8), also called "Arcadian Shepherds," after an earlier version by Guercino (1618-20), and quoted by Twombly as a *memento mori*, evokes the melancholy and fleetingness of life's passing, as well as the meaningfulness and enduring value of art in creating lasting images of beauty and pleasure—even in the shadow of death's presence. On the 'Autumn' version of 'The Four Seasons' which resides at MoMA, he writes in pencil the name 'Bacchus' at the mid-point and far left of the canvas, and 'SILENUS' quite near the bottom, thus bringing these masterworks well within the Dionysiac force field.

The multiple, circularly painted orbs, vortices of vermillion and deep violet, ejaculate bright red or black spurtings towards the right. The phalluses of the '70s have become, by the '90s, inseminating/ shooting balls of energy, nearly covered over with gobs of black and purple paint, still aggressively and powerfully applied. In both the Tate and MoMA versions of the 'Autumn' panel, the whole extreme left-hand sides, in the New York version, only from the middle down, and in the London cycle, from the top to the bottom of the canvas, close to the left edge, run and drip with purple, black, brown, and green streamings of wet paint. Again, the grapes' blood flows freely in these works. Pressed blotches of purple, exuding painterly juices, keep reminding us of the artist's vitality and his bountiful wellspring of earth-grown and archetypally supported sources.

Autumn has always been the special time of year for Bacchus in Twombly's painterly mythologies. The summer's sun stored sweetly in the grapes is ready for harvesting and pressing. The variegated hues of rich, concentrated wine, the fall season with its sharp tang and decay, and vine and grape leaves streaked scarlet and gold, overflow the artist's goblet and palette and fill painting after painting with the energy gathered in summer's heat. The Phoenician purples of sea shells, Tyrian dyes, the robes of raving Roman emperors and bottomless cups filled deeply with rich crimson wines, run, dash, stain, and blot with fluid washes many of his large canvases of the '90s. The fall season, falling in love, falling into depression too, and just plain falling, a willingness to sink into the earth, all seem to stir up images of deeply interior passions needing to go even further down to meet their origins. Both series of 'Seasons' started in Bassano during the wine harvest, conjoin images and feelings of aging, ripening, and turning inwards. Burton, writing in his *Anatomy of Melancholy* in 1621, says that Autumn is the most melancholy age of man and that this emotional down-turning comes naturally with the increasing years. Melancholy, mistiness, madness, and creativity, merge darkly, especially in the two 'Autumn' panels of the 'Four Seasons' cycles. Particularly in the Tate version, there is much black, though red still predominates. The red and black colors together lend a decidedly aggressive, violent and slightly hysterical edge to the autumnal brooding, wine drinking, and darkening emotionality.

Also, skittishly written in red crayon and overpainted on these large canvases, are the names Pan and Priapus. These are both figures, as we have seen before, who are closely associated with phallic sexuality. Pan, the unpredictable god of nature, is the spirit of the landscape, woods, and wilderness, that is at once exciting, unsettling, anxiety-provoking and meaningful in his symphony of uncanny rustling, chirping, and crashing sounds which sometimes can also arouse pan-ic. A favorite subject for Twombly, as can be seen in two beautiful drawing collages from 1975, and in a sprawling seven-part painting/drawing from 1980, Pan also appears as a classical sculpture in a four-part series of photographs, "Detail of Pan, Bassano in Teverina, 1980." The yellowish white surfaces of his marble skin are disturbingly punctuated, however, by the stigmata of nails pounded into the stone and plaster torso. Also from 1985, Twombly's sculpture "Untitled," clearly depicts Pan's pipe, the syrinx, the shepherd's instrument named after Pan's chasing of the nymph named Syrinx, who, transforming into a reed to escape the demi-god's mad lust, he in turn vengefully made into a musical instrument for posterity.

Priapus, as we have mentioned, is such a grotesque and distorted figure in his exaggeratedly sexual physical characteristics that his own mother, Aphrodite, goddess of eroticism and voluptuous beauty, repudiates and disowns him. Priapus, like Dionysos, has also always been mythologically associated with the fig tree and the fig-wood phallus. Horace in his *Satires*, has Priapus declaim: "*Olim truncus eram ficulnus*," "I was once, long ago, the trunk of a wild fig tree" (Horace 1959, p. 70); and later he refers to his own anatomy: "*diffisa nate ficus*," "cleft buttocks of fig tree wood." In this 'Satire' (I,8), Priapus also describes his own terrifyingly phallic appearance, "with the THING," "with the pole that projects long and bloody red from my frightful middle," as "my worst of all possible parts" (ibid.). During his own phallic and priapic profusions from 1959-1961, Twombly also did a series of three drawings in 1960 in Rome with both colored and graphite pencil, wax crayon, and ballpoint pen entitled "Priapus" (Twombly 2012a, pp. 208-11).

The name 'Silenus' which appears in the MoMA 'Autumn' panel, (as well as elsewhere through Twombly's *oeuvre*), refers to the teacher of Dionysos. Like Priapus and Pan, Silenus (*Silenos*) is a decidedly phallic figure, and as such, is a mentor and an initiator for the god into the realms of sexuality, fertility, unabashed masculinity, *and* fecund femininity. Mythographers, especially in the eighteenth-century, considered Silenus to have been fathered by Pan with a woodland nymph. Silenus has also since antiquity been portrayed as a gently fathering figure for Dionysos from his early infancy in Nysa in numerous tender vase paintings and sculptures. In these portrayals, Silenus as mentor often receives the child from Hermes and prepares to rear him with the nymphs. The *Silenoi* taken collectively, are like the Satyrs (*Satyroi*), a group of half-animal, half-man, ithyphallic creatures who often appear as consorts and revelers in the rousing train of Dionysos. Close associates, lovers, as well as rapine pursuers of the nymphs and maenads, they are usually characterized by an unruly, snub-nosed mien and sport pointed faun's or goat's ears, hooves and horses' tails. They are often depicted dancing, drinking, or drunk, initiating novices, or chasing nymphs, maenads, muses, or any other available women; and with their erect phalluses, appear as always randily ready to consummate their overtly libidinal urges. They are images of unbridled natural urgency.

The rampant, pan-sexual nature of these figures, Twombly's familiars, when literally writ large on his canvases, clearly connote the powerful erotic energy which imbues so many of his painting performances with an undeniably sexual jolt. The sheer physical stamina, strength, desire and libido needed to conceptually conceive these grand painting projects, and then to tirelessly work on and satisfactorily complete the extremely large canvases, day after day, year after year, honor these deeply embodied sources of the artist's actual creative and erotic energies. Pan, Priapus, Silenus, the Satyrs, the Maenads, Ariadne, Aphrodite, Eros, Bacchus, and Dionysos, his ensemble and *komos* of mythical colleagues and collaborators, all these lively figures, constitute a veritable pantheon of archetypal forces which clearly accompany Twombly and his work energetically, powerfully moving in and through him and his transforming *poiesis* into a ravishing, splendidly realized and accomplished art which spans many ages in its far-flung, richly-embellished, and scintillatingly bejeweled net of associations and meanings.

VI

BACCHUS AND THE FOLDS OF THE WORLD

In terms of the arc, sweep and scale of the major large series' of paintings that Twombly was working on through the 1990s and into the new millennium, we find the specifically Dionysiac propulsion which had already guided him for so long reaching its grandest visionary climax in 2005 with the exhibition opening in November of that year of the 'Bacchus' cycle. The suite of eight monumental paintings shown at that time, and in fact created with the prospective exhibition space of the Gagosian Gallery on Madison Avenue in New York clearly in mind, opened replete with its full title: 'Bacchus Psilax Mainomenos.' Bacchus, 'the enlightened' or 'initiated one'; Psilax, 'the winged one'; Mainomenos, 'the mad' or 'raving one.' The bipolar god Dionysos, doubled, split, two in one, embracing the divergent poles of ecstasy and madness, then burst upon the art scene at full throttle.

Acting in the role of Bacchic herald and avatar, Twombly, with this exhibit provides the performative medium of painting as an operatic stage for a fully participatory event. The installation of these eight large paintings, rather than being just 'another art show,' created a space of multiple possibilities for an actual initiatory enactment of the god Bacchus himself, for his most up-to-date appearance and 'happening,' for real in the new millennium, right there on Madison Avenue. Transforming the gallery into a magnificent ritual dramatic theatre through the sustained elaboration of painterly movement and thematic continuities within the schematic grandiosity of the works themselves, Twombly facilitated a totally contemporary live *experience* of Bacchus.

Called or not called, the god was definitely made manifest in rhythmical painterly motion. The effect was powerful, puzzling, astounding, and nearly overwhelming, for its sheer positioning of a universe of questions, absence of answers, openness, and both lack of and defiance of closure within a completely resolved, near-perfect painting cycle. Bacchus was indeed fully present, and yet at the same time, was also thoroughly hidden, and, needing to be discovered by each individual viewer, anew, on their own particular terms, and in the light of their own unique life, its transiency and poignancy, and their patiently awaiting death.

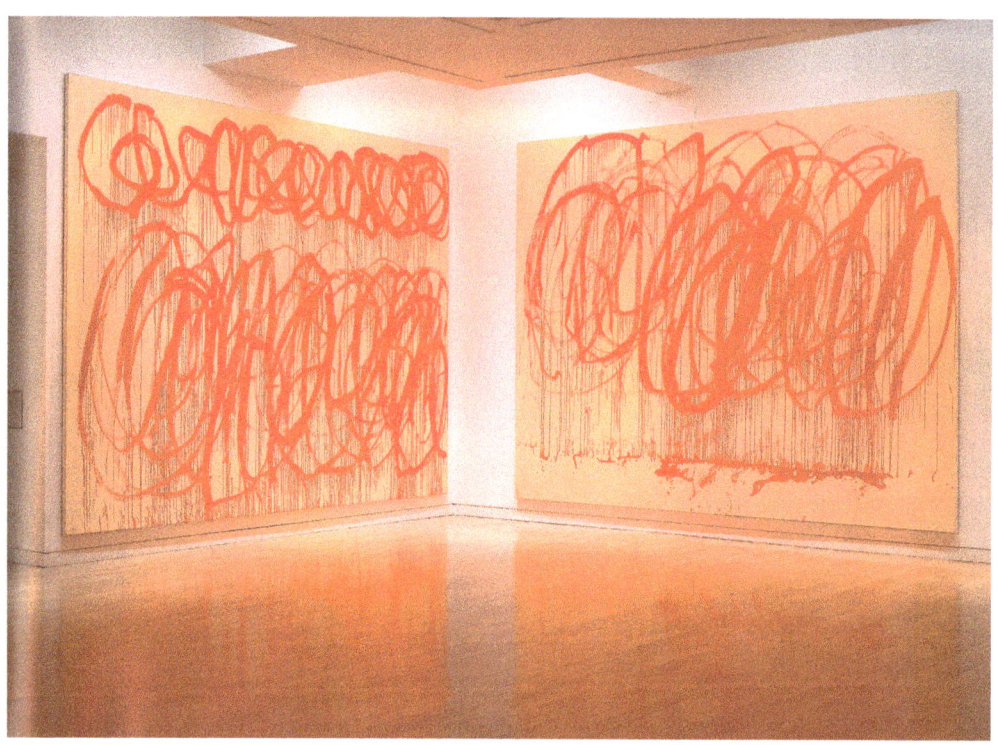

22.   Cy Twombly, *Untitled*, installation view Parts I and II, 2005.

At age 77, with this culminating 'Bacchus' cycle, the artist reveals himself at the very top of his form. In the presentation of the god nakedly unleashed in painted frenzy, Twombly holds nothing back. He gives away everything in each and every one of these eight canvases, making his own devotional offerings to Bacchus right there on the altars of the lavishly realized and radiating surfaces.

While all the canvases are uniformly 124 to 128 inches high, they range in size from 158 to 194 inches wide, so that there are in three of the eight pieces, over three-foot differences in width. By any standards of contemporary art, especially as one thematically cohesive cycle of paintings concerning essentially one 'figure,' albeit a 'god,' the 'Bacchus' work is both literally huge and perhaps the most significant artistic testament to a divinity in our time. Taken on its own aesthetic terms, the entire suite can fairly be seen as a spiritual *Gesamtkunstwerk*, a total, all-inclusive and self-contained world and work of art, from conception through execution, to presentation and reception.

Though individually 'untitled,' the eight paintings when seen together provide a gesturally enfolding and unfolding series of stories, stages, phases, aspects, or even stations, in a Dionysian mythodramatic experience. They constitute as an ensemble, a genuine initiation into the mysteries of Dionysos, with the person of Twombly as a self-absented psychopomp, and they are themselves both a mystery play and a passion play. The paintings taken one by one are each individual circumambulations of a particular *mysterium*. From *myein* in Greek, 'to initiate into religious rites,' they are the works of a *mystēs*, an 'initiate', into the transformative and renewing powers of art. They are episodes in an ongoing, unfolding journey, undulating moments which carry us along an unknown path with no definite final goal or destination, other than the quickening and enlivening pulse of heightened adventure, restrained excitement, and continuously creative discovery at their core.

The eight large paintings encompass and deluge the viewer in an abundance and virtual excess of sensations. They are incredibly sensual and erotic. Their vast size, bold slashes, and looping drapes of viscous color, and the concentrated conceptual force of their wrap-around intensity, threaten to overpower the viewer. Yet despite their palpably formidable and looming presences, the 'Bacchus' paintings hold us fast and securely in an immense, confident, and deeply gratifying embrace. They dazzle, daze, and hypnotize with an effulgent brilliance and warmth, reflecting and bouncing off each other, our eyes, and the polished shiny wooden floors of the gallery. The viewer is held captive by the gaze of the paintings themselves. Permeated with soul, these works look directly back at us, wide-eyed. We feel their urge to speak, however mysteriously, to yield up their secrets in an intimate exchange. We are held hostage in the fascinating surround of their strange and violent beauty.

It is as if Twombly, in this grand cycle, has refashioned from within the veritably fleshy folds and fiery desires of Bacchus himself, and portrayed with his own iconographical swoops, the very image of the multivalent god *incarnate*. In and through the paintings, an "'incarnate principle' of doubling, difference, and desire crocheted in to all that is *there*" (Johnson in Merleau-Ponty 1993, p. 50) spreads out before us, "its oneiric universe of carnal essences, actualized resemblances, mute meanings" (Merleau-Ponty 1993, p. 130). These paintings unabashedly reveal and proclaim that self and 'things,' like these very art works, are "reciprocal dimensions of the same Being." They are made like the world of the very same "stuff as the body" (ibid., pg. 47), and they present this "original unity of embodied self and sensed things as 'total parts' of the same carnal, corporeal world" (Burch in Merleau-Ponty 1993, p. 357). All of this Twombly precipitates through *poiesis*. "The world is made of body's own stuff" (ibid.), Merleau-Ponty writes, and "things are the secret folds of my flesh" (ibid., p. 259). These great-souled, phenomenal images are themselves actual material bodies that *look at us*, as much, and as intently, as we may look at them.

Louis Marin, in describing the sublime in Poussin's paintings of storm, lightning, fire, fear and passion, could just as well be delineating the shattering birth and eruption of Bacchus out of his mother's lightning-struck womb, or the hierophanic burst of Bacchic immediacy we feel in the thundering presence of these paintings as they appear in what he calls:

> the punctual present of the instantaneous, which, far from totalizing the flow of duration, divides it so as to *reduce* the present and *dissipate* it in the infinitesimal instant of the "sudden" ..."now" ... become the "suddenly" ... an unthinkable, unrepresentable, dimension, since it is the pure emergence of an accident-event with no beginning or end. The instant as instantaneousness is an incommensurable element.
>
> (Marin 1999, p. 138)

These are not paintings that we can either immediately grasp or easily comprehend. They are too big, and the idea of them is too grand, too far beyond the as-yet perceptible. Neither are they 'about' anything that we know, that is specific, clear or familiar. In their entirety, they even remain somewhat eerie, dangerous, threatening, and uncanny. They retain their own autonomy and 'otherness.' They do not represent, 'stand for,' or 'mean' anything in any particular or conventional sense, as much as they simply and rhythmically just remain *there*, before us, present, moving on their own self-prescribed terms, as subject/objects. They vibrate, pulsate, and convey intense thought and emotion through their many layers of dynamically built-up marks, which overflow the borders of their frames. We are absorbed by them. They are not narratives; they are events. They are both vehicles as well as broad depictions of an entire world view, a *Weltanschauung*, a particular universe, a certain attitude, experience and outlook on the world, perhaps even over many parallel and simultaneously occurring worlds.

The paintings defeat our attempts and desires to take in so much splendor all at once. They take time and resist all efforts to possess them. We are overcome by their scope, and forced as spectators into a 'letting go' of all personal strivings, aspirations, and perhaps of all rational, conceptual thinking altogether. That may indeed be their underlying aim. They are visceral and strike deeply into the subterranean poetry of life's bloodstream.

"I'm a painter," Twombly says, "and my whole balance is not having to think about *things*. So all I think about is painting" (In Sylvester 2001, p. 179).

The paintings physically dwarf us as individuals with their utter size and power. They are uncontrollable as are our own reactions and responses to them. We are forced instead into an ecstatic submission to them as 'totally other', and thereby, into a heightened awareness of the moment itself, just purely being present, sensuously looking and feeling; immediate, fleeting and infused with pathos. Through them, it becomes possible for us to emigrate and open up, to go out of self and into the world as 'the outside', as "'the other side' of its power of looking" (Johnson in Merleau-Ponty 1993, p. 47, and Merleau-Ponty 1993, p. 124). Before the 'Bacchus' paintings, seeing itself becomes an activity of seemingly infinite depth and sheer wonderment at the extent of just what is going on materially before one's eyes. The many transformations and permutations of the materials, and the changeability of matter itself, keep us, our eyeballs and entire bodies, moving, back and forth and around the panoramic picture planes, dynamically continuing and furthering them. So many incidents, events, spatters, and strokes. We swim, move, immerse, and step into, out of and around the picture's frame, surface, and depths. A reciprocal loop of movement is set up where both viewer and painting are participating and observing each other in a mutually gratifying process. In contrast to cinema, *we* move in front of these canvases and physically recapitulate aspects of their making, so that the paintings are still 'working,' and are very much in themselves works-in-progress, and *in-process*. Viewing them is to engage in an ongoing rhythmical, dialogical and dialectical *activity*. We become so captivated that, "the seer and the visible reciprocate one another and we no longer know which sees and which is seen" (Merleau-Ponty 1968, p. 139).

Like the slender and supple movements of the god Bacchus himself and his lively entourage of revelers dancing across an ancient vase, the paintings themselves seduce us into fantasy, imaginal journeys, endless reveries and polyvalent openings into the world of the 'other,' 'otherness' itself, and the world of matter at play. These images present *physis*, substances, materials, matter itself come alive. The mind is quickened, yet the body too is just as strongly stirred and touched. The work beckons to us to come out of our usual, everyday and cognitively bounded selves, to come forth and join the dance. The paintings ask to enter our bodies and for our bodies to interchangeably inhabit *their* spaces, to disappear into *them*. We move rhythmically *with* them. They invite us out of our normal ideational patterns and into a more boundless space where we do not any longer *know* or *have to know* what is going on, or even where we are. They aerate our usual bodily space-time coordinates. They dare and gesture with their colors and forms, and call to us to come out and play, to come outside of ourselves, to be alive in the world, to move as the world is moving.

In their immense and containing presence, we can finally relax and allow ourselves to slowly dissolve and just give in to the luxuriance, breadth, and generosity of spirit with which they were so clearly created. Our tightly-held individualities can loosen and collapse before their cascading furls and rivulets of crimson as we are set joyously adrift on expansive seas of emotionally buoyant color. Carried on their exuberant waves, we can delight and trust in the enthusiastic pleasures of painting itself. We *feel* these works and simultaneously sense the physical vitality of our own selves as a body that moves in space and time, *and* can also create. We become aware of ourselves as the ciphers and hieroglyphs of a boundless *poiesis*. We directly sense and intuitively grasp ourselves as a body and soul that is, by definition, creative, a poetry in rhythmical, streaming motion. As pure expressions of *poiesis* in and of themselves, these 'Bacchus' paintings inspire us as moving bodies and as 'makers.' They gently urge us towards *poiesis*; they tenderly usher us out into an individually erotic creativity.

These paintings at the same time, however, have no need to persuade, convince, argue or teach. They are not in the least didactic or pedagogic. Though in their facture, facticity and transparency they are anything but simple, they are also very down to earth, workmanlike. They embody a human craftsmanship and genuine caring for the material world. They make us aware of our basic common humanness, sameness and similarities as indivisible beings, individuals, breathing the same air in the same gallery, museum, city street, forest, or living room, equal before art. Bacchus *demotikos*, the god 'of the people,' levels the playing fields of perceptual experience. The selfsame visible world opens to all.

In the same movement as the paintings seem to democratically unite us and inclusively join all viewers in a collective whole larger than our own isolated, discrete, and separate selves, they also offer themselves as a *temenos*, a sacred sanctuary and support for our own deepest idiosyncrasies and individualities. They forgive and accept all comers. While they erase hierarchies and distances with their bold freedoms, muscular strengths, and sinuously rippling energies, they still remain inherently reserved, restrained, and unto themselves. Tolerant, respectful and accepting of all differences, they provide a numinous precinct for our most intimate inwardness and inviolate vulnerabilities. Honoring our singularities, we can be totally open before them, trusting, safe, letting down, letting go, and grateful for the gifts of quietude and calm at their center.

Almost as a kind of rehearsal or warm-up for this monumental series in honor of *poiesis*, and painted a whole year earlier, Twombly completed a cycle of six large paintings in 2004 which are also called, "Untitled," or, "Bacchus 1st Version." This earlier series appears retrospectively as a first major run-through of the 'Bacchus' theme, in its format, style, and coloring, and they contain all the predominant motifs found in the more developed and mature mastery of the 2005 'Bacchus' cycle. Considerably smaller in scale, size and number, more tentative, less assertive and assured, the first version of 'Bacchus' nevertheless still presents a powerful gathering of the same performative Dionysian aesthetics.

The red loops and drips are all there. The yellow grounds provide the same backgrounds and stage curtains for the dynamic vermillion sweeps and swoops. They are still the flesh-colored skins and the body-grounds of Bacchus crisscrossed by relentless strokes and gashes of blood-red paint. And sometimes the creamy pale yellows even come forth to fold over the surges, thrusts and dominating wettened red swaths of paint-laden brush strokes. In this earlier series, the red draping forms themselves, the kernels of the god's dance movements, are tighter, more controlled and bunched together. The coils and bundles have yet to open up fully and expand. Yet they are all still there, wound up and brooding inwardly, poised *in nuce*, not yet convinced of their own power to emerge. They bristle with tension and ripple, ready to crack apart and burst open.

This first version of Bacchus duplex, *Psilax* and *Mainomenos*, was shown by the Gagosian Gallery four years after they were painted, in an exhibition entitled, 'For what you are about to receive,' six paintings and one sculpture, at the Red October Chocolate Factory in Moscow in 2008. All six of the paintings are the exact same size, 98 ½ x 74 ¾ inches (250 x 190 cm.). Quite unlike the later series which followed, every one of the six 'untitled' paintings is in fact, named, so they *are* actually titled, written on at the top of each canvas. First off, they are all labelled 'Bacchus,' in small, scratchy, and slight lettering, all on the top left. 'Psilax,' inscribed much larger, redder and either more centered or slightly off to the right, also in crayon, essentially 'names' the tops of versions numbered I, II, III, and VI. 'Mainomenos,' writ large and thickly on the more intense and crazed versions, numbered IV and V, appears aptly designated to make these two paintings of the six, strongly stand out from the rest.

It is of particular interest that the way this first version of 'Bacchus' in six paintings was installed as an ensemble in Moscow, differs significantly from the way they were originally numbered, which may in fact be the order in which they were painted. As a result, they were initially hung in real time in a very different sequential order from the way they are actually numbered in the *Catalogue Raisonné*, Volume V (Twombly 2009, p. 125). Graphically arrayed at the exhibit in Russia as a dynamic cycle, they progress as a group in an entirely coherent and thematically compelling arrangement. The two 'Mainomenos' paintings are meaningfully and symmetrically interspersed with the four other 'Psilax' pieces to provide affective emphases. They can thus be read on the wall from left to right as Versions I, IV, III, II, V, VI. With the 'Mainomenos' pieces placed second and fifth, and 'Psilax,' first, third, fourth and sixth (or last), a very different and symbolically specific rhythm is set up. This way of grouping them for presentation definitely has a strong emotional resonance, a pictorial and mythical logic, and a clearly patterned aesthetic order which the cataloged numbering completely lacks. Here the two 'mad,' 'raving,' *Mainomenos* canvases percussively punctuate and animate the whole surrounding series of the six Bacchus pieces as an entire ensemble.

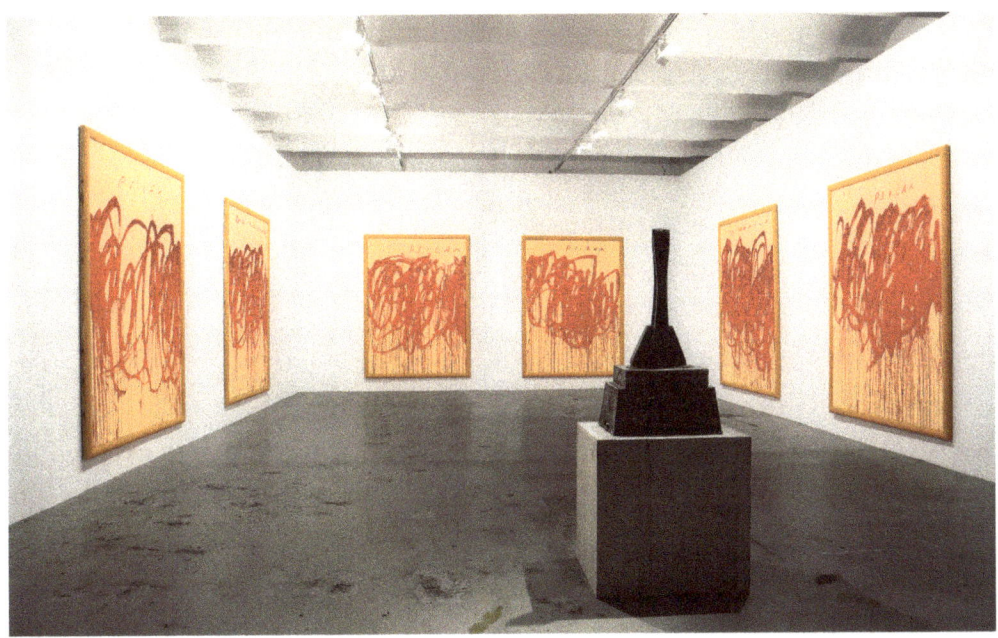

23. Cy Twombly, *Untitled (Bacchus 1st version)*, 2004, installation view, 2008.

Synchronistically, it appears that the rhythms of these six Bacchus paintings as they were exhibited, numerically and thematically form a hexagram, which is straight out of the Chinese 'Book of Changes,' the *I Ching* (Wilhelm/ Baynes 1950/72). The order in which the paintings are hung for actual showing exactly corresponds to the identical six lines in the same order found in a particular *I Ching* hexagram:

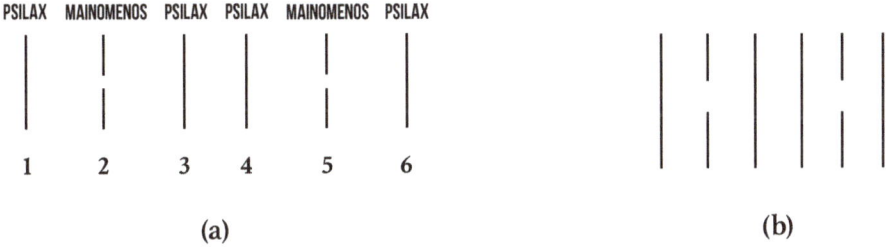

or horizontally, as they would actually appear in the 'Book of Changes,' built up from bottom to top:

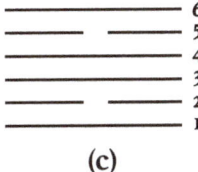

In this divination system, the unbroken solid lines are odd-numbered and are therefore considered to be 'masculine'; and the broken lines are evenly numbered and archetypally 'feminine' (ibid., p. 118). This configuration above, figure (c), is composed of two identical nuclear trigrams,

_____ _____   , stacked one on top of the other in the *I Ching*, as in figure c,
_____   or, arranged like the paintings are exhibited, side by side, as
(d)   in figures a and b.

In terms of the original Chinese text, this 'Bacchus' ensemble is a presentation of the trigram 'Li,' doubled, 'Li' and 'Li,' or 'Li' over 'Li,' or visually: 'Li'. This produces hexagram number 30, 'The Clinging Fire.' The 'image' is 'Li' thus of 'fire' doubled, fire upon fire. This very specific image is created by just this one, and only one, possible random arrangement or placement of six individual lines, or paintings, in this exact correspondence with each other, out of potentially 64 different combinations, each of them having their own unique 'image,' 'judgment,' interpretation, context, commentary, history, and genealogy, in the long cultural tradition of reading, studying, and practically using the *I Ching*.

In the traditional scholarly commentary on the hexagram, which derives from ancient Taoist and Confucian texts, the sources speak of this image, 'Li,' 'The Clinging Fire,' as a presentation of 'nature in its radiance' (ibid.). They further state that:

> Human life on earth is conditional and unfree, and when man recognizes this limitation and makes himself dependent upon the harmonious and beneficent forces of the cosmos, he achieves success... By cultivating in himself an attitude of compliance and voluntary dependence, man acquires clarity without sharpness and finds his place in the world.
>
> (ibid., p. 119)

The 'message' of this hexagram is thus, that through the persevering light of fire, the darkness and all the material substances around the fire, including the air itself, become illuminated, burn more brightly, and/or become consumed in the flames. Analogically, in the ensemble of these six paintings, and in the way they are designed to be viewed, the two 'Mainomenos' pieces, two and five, can be seen as the unquenchable forces of 'raving madness,' that is, the fire itself, which animates and energizes the four other 'Psilax' paintings, the aerial elements surrounding the fire, one, three, four and six, making them blaze up and burn more clearly and brightly. The redness of the fire, 'madness,' *Mainomenos*, would also in this context be associated with the 'feminine' powers and energies of the unconscious, the psyche *in* nature, the very soul of nature, making it enlivened and flare up (Fierz-David 1988 and Hall 1988).

We have already seen Twombly exploring this aspect of Dionysos/ Bacchus as 'Psilax,' the 'winged one,' 'of the air,' light, and thereby spiritual, even when 'wing' was affixed to representations of Dionysos as the phallus, as well as in the 'Wings of Madness' series, in the fiery 'Summer Madness' paintings from 1974, 1984, and 1990, and in the aerial 'Petals of Fire' (1989). Already even much earlier, he had created in 1972 and again in 1979, multiple series of drawings titled with some version of 'wings' with classical Greek references (In Twombly 2016). Also, we find in the two very large, beautiful paintings, "Untitled," (92 ⅛ x 67 ⅞ in.), both from 1992, that Twombly quotes a line translated from Baudelaire's *Journaux Intimes*: "I have felt the wind of the wing of madness" (Leeman 2005, p. 291). The poet Emily Dickinson of whom Twombly was quite fond and also directly quoted in a late painting, writes: "Inebriate of air-am-I" (Twombly 2014, p. 290). The very same 1992 "Untitled" paintings mentioned above, also contain the quote from Rilke's 1918 poem, "On Music": "outside, as amazing space, as the other side of the air" (Rilke 1981, p. 169). For Rilke, this "other side of the air," is, in the poem, meant to signify not only music, but "the silence of paintings," and the "Language where Language ends," three very different and singularly powerful notions. The concept of wings as aspects of divinity, inspiration, and divine possession, or the heaven-sent 'madness' instigated by a god, are themes which are frequently found conjoined in ancient art and literature. The actual images of *'psyche'* itself, the 'soul,' as both essential life breath and as a small winged being, human figure, or butterfly leaving the mouth and body of the deceased at the time of death, is often found concretely depicted on classical Greek tombstones and on *lekythoi*, the fine, ancient white-ground funeral vases buried with the dead.

Plato, in his unparalleled discussion of the philosopher's vocation in the *Phaedrus*, says there that the *psyche*, the soul of the philosopher, must *re-grow* its wings in order to once again reunite with the god or gods from whence it has come. This form of madness, "divine possession," he says, is reserved for the lover who yearns to fly with his belovéd (Plato 1973, p. 56). Furthermore, he claims that both the lover and the belovéd must recollect, discover, and see in themselves and in each other, the traces, traits and attributes of the particular god whose divinity they belong to, partake of, and then essentially must honor with their lives (ibid., pp. 60-1). When the avid Greek geographer, historian, and inveterate traveler, Pausanius, went in the second century A.D. to Amyclae, a village in Laconia, he found that the local people there worshipped Dionysos *Psilax*, which means 'beardless' and refers to the god in his youthful or adolescent form. *Psilax* is also Doric Greek, for 'winged' or 'the winged one,' and clearly points to the god who takes us inspirationally away and aloft, and to an 'other' realm (Bull in Twombly 2005, p. 55).

In this same archetypal/Platonic vein, we can now see that Dionysos then leads those who follow him in his train and through his flowing motions, into a becoming one with the god, a joining with him in both body *and* soul. The dance of Dionysos and his followers is a sinuous, flexible and fluid movement, a rhythmically supple waving and weaving, an effervescent flight of spirit and imagination. *Lysios*, in liberating the psyche, facilitating its release into indeterminacy and freeing the soul, allows the soul to re-gain its wings, that is, its psychological freedom, mobility, and movement, so that it can fly from the literalness, practicality, and concreteness to which it is ordinarily bound by life's mundane daily concerns. The soul has its own spatio-temporal laws, however, comprising an altered and alternative universe with its own quintessentially *psychical* dimensionalities. Psyche gains its true orientation in this invisible and ineffable realm of soaring heights *and* unfathomable depths. It is Heraclitus once again, who in fragment 45, "first brings together *psyche*, *logos* and *bathun* ('depth'): 'You could not find the ends of the soul,' he says, 'though you travelled every way, so deep is its logos'" (In Hillman 1979, pp. 24-5).

In both of these major 'Bacchus' series, Twombly indeed honors and appears to align himself with the retinue of that god who is doubled, dualistic and duplex, aerial *and* fiery, clear and spiritual, *as well as* mad, raving, and raging. This god flies to the suprasensible aethers of eternal Olympos, and descends when necessary to the chthonic underworlds of water, Hades, and death.

In both of the 'Bacchus' series, there are also basically only two groups of colors, reds and flesh-colored yellows, red upon yellow. Likewise, we find in the *I Ching*, in the same hexagram of 'The Clinging Fire,' it is said once again that it is the *twofold* clarity of man that clings to what is right and can therefore shape the world. Our nature *is* twofold, our consciousness split, and we must constantly embrace both sides in order to consciously choose, pick, and mindfully decide for the one or the other. This acceptance of our doubleness, mortality, and the judgements, choices and consequences they entail, and the wisdom to decide between these often gaping opposites, is conveyed in Rilke's gravid poem, "The Apple Orchard," written from Albrecht Dürer's woodcut, "The Fall." The engraving shows the entwined figures of Adam and Eve receiving the apple from the serpent, himself wrapped around the tree; spirals everywhere. Rilke writes: "...all must be/Harvested and yielded, when a long life willingly/Cleaves to what's willed and grows in mute resolve" (In Jacobus 2012, p. 38). This is a concordance of living with our innermost nature, our doubleness, separated from our self and yet still holding the divide, intentionally embracing our internal divisions.

It is the divine madness of Bacchus, our *Mainomenos* nature, that provides the fire. This raving core at the center of human personality *is* our uniqueness and individuality. We are all divinely mad. It is our transpersonal legacy from Dionysos/Bacchus, the innocently playing child god, dismembered and eaten by the Titans who are then smote by Zeus' thunderbolts, incinerated on the spot and turned into ash. In the Orphic anthropogony, out of this still smoking *stuff*, Zeus creates nothing less than the human race itself. The riven and split human beings that we are, arising out of this gruesome Orphic creation myth, must thus bear forevermore the brutal, Titanic and earthly aspect of our nature, which the Orphics and we ourselves until this day call the 'body,' the *soma*, as well as contain the divine spark and god-like parts of the devoured Dionysiac infant within, the *psyche*, our immortal portion, the human 'soul,' boundless and transcendent.

The original self as the wisdom residing within the objective psyche, in both inner and outer nature, is indeed mad, and impelled to perceive and attempt to create an altered and radically transformed world. Twombly embraces and channels this vision of dedication and commitment to total, uncompromising, revolutionary change, in his own way, quietly yet relentlessly, in and through his work.

The artist remained implacable until the end and to the very last paintings he touched, in staying with and following his own Dionysiac thread, the thin red stream of pulsating life impulse which had guided him throughout. After the great 'Bacchus' cycles of 2004-5, it is possible to discern at least three

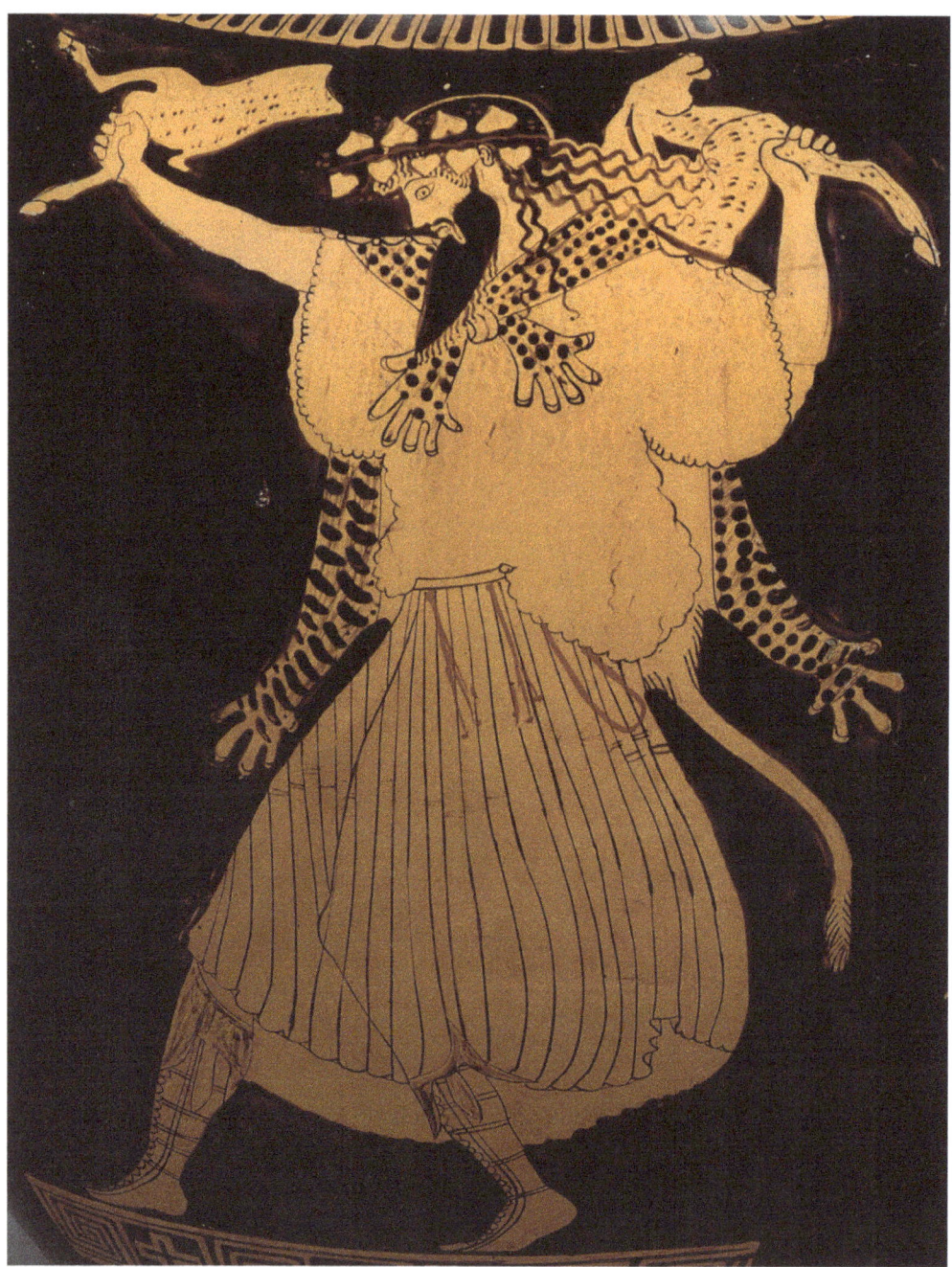

24.   *Dionysos Diasparagmos, Paroxysm of the Ecstatic Crisis*, detail, c. 450 B.C.

distinctly different directions towards which the Dionysiac energies flowed in Twombly's efforts to complete the great 'book' of his life's work, which he always at the same time very well knew would remain unfinished, open and ongoing, even with his own death. The primary continuation, link and indivisible *telos* or goal of the 'Bacchus' series after 2005, and where those paintings directly attained their fullest resolution in bringing to a culmination this one grand sweeping valence of pure energetic expression, is to be found with the three "Untitled (Bacchus)" canvases commissioned by the Tate Modern in London, and now residing there as part of their permanent collection. Twombly completed the three paintings in 2008 and they were gifted to the Tate in 2014. These three masterworks of his late style, summing up the 'Bacchus Psilax Mainomenos' series, appear as the seamless extension and as the inevitable final successors to the eight 2005 pieces. Without missing a single stroke, the three paintings reflect Twombly's performative grappling and engagement once again with the dynamically dancing figures of Bacchus, working on them over an additional three years, from 2006 to 2008, in a continuous and conclusive unfolding of this one majestic theme and image. These three Bacchus works arrive to unfurl themselves as the capstone and coda to the great 'Bacchus Psilax Mainomenos' series, and as the resolved and harmonious pendant to the frenzied and bloodied madness of the earlier works. Here both Psilax and Mainomenos are finally integrated into a wholly embracing and calmer Bacchus. Composed and created in the exact same size and format and with the identical pigments, finishes and palette as their august predecessors, these three canvases still embody all the forcefully propulsive arcing, rolling, looping, and energetically sweeping ecstatic energies of the magnificent cycle to which they belong, but bear on their compelling surfaces in addition, a more pure, starker, streamlined and reduced simplicity which the earlier pieces had seemingly set out precisely to disrupt and destroy. Gone are the jagged intensities, sharply cutting edges and violent stabs and slashes. Gone are the baroque and limitless excesses, flamboyant flourishes, and wanton mayhem. These three monuments to the glory of Bacchus resound instead with a symphonically orchestrated grace and unabashed beauty. The furious agitation, aggressions, and urgencies of unmet desires have given way to a magisterial expansiveness and ease. The great spirals and loops have softened and have become folded into the whole Bacchic cosmos of the work's generous span. The pieces carry themselves with a more stately grace, slower momentum, and a more gentle demeanor as the vermillion gyres now slowly sweep, surge and slide, still cascading their streaming drips as they move from left to right across the broad reaches of flesh-colored canvas. They progress in their dancing movements with a refined processional dignity and a nobility of carriage and bearing. Though still powerfully expressive and inimitably emblematic of his totally contemporary and visionary grasp and 'take' on the dynamisms of the Bacchus mythologem, there is also inhering in these three later works a genuine wisdom and an assured acceptance of the many complications and contradictions of human life. They represent the *summa* and apex of Twombly's specifically Dionysiac directionalities. The god's fury has abated, aged and mellowed along with the artist. The wildness, raving intoxication and boundlessness have seemed in the short space of three years to have resolved themselves into a kind of peace.

Bastian writes of the whole 'Bacchus' series that:

> These glowing red arcs of rhythm pursue their form in a manically charged thought-image, which is not a retrospection but the path into the absolute fathomlessness of a free form. The amplitude opened by these pictures is the expansion of the painterly gestus that relies solely on its own syntax and sensuality. Without a doubt the Bacchus paintings suggested the eruption into an unbound spatio-temporal form, the risk of the 'attainability of the unknown.'
>
> (Bastian in Twombly 2014 b, p. 28)

In his finest hours, Twombly is always leading us to the brink of risking and leaping toward the 'attainability of the unknown.' The particularly Dionysiac forcefields and rolling, enwrapping strokes of brilliant redness, with their great circles, loops, coils, and momentums which appear in Twombly's other late great works, all reveal the echoes, resonances and many of the same basic impulses of these 'Bacchus' pieces, but they also at this point, all at the same time, diverge in a quite different direction, guided by yet newer urges and ambitions, toward now pictorially reconciling forms of writing, language, speech, gesture, poetry, calligraphy, and color into a visually unique rhythm which was to constitute the final burstings and flowerings of his entire artistic trajectory, beyond even his own self's imaginings. The group of works that begin to veer off from the immense panorama of the 'Bacchus Psilax Mainomenos' cycles, while continuing the blood-red theme of instinctual erotics, include the six "Untitled" paintings from the Lexington studio shown at Thomas Ammann Fine Art in Zürich, and additional "Untitled" all done in 2006, two "Untitled" pieces from the 'Blooming' series (2007), and the four additional 'Bacchus' paintings, all made in Gaeta in 2006-8. These significant works and recognizably literal extensions of the Dionysos-Bacchus mythologem all directly presage and formally herald the final carmine-tinged vectors of his entire life's *oeuvre*, the "Camino Real (I-V)" (2009-10) cycle, and the eight "Untitled (Camino Real)" (2011) group of very last paintings, as Twombly, at his ultimate end, turns the *viriditas*, the 'greening' and 'greenness,' and the *rubedo*, the 'redness,' and 'reddening,' into the pure alchemical gold of blinding realization.

VII

The *Rubedo, La Véraison,* the Reddening

Returning now to Twombly's earlier work once again, this redness of the fire and the blazing force of both its creative *and* destructive potentialities is not at all new to his concerns as in the 'Bacchus' paintings. Throughout the course of his *oeuvre*, it is more often the violent, aggressive and blood-tinged reds which take center stage and stand as signal and warning to the powers that lie within the psyche, waiting and ready to be either blindly released and acted out, *or* purposively harnessed and canalized, depending upon our relationship with Dionysos/Bacchus, this dual god.

In the early sixties, it would appear that Twombly himself was furiously grappling with this basic human split, examining the nature of madness, rage, and destruction; and that within the mediums and container of his art, he could eventually find a way to successfully negotiate between the twin warring poles of creativity and violence within himself. His conjunctions of the color red with themes of rage, rape, murder, and madness, found its most continuous and consistent expressions in nearly a hundred, large, blood-flecked canvases, ranging from the explosions of dismembered body parts and organically shooting fluids in the "Ferragosto" paintings of 1961, to the culmination of this cathartic effort, in the 1963 painting in nine parts, "Discourse on Commodus."

Beginning in 1962 alone, Twombly painted numerous, passionately aggressive versions of "Leda and the Swan," all of which spurt blood and more or less book-end by late 1963, several other series of paintings, also taking up themes of violent rape, murder, mania, and death. The motif of the Grecian princess Leda being raped by Zeus in his theriomorphic form of a swan was extremely popular for painters and sculptors from antiquity right up through the Renaissance and into the Baroque period. Indeed, many famous Italian master versions of this mythological event were easily available to Twombly for viewing just in his adopted native Rome alone. Out of the forceful divine coupling depicted in these mythologically-based images, Leda bore further disaster for mankind, however, since her offspring was the radiant Helen, the ostensible 'cause' of the Trojan War, the beauty whose beguiling body and ravishing, demi-divine face launched a thousand ships. Twombly painted no less than five large stagings of this furious conception and copulation.

During this one year, Twombly also painted many versions of the "Death of Giuliano de Medici" (1962-3), in at least six variations, all of them spotted and streaked with bloody red clots and gashes, as well as creating numerous drawings on the same theme. Likewise, the "Death of Pompey" (1962) repeats the form of a 'human-like' rectangular structure surmounted by globes (heads?), which the artist then attacks with palette knives and messily applied crimson pigments. "Catullus" (1962), also split and doubled forms, runs red with circular swirls of blood-stained vermillion. "Venus"(1962), a vortex flying off in different directions, mythologically recalls the fabulously-endowed lover of Adonis, Asian Aphrodite, and her bloodied birth out of the severed genitals of her father Ouranos, which Kronos flung into the sea, thus inseminating her voluptuous aquatic beauty and fluid sexuality with the foam and sea spray of her undulating waves. Many drawings of "Venus," including numerous versions of the violent "Birth of Venus" and "Venus Genetrix" were also done that year (Twombly 2013 b).

Each blood-tinted large painting follows one right after the other in this amazingly prolific year. Next comes "Achilles Mourning the Death of Patroclus" (1962), two 'figures' furiously painted red, tainted and tinted by their battle-spilled lives, emitting, seeping, and gushing pigment, while they themselves are disintegrating into violent whirls. The painting "Study for Vengeance of Achilles" (1962) precedes the dramatically symbolic, "Vengeance of Achilles" (1962), a huge blood-drenched, phallically vertical sword blade. In fact, the shape of the blade mimics the letter 'A,' which for Twombly clearly has "a phallic aggression" (In Sylvester 2001, p. 178). Sharp and triangularly-shaped, it points upwards, the whole top third of the image painted and streaked with very bright, still-glistening red. From the end of 1961 well into 1962, he also completed at least 13 drawings entitled, either "Vengeance of Achilles," or "Study for the Vengeance of Achilles," several of which are essentially analyses of the transformations of the letter 'A' into a crimson-scribbled, bloodied sword point (Twombly 2013 b). The year 1962 finally ends with the painting, "Ides of March," as drips of scarlet gore commemorate the assassination of Julius Caesar at the hands of his erstwhile friends, Cassius and Brutus.

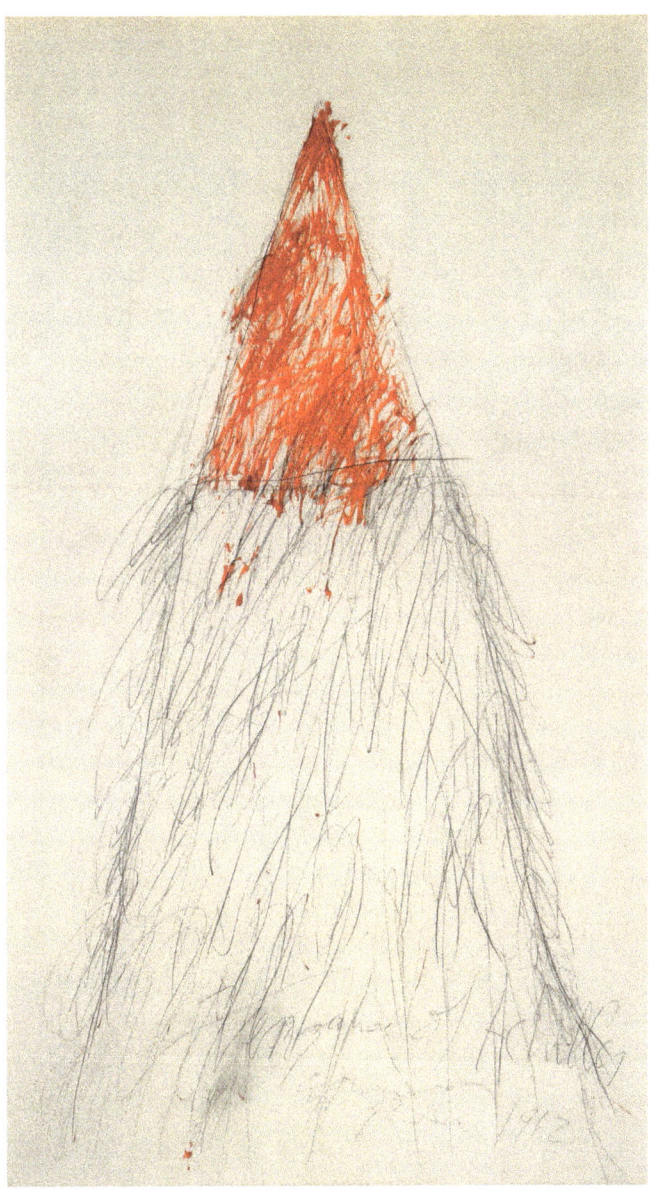

25.   Cy Twombly, *Vengeance of Achilles*, Rome, 1962.

Following the bloodied red thread of violence into 1963, we come to a series of paintings that can be seen as the summation of this difficult and conflicted portion of Twombly's life on an individual/personal level, and perhaps also collectively/archetypally. When the nine-part painting, "Nine Discourses on Commodus" (1963) had its inaugural showing at Twombly's first exhibition in a while in New York City, again at the Leo Castelli Gallery after a four-year hiatus, the piece was presciently described by one critic as "a landscape of delirium" (Twombly 2008, p. 125). It remains to this day as perhaps the quintessential exposition in contemporary art of an historically-based and personified descent into the reddened madness of a truly psychotic process.

The deranged Roman emperor, Aurelius Commodus, reigned from 161 to 192 A.D. Priding himself as a man of combat, he singlehandedly slaughtered untold numbers of wild and exotic animals, as well as poorly-armed and enfeebled slaves, prisoners, and gladiators, all with his own hands before the cheering throngs in the Colosseum. A cruelly paranoid megalomaniac with an unimaginable and brutally literal lust for blood, he himself finally had to be murdered, put down like a mad dog, by a collaboration of his fellow statesmen, close family members and his major military leaders, in order to prevent him from exhausting the entire Roman treasury on his exorbitant, self-aggrandizing exploits and excesses, which included unlimitedly minting his own money with his picture on it.

One can imagine the slide into further and deeper levels of madness and psychic deterioration that overcame Commodus as we follow Twombly's progression, or more accurately, re-gression, in and through the nine panels into more and more primitive modes of mark-making, as we wend our way downwards to the heart of darkness through the nine paintings of the cycle. Like many of the canvases just discussed from the year before, the 'Commodus' series of these nine works all contain some ruled lines, traces of graphs, rectangular figures, numbers, and one or two horizon lines, all drawn in very faint, spindly lead pencil on gray paper or canvas. Superimposed upon the background of fragile pencil lines which act as barely visible grids with their thin frame-like lines, are wildly smeared gobs and crazed jabs, gouges and slashings of mainly red and white paint. Organized into two globular circular forms, the two 'figures' or orbiting swirls, the mad emperor Commodus frantically split and doubled within himself, drip, emanate, and throw off paint from their flailing, madly-wound and whorling centers. Twombly here lays bare the crazed dissociation, disintegration and decomposition of both a human being, a mind alienated and at war with itself, shattered and torn in body and soul, as well as the ultimate nature of all forms and physical materials themselves, the inner *telos* of matter and the material world tending towards entropic dis-solution.

The split into the two orbs so frequent in many of his works from these years, points to a polarization, a twinning and divisive decompensation or psychic mitosis occurring within the artist's own life and personality. The fact that he returned to this doubling motif so often and so forcefully, essentially making portraits, and in reference to historical personages as well as mythical characters, many of whom actually met violent deaths, points to his own deep inner need to work through the rending splits within himself, urgently attempting through innumerable drawings and painting after painting, to hold their unbearable tension and resolve their conflictually rending oppositions.

In the later 'Commodus' paintings, the barely discernible, pencilled background structures, horizon lines and grids, all seem to serve as sort of hints of a stage or platform upon which the dramatic and bloody tragedy of madness and violence plays itself out in body-spilling, living color in the foreground. The two prominently centered forms are eviscerated and torn apart against a rationally conceived and lined background of gray logic and order which cannot begin to contain the physically and emotionally tortured forms. The geometric orientation lines are the barest vestiges remaining of a linear, logical, rational framework upon which human savagery is boundlessly and gesturally performed.

The Roman imperium which brought us the urban grid, civic organization and roads, our number, decimal, and calculating systems, as well as most of our modalities of social, political, judicial and linguistic organization, also sowed the terrible seeds for its own violent demise. The civilization of ancient Rome was ultimately undermined by its own disconnected, split-off brutality, barbarity, greed, and basic inhumanity. The 'Commodus' paintings bring to the fore Twombly's meditations on power, consumption, civilization, and culture, all imagined against the backdrop, and in the face of, sheer, vertiginously spiraling, out-of-control madness. The fragile and fleeting remnants of psyche, creativity, and community, he seems to suggest, may not be adequate to the task of containing or ordering the upsurges of chaos and destructiveness which well up from within, especially when a culture or society is so out of touch with its own inner and outer nature, so divided and alienated from itself, that it cannot manage or bind the erupting violence. The grandiosity and inflated emphasis on mindless consumption and 'commodities,' whether in Rome's 'bread and circuses,' or in our own media-driven or online simulations of reality, and the consequent lack of limits, boundaries, purposes or symbolic meanings which would guide a civilization, a 'polis,' a collectivity, points to the unavoidable crumbling and degeneration of psychic values within, as well as to the decline of a sustainably healthy culture and facilitating environment without. A materialism devoid of soul values rushes in to fill the void and threatens to reign supreme.

Twombly was creating these works at the height of the Cold War; the civil rights movement was boiling and blazing in the South; the Bay of Pigs disaster in Cuba, and threat of nuclear war with the Soviet Union loomed large; the greed for oil continued unabated in both the Near and Far East; John F. Kennedy was assassinated that November; and the United States was becoming increasingly involved in Vietnam with an escalation of troop deployments and aerial bombings. This urge to violence and the rapine domination of people and nature, the artist seems to caution, will be our undoing, as it was for the Romans, and is undoubtedly for every major civilization throughout history. Archetypal forces and gods back these violent and rageful stirrings within us, and they cannot be easily appeased, much less denied or disowned, but only respected, embraced, honored, and in the best of all cases, transformed through creativity and *poiesis*.

Spanning these epochs from the mid-'60s right up to the 'Bacchus' paintings of 2005 and beyond, Twombly continually relied upon the touchstone of ancient Greek culture and civilization as a kind of psychological, spiritual, and ethical compass to guide him through the winding and evolving labyrinths of his own artistic practices. Towards the end of 1964, before Twombly's work veered drastically into the realm of black, gray, and white, austerely devoid of color altogether, the period of the stringent 'blackboard' paintings, he completed one large triptych, picking up once again on the bloodsoaked Homeric theme of the *Iliad* which he had already explored with the 'Achilles' works. In "Ilium (One Morning Ten Years Later)" (1964), we find all the names of the gods and heroes, phalluses spurting and marching left to right across the battlefield of canvas amidst bisected circles, six-spoked wheels, squares, numbers, buttocks, X's, and a dense whitish ground completely painted over and marked with scratches, scribbles and smudges. The painting's surface has become a veritable field of struggle, a record of days and weeks spent engaging with a world of tragic, disturbing, inexorable conflict. And there, remarkable to behold, amid the welter of names, marks, signs, jabs, and gouges, the general carnage and streaks of phallic aggression, on the extreme right-hand border of the central canvas, we find for the very first time on a painting, in small lettering: 'Dionysos,' the name written out and ascending upwards from left to right. Just over it in the same slanting script is the word 'Nyseian,' perhaps indicating the god's nativity, born in Nysos, Dio-Nysos. Even in the midst of all this bloodshed of the Trojan War, we also witness this ecstatic god still keeping his company with the 'Maenads,' his raving women followers, whose collective name also appears right there on the same panel with his own and 'Nyseian' to complete the trinity of the god, his *topos,* and his devotees as well.

As the wilder red colors and color in general nearly vanished completely from his art, from 1965 through 1971, and his expressive range diminished, or he purposively reduced his practice to a minimalist vocabulary once again, of describing lines, pencil and white crayon drawings, circles, endlessly repetitive strokes and loops, and a severely reductive period of graphically marking time set in, so too then in 1972 did his actual production of paintings plummet to an all-time low of just four recorded pieces in the one year. Over the next four years, through 1976, Twombly appears to have created a total of just four more paintings, at least according to his *Catalogue Raisonné* (Twombly 1995), an extreme drop-off from an artist who was making nearly up to 100 large paintings in a year, not including numerous drawings and various works in a variety of other media.

In 1977, Twombly started once again using color, and this return to painting was marked by his simultaneously and unsurprisingly picking up the emotionally-charged leitmotifs of the soulful and ancient Mediterranean world he loved so much, classical Greek mythology, poetry, philosophy, the writings of Plato, and particularly, the *Iliad.* Inspired by Alexander Pope's translation of the Homeric saga, he began work that year on "Fifty Days at Iliam," completing it in 1978. He especially appreciated Pope's 1715 version of the classic, in particular, he said, for "its frenzied energy" and "headlong, forward rush" (Twombly 1994c, p. 45).

The title of this ambitiously coherent and awe-inspiringly large body of work, Twombly says interestingly, he "spelt":

> I-L-I-A-M, which is not correct. It's U-M. But I wanted that, I wanted the A for Achilles; I always think of A as Achilles; I wanted the A there and no one ever wrote and told that I had misspelt Ilium.
>
> (In Sylvester 2001, p. 177)

The A in 'Iliam' and the A for Achilles, the shape of the letter A, and images of the repeating, sharpened sword points in the 'Vengeance of Achilles' series of drawings and paintings, all obviously carry a "very aggressive" energy for Twombly. The idiographic form is "more like a rocket," he says.

> It's pointed... My whole energy will work, and instruments and things will have a very definite male thrust. The male thing *is* the phallus, and what way to describe the symbol for a man than the phallus, no?
>
> (ibid., p. 178)

With this monumental ten-painting cycle, which we have taken up earlier in regards to the imagery of the phallus, Twombly comes back to the color red and the symbolic use of 'redness' with a vengeance perhaps unmatched in modern art. Beginning with the red-centered swirling orb of 'Shield of Achilles', red appears in each of the first six paintings of the series, and especially in connection with portrayals of the Greeks themselves, the 'Achaeans,' and specifically in reference to the greatest hero of them all, Hellenic Achilles.

Nowhere in his own vast body of work, however, does the color red appear to roar and rage with the same fiery fury as it does in the massive 'Part V' of "Fifty Days...," an oil painting measuring 118 ⅛ x 75 ⅝ inches. Under the looming destructive forcefulness of its monolithic blaze of bright red paint, covered and mixed increasingly as it moves to the right with deadly black, until it disappears completely, its rush and razing terror cut off only by the edge of the canvas, Twombly inscribes a line from Pope's Homer with scratchy red crayon: 'Like a fire that consumes all before it.' He has this time truly portrayed a furnace of fire that engulfs everything that dares to stand before it, all the warring participants, bystanders, families, spectators, everyone and everything, Greeks and Trojans alike, any semblance of life, all annihilated in a ferocious holocaust. Rage, the maddened frenzy of killing, human butchery, and savage blood-letting destruction reaches its acme in this image of a mindless inferno. Confronting the martial codes of our foundational Western civilization at their roots, he places before us the inescapable and encompassing reality of our basic human instinct, essentially, *to kill each other.* Here in a massive field of crackling red intensity, Twombly lays bare our constant urges towards murder, madness, self-obliteration, and destruction.

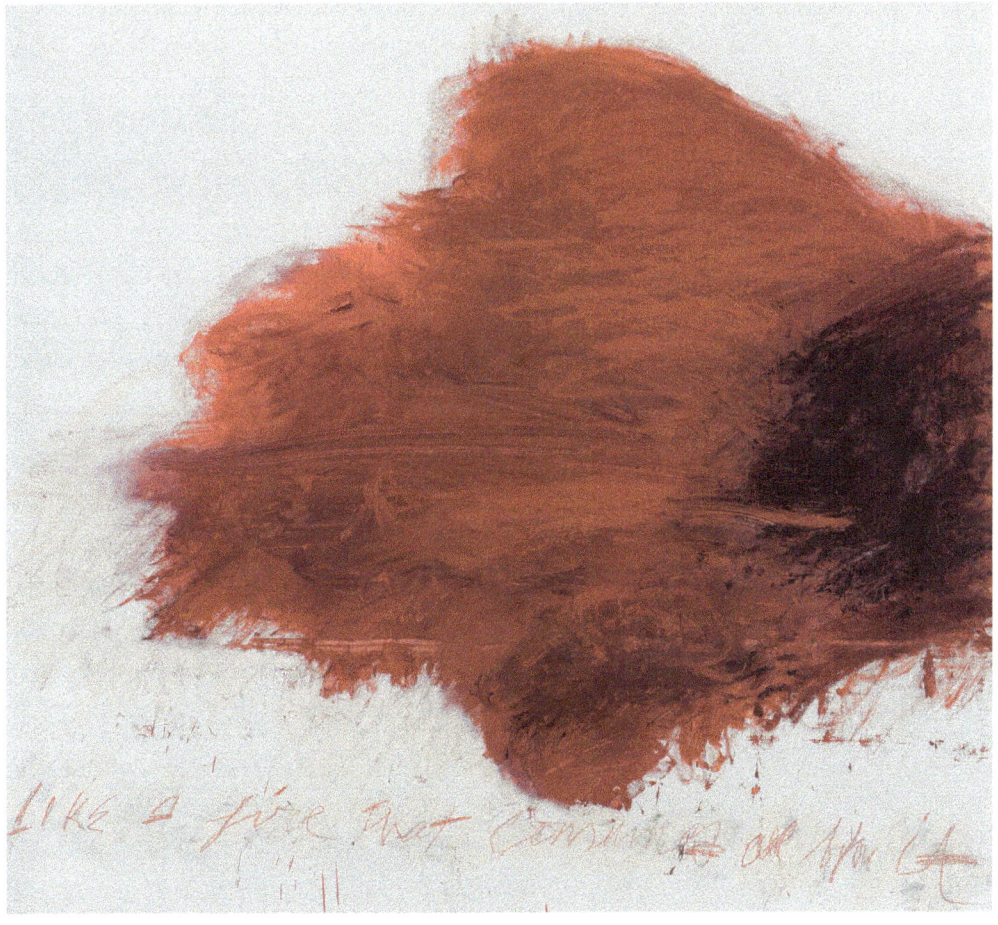

26.   Cy Twombly, *Fifty Days at Iliam,*
Part V: The Fire That Consumes All Before It, detail, 1978.

Warfare and the intensified aggression it reflects is an instinctual reaction that as humans we all obviously share, a desire to lose control and collectively submit to a greater archetypal power, again a 'divine madness' as it were. We are driven by both biology and destiny to become *mainomenos*, possessed by mania. As humans, we *are mainomenos*. We are mad—we are maddened, raving beings. There are gods, Twombly says, however, and following Homer, he writes their names on these canvases, who are behind our death-dealing impulses to murder one another. Taking another's life, he acknowledges, without mitigating the horror, is a numinous activity. It is the dark side of holiness. It wells up in us from our earliest paleohominian ancestors. It encompasses both of the extreme poles of our human being, from the very lowest urges to the highest ideals and values. It is, as Jung would say, *both* instinct and archetype.

The totally unrestrained Titanic powers of masculine rage that tear across this canvas in a convulsive whirlwind, have nowhere before been so clearly imaged, except perhaps in the *Iliad* itself. Relentless, implacable blood-lust is the real subject of both Homer and Twombly. The forces of Thanatos, the organismic death instinct in all human beings, as Freud soberly predicted, is the nemesis of our human civilization itself.

The Greeks knew well that the act of killing is itself an ecstasy, an orgy of emotion. Sweet victory and vanquishing the 'other,' the sworn foe, becomes as a result, a supreme value in Western culture. The momentary triumph and control over death and non-being bestows a god-like power and exultation in the perpetrator's taking away of another's life. One is blinded by impulse. It is one of the very few avenues we humans have open to us for experiencing this aspect of a dark and cruel divinity. This transient conquest and super-human overcoming attained through sheer brute physical strength, will, tenacity, focus, discipline, endurance, training, and perseverance—and a harnessed hate and rage—is at the heart of all male competition and struggle, the many militaristic agons of sports, athletics, politics, the killing fields of war facilitated by a de-humanized and weaponized technology, the compelling addictions to mastery, control, domination, and finally, culminating in death itself, the blissful submersion and dissolution of individual identity and personality. This urge still strongly roars in the ears of the collective and among nearly all societies, drowning out any respect for the voices of basic human dignity, integrity, ethical or moral feeling values, or the engagement in meaningful discourse, speech and language. It is perhaps *only* language, verbal expression and words themselves, which would have the precarious power to curb the ferocity of our innate destructive urges and instincts. Speech and the many forms of *poiesis* or 'creating,' are the only fragile membranes remaining that we have to separate ourselves from our own animalistic savagery.

In the very next panel of the 'Iliam' series, 'Part VI,' the bloody theme continues, somewhat abated or sated, but here in this panel, it is only mollified by death itself. 'Shades of Achilles, Patroclus and Hector,' the three great heroes now all equal in Hades, residing in the underworld, remain eternally and triangularly linked in this largest painting of the cycle, 118 ⅛ x 192 ⅞ inches. The three male figures, bonded in fated love, lust, hate and death, are now arrayed equally, side by side, as three discrete, bounded, quadrifoil emblems spread across the panel. No longer proud, pointed phalli as they were depicted in life, love, and war, they are now wispy shades in the gray, indeterminate, murky underworld realm of depth and death. Inhabiting an imaginal space of the afterlife, they have passed on. They are now bodiless and bloodless, rosettes, flowers without stems, ungrounded. All three heroes are portrayed as bounded geometric wholes, static and self-contained, lacking energy, movement or directionality. No longer do these once-virile warriors have purpose, animation, force, or spirit. They have become symbolic, emblems of themselves, and mere signs of their flashingly brief and blazingly meteoric lives.

The first of the deceased heroes, Achilles, does, however, continue the theme of riotous red paint, now scrawled even more darkly, mixed with an impervious black. The *nigredo*, an ashy alchemical blackness, contaminates and stains the fiery reds of passionate life now fled and burned-out, with the blotting intimations of death and the earthy darkness of the tomb. The figure of Achilles also contains a black 'X' within it, marking his chosen fate to die fighting, cancelling himself out. As in the *Iliad*, nullifying and crossing out himself and his existence, Achilles opts resignedly for a glorious death at the height of battle instead of a longer life of peace and domesticity; and he does go out fighting in the fullness of his warrior's powers.

The story of the Trojan War *is* in large part, the story of Achilles' reddened rage. In Twombly's encompassing series, it is usually the Greeks, the Achaeans, who are tinted with the sanguine shades of red, while the cooler and more rational Ilians, the Trojans, are portrayed in a haze of cloudy blues and whites diffused over the sprawling canvases. Homer begins his epic:

"Rage—Goddess, sing the rage of Peleus' son Achilles" (In Fagles 1990, p. 77). The whole first chapter or Book One is called, 'The Rage of Achilles.' The fact that when the god Dionysos re-emerges for Twombly in the 'Bacchus' series 28 years later, in unadulterated, pure, joyous sweeps and folds of red, shows both the manifold connections and the unbridgeable distances that the figures of Dionysos/Bacchus and Achilles have travelled together through time and share in a common subterranean context for Twombly regarding his iconic use specifically of red paint.

An additional underlying mythological connection between Achilles and Dionysos/Bacchus is also to be found in the *Iliad* itself. The fates of Achilles' choosing, either to die on the field of battle before Troy, or to return home to Greece and age gracefully, comfortably ruling over his fiefdom, are laid out and foretold to him by his own mother, Thetis, early on in the tale, in Book One. Thetis herself makes an inscripted appearance in 'Part IV' of "Fifty Days...," reverently spelled out in Twombly's skittering hand. The single reference to Dionysos in the *Iliad* comes in the interjected story in Book Six about the son of the Thracian king Dryas, Lykourgos, who chased Dionysos and his nurses, the Maenads, attempting to kill them, and forcing the god himself to dive into the sea and seek refuge there at the bosom of the sea nymph and goddess, Thetis. She in turn protects Dionysos there beneath the waves for nine months, becoming his foster mother, while the rageful aggressor Lykourgos is venge-fully blinded by the gods, and thinking he is hacking his vines, chops his son to death before taking his own life. Achilles and Dionysos thus spring from a shared maternal matrix and mythologem. Both claim Thetis as mother.

In a ritual reenactment of this mythical event retold by Homer, in later centuries, priests of Dionysos would performatively chase his female devotees, the Maenads, with a double-edged, bull-slaughtering axe, making them scramble for safety, as the god himself, acted out by one of his worshippers, would escape into the water. Plutarch also tells us that the women priestesses of Elis in the Peloponessus, would then sing, urging the god to return from the watery depths where he had sought safe haven with his foster mother Thetis:

> Come, Hero Dionysos
> to the temple by the sea
> with the graces to the pure temple
> raving with the bull's foot.

> (Kerenyi 1976, p. 182)

Dionysos is a red, righteously maddened bull raging from the sea, "bull-faced,/warlike, howling, pure" (In Athanassakis and Wolkow 2013, p. 27). Spurned, his fury knows no bounds. Again, the combustible conjunctions of fiery red madness, rage, blood, wine and water, fuse and ignite into imagery. In Euripides' *Bacchae*, young king Pentheus, delirious, deluded, hallucinating, struck mad by the angered Dionysos, his first cousin whom he has unwittingly dishonored, sees the god as a bull leading him through the streets of Thebes. Pentheus also sees two suns in the sky, again the doubling motif of madness, the madness of the dual god, "primeval, two-natured" (ibid.), who can bring either ecstasy, blessings and joys, or psychotic rage, disaster, dismemberment, and terrible death.

There are literally dozens of references in the *Iliad* to the conjunctions of the redness of fire and the divinely raging fury of battle. The three figures: Achilles, as well as to a lesser degree, all the other Homeric heroes from that saga; misguided Pentheus, who says: "The frenzy of the Bacchantes rages like fire at our gates" (In Twombly 2005, p. 53); and the maddened Lykourgos, are all three, however, only normal mortals. In all the stories and legends from antiquity, they are clearly not fully gods. Half divine is not good enough to save Achilles from his own unbounded emotionality or his predestined death. Dionysos/Bacchus, on the contrary, *is* very much a god; and for humans to experience the archetypal emotions reserved for the immortals is always to court catastrophe, and to risk the greatest tragedy. This hubris, overstepping, or inflation, is, in fact, the *sine qua non* and very stuff of all tragedies in general. To mix what is infinite and suprahuman with the limited and finite, without clear borders, produces both psychosis and madness, as well as the materials of all tragedy. Human nature, Homer is clearly telling us through the centuries, *is* intrinsically tragic.

The *Iliad* makes the invisible visible by showing us the gods, Ares, Athena, Zeus, Artemis, Poseidon, and all of the others, the archetypal powers who are behind and controlling all the actions of the heroic, though doomed protagonists, while simultaneously clarifying and sharpening the divide between humans and the gods, by delimiting differences and borders, and sharing out portions. This is the fundamental prescriptive morality and psychological balance that Homer's *Iliad* puts forth as valid and binding nearly three millennia ago, the limits, rules, and boundaries of human and divine contact and conduct. Twombly, like Homer, furiously and gloriously images the implacability and necessity of either adhering to these basic archetypal laws, or suffering the rending consequences.

Linking the redness of rage, the phallic aggression of war, and the transformations of destructive energies into more differentiated forms, at the same time as "Fifty Days...," Twombly also worked on a series of drawings entitled "Shades of Night" (1978). There, more like the red quadrifoil emblem for Achilles in the underworld, and the amorphously shaped red of 'Iliam's Part V', we sense the necessity in the artwork itself for such overwhelming anger to go underground, back to the unconscious for a while, where, sublimated, it can be once again re-formed into more finely-tuned and creative directions, after having been so fully blown and elaborated in the awe-inspiring installation of the *Iliad* cycle.

In the first grouping of the 'Shades of Night' drawings, the forms are intensely black-blue quadrifoils, with unmistakeably nocturnal depths of vigorously darkened paint. Later, in this same year of the 'Iliam' installation, he made a five-part series of red 'Shades of Night,' dated January 8-August 1, 1978, cloudy masses now come alive with bright cadmium color and indicating a resurgence of purely fiery and libidinous energies (Twombly 2016, pp. 252-6).

Between "Fifty Days at Iliam" (1978) and 'Bacchus' (2005), there is only one other major group of work where Twombly has forcefully massed so much redness in a particularly Dionysian context to such astonishing effect. Like both "Fifty Days..." and 'Bacchus' too, he has appeared on these occasions to use various red pigments in the service of expressing highly-charged and passionately colored depths of emotional and spiritual experience. Beginning in August 1981, he started the 'Suma' series with two very loose drawings. In August of 1982, apparently within a couple of weeks in his studio in Bassano, he completed a series of about fifteen more pieces on paper, entitled collectively, the 'Suma' drawings. One set titled, "(HRIH)," the first of the group, is in four parts. All of these works on paper are furious whirlwinds of oil paint, oil stick, and crayon, bundled tightly into dense swirling balls. They are all basically circular forms of maddened, aggressive scribbles, thickly layered round and round with a variety of media into vortices of intensely red slashings. There is so much pigment applied to the surfaces that they practically stand in relief off the sheets. They range in size from 39 ½ x 27 ½, to 79 ⅛ x 59 inches.

'Suma' means 'flower' in Sanskrit, and *padma* is the solar lotus flower in particular; and over the two largest pieces as well as some of the smaller ones, he has also written, 'OM MA NI PAD ME HUM,' the yogic Tantric formula and widely-known mantra for chanting meditation which translates as, 'the jewel in the lotus,' or as translated by Schulz-Hoffmann: "I bow down before Him who sits in the Lotus blossom" (In Twombly 2006, p. 103). He also much later drew that same chant in striking blue crayon on a sculpture, "Untitled ('Om Ma Ni Pad Me Hum')," in 2000. He initialed and dated all of these pieces, inscribed 'SUMA' on many of them, and 'HRIH' also on several. Although Twombly did visit India in 1973 and all of these five pieces clearly reflect certain aspects of Hindu and Buddhist religious tradition and practice, and furthermore, quite explicitly express those feeling values and East Asian sensibilities which appear throughout his *oeuvre*, the 'Suma' works still almost bear more in common iconographically with his longer-standing fascination with flowers, wheels, solar discs, whirling dervishes, and most primordially, the fundamentally circular energy centers, mandalas and symbolisms of the spiritualized and expressive body which he discovered for himself first experientially, and then undoubtedly later confirmed imagistically throughout a variety of cultures.

These pieces are mystical invocations in paint of an active and physical spirituality. They also bear some relation to his art work concerning Rumi, the mystical poet of Sufism (1980), as well as to other pieces figuring images of orbiting circles, chariots, cars, carts, solar barges, the lotus and the ecstatic whirlwind which surrounds the sublimely centered devotee engaged in Tantric meditation practice. The 'Suma' works could easily be themselves construed as 'yantras,' that is, as pictorial images used to visually concentrate purposeful meditation and contemplation, visible vortexes for accessing altered states of consciousness. The letters 'HRIH' on the works, allude to the Buddhist seed syllables of 'great compassion,' which are again chanted by practitioners in order to facilitate communion with the Amithaba Buddha, the 'Buddha of infinite light.'

Four of the 'Suma' pieces are fairly loosely-scribbled, spinning, wildly winding, jangling reds with admixtures of black. But the next to the largest of the group, with the 'OM...' chant written at the very top in small thin lead pencil, and then with the word 'SUMA' thickly lettered in paint just below that, is an unparalleled, fiercely passionate ball of crackling red intensity, painted and drawn in oil stick harder and harder, over and over, till it attains a specific gravity, density and energy entirely its own. It dares one to enter its field of centrifugal attraction. For all of its madly-inspired physicality and incredible hand pressure, it nevertheless approaches a pure and perfect stillness at its center, as if it contains within itself the third eye of its own crazed stormings which vibrate electrically round and round a core quiet and profound peacefulness. It remains hypnotic in all of its meditative concentration and forcefully scrawled wildness, carefully focussing round a still point. The work, in fact, performs and *creates* a deep and blissful calm. The circular ferocity coagulates and condenses the utterly mad materiality of its making into a numinous space of distilled fullness. It defines a feeling of 'redness', and itself embodies and projects the essence of the color *red*, full, passionate, and weightily substantial.

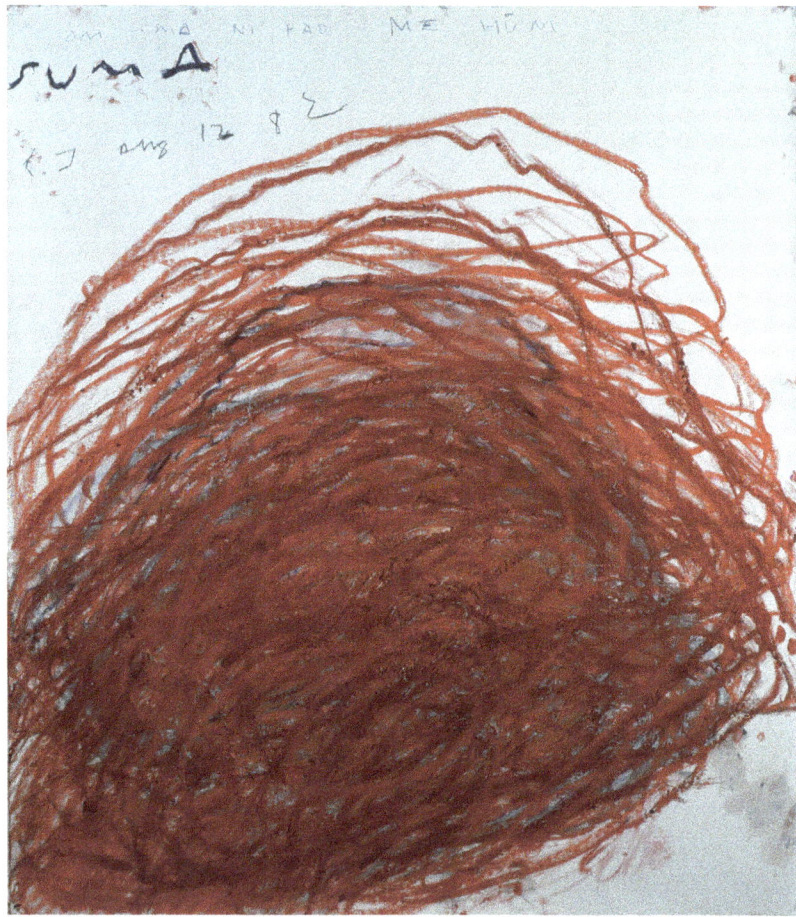

27.   Cy Twombly, *Suma*, 1982.

Much of the drawing had completely veered off the lower left and bottom edges of the paper in its transported making, yet it remains the vehicle of its directly experienced feelings of centered wholeness and physical well-being. In this piece, the red nearly shouts with triumph, exultation and sheer joy in its victory over the underlying violet and black scribbles. Unsullied and unapologetic, pure heart-pumping red just about screams out artistically its love and devotion to enthusiastically-lived life, inspired and throbbing wildly in the moment of its own self-expressiveness.

The largest of the five 'Suma' works returns us to a theme that Twombly had been working with right along, but now brings into direct syncretic contact with the motifs of Asian religions, and that is Dionysos, Bacchus, and grapes. Of course, Alexander the Great, the Macedonian with whose life and exploits Twombly's art had intersected at several different points, historically returned homewards victorious from his conquests in India, and had actually and posthumously assimilated the imagery of a triumphant Dionysos/ Bacchus, the spiritual/military conquerer, to himself and to the entire procesional march of his westward returning army, thus knitting together India and Greece, east and west, with mythological and archetypal significance. The spiritual ecstatic bonds between east and west were literarily established in the fifth century A.D. with the *Dionysiaca*, the longest epic poem in existence, written by Nonnos of Panopolis (Egypt) in which he completely identifies Alexander's Hellenizing mission to India with the conquering god Dionysos spreading Greek viniculture and civilization across Asia, while returning with the ancient wisdom teachings of Hindu mysticism.

In this looser, less intense version containing the 'OM...' chant lettering, 'SUMA' and 'HRIH,' he covers over circular black, gray, and violet scribbles with red, but then on the very top center of the large sheet, he also collages the same photocopied reproduction of a botanical illustration of a grape cluster that he used in the third of the three 'Bacchus' (1981) paintings from a year earlier. The only difference in this collaged addition is the tighter cropping and browner shading of the grapes, rather than the purplish tints of the '81 'Part III' of 'Bacchus.' The correspondences between the Indian deity Shiva and the Greek god Dionysus were elaborated at great length in a book by that name, *Shiva and Dionysus*, which also first came out in an English translation the very same year as the 'Suma' drawings, 1982 (Daniélou 1982). All in all, between 1981 and 1989, Twombly made approximately 130 drawings, many in larger scale, in which the color red absolutely predominates.

The motif of conjoining the redness of fire and water upon the sea recurs time and again through Twombly's work. In a number of pieces on paper from 1983-5, variously titled, 'Proteus,' 'Protea,' and 'Proteas,' we can see him interestingly intertwining fiery red floral motifs, the protea flower itself bursting and blooming into flame, with the figure of Proteus, a pre-Olympian Greek deity and sea god who was said to reside on the Egyptian island of Pharos. *Proteus*, the 'Old One of the Sea,' is also portrayed in Greek myth as a master of metamorphosis, interchangeably transforming himself into different animals, and especially from fire to water and back again, in his fabled battles with the Homeric hero Menelaos who tries to dominate him. These works themselves, of a red Protean blossoming, give substantive form to Twombly's notion of art as an "actioning," "a doing," and a "becoming," in the shifting and changing performative processes of *poiesis* (Staff 2011, p. 50).

Several versions of floating 'Petals of Fire' in 1988-9, the red blotches staining the besieged boats in the "Naumachia" drawings (1992), and numerous large untitled paintings and drawings of burning boats (1992-4), lead him to the challenge of paying homage to two of Turner's greatest elegiac paintings of blazing ships, naval warfare, the tides of history and the wistful passing of time itself. Twombly confabulates Turner's, "The Fighting Temeraire Tugged to Her Last Berth to be Broken Up" (1839) and the astoundingly poetic, "Peace—Burial at Sea" (1842), with its fire, smoke and limpid water, (as well as possibly Manet's "Battle of the Kearsarge and the Alabama") (Leeman 2005, p. 254), to produce, "A Study for the Temeraire," a painting in three parts which he completed in 1999 as a celebration honoring his distinguished predecessor, J.M.W. Turner.

This theme of fire, water, and death not only continues, but takes on greater archetypal and pictorial depth and ritual significance the very next year with one of his grandest cycles ever, the "Coronation of Sesostris" (2000), a majestic solar lyric of Egyptian myth in ten very large panels. Having done numerous drawings of the solar barge of Sesostris in the 70's and throughout the 1980s, he begins these paintings first of all with a dedication to images of the sun in the first four huge panels, and then moves on to fire, flowers, and sun-and-flame-drenched ships. Several paintings of this gripping series feature one or more large antique sailing vessels or barges lined with oars and soaring to oblivion in streaking red paint from burning masts and torch-lit hulls.

We can further see the running rivulets of flaming red paint, as well as cascading, streaming, fiery flowers flowing from masts and hulls, becoming even more destructively amplified in the very next year as entire fleets of ancient ships brightly burn in the sea battle and streaking carnage of the fantastic "Lepanto" cycle (2001), created specifically for the 49th Venice biennale in 2001 and reflecting the spirit of Venice as the long-reigning empress and protectress of the Mediterranean. Numerous gaily-colored ships and barges flaming in battle also sail darkly across grayish-white canvas seas in the 'Spring' and 'Summer' panels of both versions of 'The Four Seasons' (1993/4). Fire at sea, blazing and burning in ghastly pyres uneasily embraces watery depths, as we can imagine all hands on board shrieking and sliding noiselessly down and disappearing into the quieting deep in these catastrophic conjunctions of fire and water. Only an archetypal image could possibly hold together in memory and mourning these impossible oppositions of flaming ships and watery depths, life and death, ecstasy and oblivion, and beauty and destruction, so definitively and elegiacally captured by the artist in these great painting cycles.

Now quickly fast forwarding beyond the 2004-8 'Bacchus' cycles to Twombly's other enduring testaments to the powers and shadings of the color red, and to the outpourings of vitality it represents, we can find that there are three great bodies of his later work where varying shades of redness actually predominate, but do so in a way energetically much differently than the wilder Dionysiac blood crimsons we have been considering. Almost harking back to the red quadrifoil form of Achilles in 'Part VI' of "Fifty Days at Iliam," quietly bounded, whole and contained, these late tremendous massings of scarlets and vermilions, carmines and alizarins, seem to retrospectively reflect an artist more at peace with himself, composed, a master draughtsman and persevering creator with *poiesis* oozing from his fingertips, observing the transience, fragility, beauty, and poetry of life itself through the prism, once again, of plant life, flowers, blossoms and petals, peonies and roses, bursting open, falling and fading in a glory of fiery numinosity and grandeur. Though now in these late works, the redness itself is radiating and streaming from deep within their essences and immensities, rather than blazing up and burning out as in the earlier fiery motifs. In three monumental series: "Blooming: A scattering of blossoms and other things" (2006-7), a major exhibition of numerous works in different media which he created with its elegant Hôtel de Caumont, the Avignon site of the Lambert Collection in mind for its opening; the "Untitled (Roses)" (2008), a series of six huge horizontal paintings of roses with excerpts of poems from six different modern poets, commissioned by and now installed at the Museum Brandhorst in Munich; and thirdly, "The Rose" (2007-8), a suite also of five very large canvases unveiled at the Gagosian Gallery in London, inscribed with stanzas of Rilke's poetry from his collection, written originally in 1924 in French, *Les Roses*, Twombly has appeared to creatively come to terms with the edgy explosive violence of redness. In the magnificently broad canvases of these three major cycles, he symbolically marshals the fantastic potency and pungency of flowers and red roses in the service of the goddess Aphrodite, whose sweet scents, tender caresses and wistful wisdom of the body, of love and of the natural world, these radiant blossomings open up to, announce, and valorize. Her charms and her securely held knowledge of the eternality and persistence of sensuous and divine beauty have seemed in these grand, multi-panelled canvases, to have quieted, subdued, and transformed the aggression, urgency and anger of the *rubedo*'s earlier ragings. The violence of redness is transfigured in these impressive bodies of works within a crucible of profound compassion and acceptance that he appears to lovingly emanate in and through the painted flowery motifs and surfaces.

Much earlier, in 1989, Twombly had already done a series of small-scale drawings in acrylic and wax crayon on paper in seven parts, "Untitled (A Rose)," which highlighted red blurry flurries of roses flying apart on each sheet. As an image of the *unio mystica*, and this profound peace which surpasses comprehension, on one of the monumental "(Untitled) Roses" paintings in Munich, Twombly inscribes the ineffable meanings that the flowering red rose holds for him, quoting and re-creating the form of the last and concluding passage from T.S. Eliot's, *The Four Quartets*:

> and all shall be well
> all manner of things shall
> be well
> when the tongues of flame
> are in-folded
> into the crowned knot
> of fire
> and the fire and the Rose
> are One.

(In Twombly 2014, p. 347)

What is it about this redness, however, of fire, roses, blood and wine, that has so fascinated Twombly that it runs like the thin red thread of life itself pulsating through his work, bursting forth here and there, sometimes in large streams of works, in different forms and manifestations? When we now go back to the classical world, as Twombly has so often done in his own artistic performances, of what Aby Warburg called *his* discipline, *Nachleben der Antike*, the 'survival or afterlife of antiquity' in the contemporary world, in themes, motifs, and images, we find at the root of redness, semiotically-speaking, that the zealous Greek god of war, Ares, is himself indeed fiery red, as is his Roman counterpart, the military and agricultural god, Mars. Christopher Marlowe, a late sixteenth-century poet to whom Twombly dedicated a stunningly beautiful painting, writes of "Blood-quaffing Mars" (In Twombly 2014, p. 256). Ares and Mars are both associated with the cultural beginnings of smelting ores and the metallurgical development of iron, especially for its use in crafting superior weapons at the end of the Bronze Age and around the time of the Trojan War. Astronomically, Mars is also the red and burning hot planet, as well as the speediest orb of our solar system to travel around the sun.

Redness, in the meaningfully symbolic sign systems of alchemy, from ancient Egypt and China through the European Renaissance to Newton and beyond up until our own time, is most often imaged by the non-metallic element of sulphur. Jung wrote extensively, of course, on the parallels and analogical connections between ancient alchemy, its materials, methods, and practical applications, and the contemporary psychological processes of individuation and the development of the personality in and through the psychoanalytical journey. Combustible red sulphur, though highly volatile, is needed during the numerous operations, however, whether material or symbolical, to tincture or tinge the impulses of the soul during the practical procedures of working with the alchemical materials and their corresponding inner psychological manifestations. The 'redness' is sometimes also considered to be the soul herself, or the bride of the male alchemist, or artist, his anima, the spiritual *anima tingens*, the inner personification of a man's contrasexual or feminine/creative feeling side, an imagistic embodiment of his unconscious. She is earned through the work. She *is* the fiery tincturing spirit within, which gives him his color, his garment, reflecting his affective tone, his outward appearance *and* inner relatedness. "He shineth in colour like a ruby through the tincturing soul, which it hath acquired by virtue of the fire" (In von Franz

1966, p. 372). This redness is the *color invariabilis*, the most precious "unchanging colour" (ibid.), which is attributed to the soul. It is achieved through an initiatory ordeal by fire, hard work, heat, and the eventual mastery of volatile impulses and explosive emotions. It is accomplished through the gradual transformations of rage, anger, and passionate feeling into art. It is so positively powerful though, that it can assimilate the body to itself and make the body spiritual, that is, make of the body a psychical, as well as a physical, substance.

The fiery, tincturing soul also imparts color to the world.

> This motif recalls the ancient idea of the soul as a coloured garment
> enveloping the material world. According to the Gnostic Basilides
> the world-soul is nothing but an "enphasis" or "colour" of light which
> has descended into matter.
>
> (ibid., pp. 372-3)

In this same context, Giorgio Agamben quotes Elsa Morante from her book on the Franciscan painter, Beato (Fra) Angelico: "Colors are a gift of light, which makes use of bodies...to transform its invisible celebration into an epiphany" (Agamben 1999a, p. 106). He goes on to say:

> The "celebration of the hidden treasure" is therefore the becoming
> visible, in bodies, of the alchemy of light. This alchemy is both a
> spiritualization of matter and a materialization of light.
>
> (ibid., pp. 106-7)

There is surely no other art form quite like painting which has this transformative power to render and memorialize light in materialized forms.

The reddening, the *rubedo* phase of the alchemical process, also often signifies the completion of the work. The marriage of the red man and the white, *albedo*, or sea-blue woman, Ares-Aphrodite, Mars-Venus, besides symbolizing the union and concord of love and war and masculine and feminine elements, is also one of the most universally common themes of artists, especially in the Renaissance and up until the present day. It represents the successful integration of an individual with their own soul, and/or the conjunction of the soul with god. It is an image of the unitary self, the two in the one. This is portrayed throughout the world's mythologies, initiatory iconographies and religious symbolisms in the *hieros gamos,* the 'holy wedding,' or, in the *coniunctio oppositorum,* or the 'conjunction of the opposites,' the *mysterium coniunctionis,* the mystical union of the king and the queen. These images point again and again, besides their obvious cultural and historically-grounded external realizations indicating wholeness, to the *intrapsychic* unification of male and female qualities *within* an individual, in their actual, practical everyday life, that is, psychically, relationally, emotionally, and spiritually.

From the Old Testament, we also have the image of the Red Sea, parted by God to allow Moses and the Jews to escape from the land of bondage in Egypt, and to begin their long exodus to the promised land of Israel. When the sea closes in upon the pursuing Egyptian army, drowning and dissolving them, early Christian allegorists would later interpret the redness of the sea as the fluid fiery medium which dissolves our sins and 'blackness' in a baptism of blood. The blood of Christ, and with it, the legend of the Holy Grail containing the blood from the crucifixion, is consequently the sanctified canonical story and religious justification of the Judaeo-Christian West in its continuing mortal struggle with the 'darkness' and shadowy 'evils' of the East. It also provides the basis for the Arthurian legends, Parsifal, Dante, the Provençal poets, the troubadours, the tradition of courtly love, the first stirrings of Renaissance humanism, as well as serving up rationale for the numerous crusades actually waged in the 'holy land' during the Middle Ages, and perhaps, still to be seen today in the 'war against terrorism,' being fought primarily in Afghanistan, Iraq, Yemen, Libya, Iran, Palestine, Pakistan, Syria, Israel, and Egypt, and in other Muslim countries of Asia and Africa.

Perhaps the most basic and obvious source for Twombly's use of redness though, to denote the inner driving forces of fire, heat, passion, rage, and love, both creation and destruction, derives from the archetypal imagery surrounding the sun itself, the origin of life as we know it. Together with the 'other' heavenly orb and source of light, at least for all earth-dwelling species, the moon, we have comprised with their union, the royal couple, king and queen, Sol and Luna, who psychically, still dominate collective human consciousness as the archetypal masculine and feminine dyad, the royal *and* parental coupling pair, the font of all creation. The fact that Twombly has consistently produced works where the color red carries an actively masculine energetic force, and the white, yellow, green and gray surfaces serve as a ground, feminine matrix, a body and receptive/creative origin, or *chora*, a container, receptacle or vessel for the forms to appear, carries forward and into a postmodernist aesthetic, ethos and futurity, both the ancient lineage and still-resonant meanings of this timelessly potent color magic to symbolize these cosmic principles, as well as his own entirely new language and vocabulary of painterly forms to convey it in his own completely unique and distinctively contemporary idiom and terms. Colors became for Twombly the basic denotative icons of his own symbolical vocabulary.

We can see that for all cultures and throughout successive phases of human development and history, color has possessed such abundant magico-religious powers in excess of its functionality so as to have made men overcome all kinds of difficulties to seek, prepare, obtain, and manufacture particular pigments, metals, minerals, ores, stains, or dyes for expressive use. For the Ndembu-speaking people in central Africa, for example,

> their three primary colors, white, black, and red, were "conceived as rivers of power flowing from a common source in God and permeating the whole world of sensory phenomena with their specific qualities," [and] "are thought to tinge the moral and social life of mankind with their peculiar efficacies."
>
> (Taussig 2009, p. 7)

In Arabic alchemy, those same three colors become responsible at genesis for nothing less than the creation of humankind:

> In Mohammedan tradition, Tabari, Masudi, and others say that when the earth refused to provide the material for Adam's creation, the angel of death came along with three kinds of earth: black, white, and red.
>
> (Jung 1963, p. 386)

Through kabbalistic influences in alchemy we learn that "Adam sometimes has three colours, red, black, and white, and sometimes four, white, black, red, and green" (ibid., p. 387 fn). The four colors correspond to the four elements and the "four stages of the process (*tetrameria*), marked by four colours, by means of which the originally chaotic arcane substance finally attained to unity, to the 'One,' the lapis, which at the same time was an homunculus" (ibid., p. 385).

In the *Pirke de Rabbi Eliezer*, it is said that "God collected the dust from which Adam was made from the four corners of the earth":

> He (God) began to collect the dust of the first man from the four corners of the world; red, black, white, and green. Red, this is the blood; black refers to the entrails; white refers to the bones and sinews; green refers to the body.
>
> (ibid., p. 386 and fn 26)

Other sources say that green refers to the skin and the liver (ibid.).

Specific colors, like red, white, black, and green, are therefore prized in many if not most societies still for magico-religious reasons, because they are seen and experienced as "alive, as *mysteries*" (Taussig 2009, p.7), and, as essentially creative *in themselves*. Color serves to jar and dislocate the everyday normal world, making it come alive and transforming it. This sacred, shamanic, mysterious, and ritually theatrical use of color, has its original sources no less in the gods themselves and in the natural world, than in the deeply organic and physiological referents of "the copulating, procreating, growing, and dying human body" (ibid., p. 8). All nature, whether human, animal, plant, or mineral, expresses itself and speaks primarily through the language of colors.

Color, Barthes writes, "is, in a way, another logic, a kind of challenge offered by the poet (and the painter) to the Aristotelian rules of structure" (Barthes 1985, p. 185). It is "morally dangerous," he says, and a transgression and violation of the purity of the page, and for Twombly particularly, even sometimes a kind of "*dirtying*" (ibid., p. 180), a spoiling and smearing with "shaky maculations, tenuous blemishes" (ibid.), and wobbly, feeble, fallible lines made seemingly in passing. His mark-making often appears cast off, offhand, abject, and discarded.

Due to Twombly's unselfconsciously anti-heroic stance regarding the project of abstract expressionist painting, even the smallest spot or slightest smudge and smear of bodily-colored, rusty red, produces a specific event at the "site of pulsion" (ibid., p. 204). Color is liberating, erotic, a gestural '*stroke*' of impulse producing a specific *jouissance*. Redness does not need to be massed in large amounts to elicit the sigh, thrill, or exclamation of pure pleasure in its happening on the canvas. For the singular stroke, streak, or even the most minute point, as it makes the color, produces and evokes an 'event' of bliss. As Riley writes:

> The force of Twombly's red is felt even when it is used sparingly. It is the concentration of richly mixed color in heavily impastoed, multi-layered moments that define its force in Twombly's work.
>
> (Riley 1995, p. 62)

For both artist and viewer, it is always surprising, "unexpected" and "new each time" (Barthes 1985, p. 166). *Color* itself, issuing forth from the crayon held by fingertips, *is* inherently "a kind of bliss" (ibid.), a deep pleasure and a passion, precisely because it is the active and actual performance and demonstration of a material fact, the colored crayon itself, as an absolute substance, appearing brilliantly anew each time and manifesting in all of its intrinsic, irreducible, inherent, and infinitely real, luminous glory.

Color as it issues forth from the body in the material mediums of art and mark-making, is an out-folding and an extension of our flesh itself, our matter, out into the reciprocating corporeal *thereness* of the world. It is a transmutation of matter into psychic flesh. *Poiesis* is a giving-birth in collaboration *with* the world of matter and with nature herself. It reveals the mystery and miracle of creatively participating in this material evolution of nature. We are *her* servants. We are here to further *her* aims. Twombly's art presents and performs an actual genesis, the birth of the visible out of invisibility, a growth into the here and now of fleshly, bodily life. He midwifes Mother Nature's *materia* and materials and brings them to a kind of fruition and perfection. The line, as Paul Klee said, is allowed to "muse." Klee referred to his drawings as: "taking a line for a walk." Line-making, he said, is "an active line on a walk, moving freely without a goal. A walk for a walk's sake" (Klee 1953, p. 16). Art no longer imitates the visible, "it 'renders visible'; it is the blueprint of a genesis of things" (Merleau-Ponty 1993, p. 143).

Merleau-Ponty calls "the world flesh, in order to say that it is a *pregnancy* of possibilities" (Quoted by Johnson in ibid., p. 51). Later he adds: "in the patient and silent labor of desire, begins the paradox of expression" (ibid.). The fiery desire of the artist is in bringing the secret lining of the world's invisibility, seamless being itself, into visibility, birthing it, delivering it in labor out of the body of the world's offered materials.

We say that a human being is born the moment when something
that was only virtually visible within the mother's body becomes at
once visible for us and for itself. The painter's vision is an ongoing
birth.

(ibid., p. 129)

The "voracious vision" of the artist, the French philosopher continues,

reaching beyond the "visual givens," opens upon a texture of Being
of which the discrete sensorial images are only the punctuations
or the caesurae. The eye lives in this texture as a man in his house.

(ibid., p. 127)

Like fish in water, our vision swims in the world of the visible. Twombly,
boldly, dives into and paints out of these 'caesurae' of the visible, these breaks,
ruptures, fissures and cracks in the shimmering and shattering globe of being,
in order that Bacchus may perhaps, suddenly, precipitously, frenzyingly, rush
out from his occlusive hiding place, and just for a moment, be reborn, miraculously appear just here, before us, in a flash, shuddering, before the eyes.

At the opening of the 'Bacchus' series in New York in 2005, the smells
of fresh paint, varnish and turpentine, permeated the large room hung with
the vertically towering drapes, soaring folds and rolling sweeps of inspired
Dionysiac redness. Huge scorings and scrawlings of red paint on fleshy, skin-
colored canvases lay spread open all around. The huge paintings reflecting in
the highly polished wooden floors of the gallery made the viewers appear to
be standing essentially in pools of blood, submerged in shiny blood-red light,
immersed, bathing and participating in Twombly's radically gestural asser-
tiveness covering the five giant walls. An extreme violence of Bacchus streaked
and soared, gashed and gushed across the large room, and anyone entering
the gallery space immediately became embraced and baptized in the red
liquid colors, and submissive, whether willingly or not, to the auratic glow of
pure bright light and color. The reek of fresh paint and the visually aggressive
rhythm of the works, all contributed to force viewers into at least a physically
proximate complicity and heightened collusion with these defiant testaments
to impassioned creativity. Bacchus loomed large in this sacralized space as a

triumph of art over death, a ritual blood sacrifice to the god performed in paint, and as a witness to the self-generative and transformative powers of contemporary art to renew itself at both its material and symbolical roots. *Bacchus renovatus.* 'Bacchus renewed.' Bacchus re-birthed in the here and now—re-born through painting's *poiesis* appeared lavishly exposed in expansive glory.

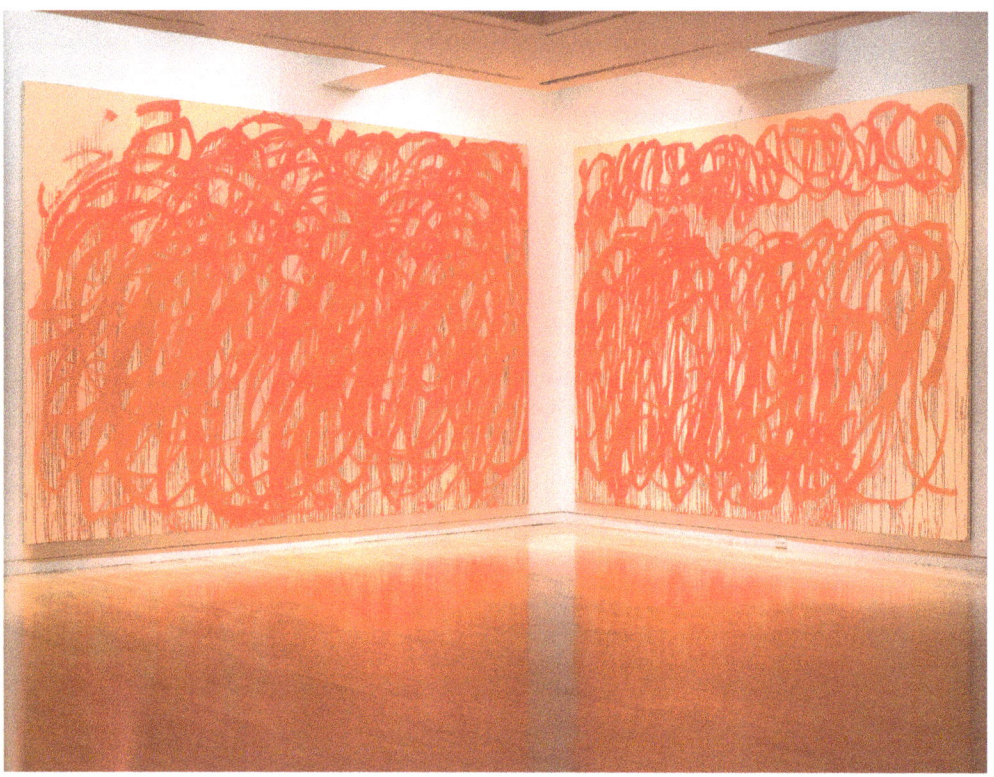

28.   Cy Twombly, *Untitled*, installation view Parts VII and VIII, 2005.

For the first time in his work, in two of the immense pieces, Parts II and III, Twombly had allowed the canvas to bundle on the floor while painting the series in his Gaeta studio. Those two parts were painted in the smaller upstairs space. So that underlying the rolling upward surges of cascading loops, streaming trails of red paint had been allowed to run down, pool, and gather along the bottom folds of the canvas draped onto the studio floor. *Solve et coagula*, the alchemist's guiding aphorism and motto was presented here in full form. 'Dissolve and coagulate,' endlessly repeating, the eternal pulse of movement and rest, upward force and downward fall, here found its own natural balance, contra-naturally, however, through art, reinforcing the fact that art itself is already an alchemical *opus contra naturam*, a 'work *against* nature.' *Poiesis* is *the* 'work against nature.' The alchemist as artist performs the 'work against nature,' however, only to further nature's *own* innermost needs and goals. The artist tending the vessel, alembic, oven, furnace, or mediums of his craft, again acts solely as a midwife to further nature's *own* most interior strivings towards meaningfulness and fulfillment. Jung quotes the alchemical dictum: "What nature leaves imperfect is perfected by the art" (Jung 1969, p. 294). Bacchus appears here in these works as the avatar of nature herself. Bacchus heralds the unveiling of nature in all of her chromatic differences, "she", as "a luminous spatialization, the ultimate language of a jouissance at the far limits of repression, whence bodies, identities and signs are begotten" (Kristeva 1980, p. 269).

As counterpoint to the rising and roiling forms above in these two 'Bacchus' paintings, the horizontally-gathered paint in the rumpled folds below provided a grounding to the onward dynamic movements ascending vertically upwards. Nietzsche's notion of 'eternal return' and recurrence, which epiphany he had while staring at a huge rock cliff in Sils-Maria, Switzerland, where he summered during the 1880's, here makes itself manifest. An earth soaked in pooling blood-red paint, displaying the residue of painting's process, Twombly's physical exertions, and the purposive laws of gravity, revealed nature and life itself returning to its foundational sources 'below,' once again, *falling*. Underneath this dynamic daylight world where we usually look at paintings, the imagined world below collected the blood soaking into the earth, absorbed by the materiality of the canvas; and now visualized, the redness continued racing through our own bloodstreams, the invisible pathways of our interiors. Nature's *own* imaginings as the literal subtext in these paintings, accident, incident, gravity, weight, and chance, gave depth and fundament to the narrative, the enacting, cursive and purposive left to right flow dominating the main portions of rolling forms on the canvases above. Through unintended drips, spatters, and streaks, the paintings escaped their own aesthetic, man-made confines, and in their excess and surplus, imaged the unbounded freedoms and creative imaginings of the god Bacchus himself at play, *Bacchus Ludens*, *Liber,* the free god, collaborating with the spontaneous and random forces of Mother Nature, *mater* herself, the feminine soul of matter and the inner life-spark of materials, to produce an art of continuously relational and reciprocal processes. The mother of Dionysos, Semele, was once, of course, a great goddess herself, and her name remains cognate with the Russian word *zemlya*, 'earth,' the mother of us all, our ground, womb and tomb, beginning and end. From here in 2005, with the announcement of this magnificent 'Bacchus' series, until the end of his life, Twombly was to paint grounded only in and out of a deep connection with the innermost interiority of this feminine nature herself, embracing the 'spirituality of matter' and applying himself to collecting the scattered "spiritual sparks of divine holiness" he found in his own environments (In Agamben 1999a, p. 108).

The universal solvent, the transforming tincture of the redness in alchemy made visible in 'Bacchus,' is, once again, manifested in action. Carrying on in his own finely-honed style the tradition initiated half a century earlier by Jackson Pollack, Twombly continues to convincingly embody nonpareil 'action painting' into the 21st century. The *aqua permanens*, the *coniunctio* of fire and water, the liquid form of the philosopher's stone appears, and stages its own hierophanies through the art of his painting. His practice, process and product, now realized as all varying aspects of the one *aqua permanens*, the 'enduring water,' are unified in his gestures. It is both the *prima materia* and the actual ordinary materials he begins and works with, as well as it is the goal of the alchemical opus itself, the *lapis philosophorum*, the 'stone of the philosophers,' the gold, the healing elixir, the actual pure substance, and the 'treasure hard to attain,' effecting a transformative experience for us as viewers/participants, taking us from one place to another.

With the 'Bacchus' paintings, Twombly too has seemed to reach certain kinds of life goals and artistic and creative re-solutions. A unity of purpose and direction permeates the work. There are no longer any hesitations or distinctions within these paintings between their physical and material facticity and their symbolic/thematic meanings and psychological or aesthetic significance. Everything has been revealed and blended into a unitary elation, a euphoria and joyous delight in life. 'Bacchus' is a celebration. Opposites of color and form come together in these great looping spirals of devotion to the superordinate principles of the painting process itself. The powers of *poiesis* are glorified as a vehicle of the individuation process. There, in the smallest of paint-streaked details *and* in the overarching conceptions of the entire cycle, we find the tracks and traces of this still powerfully resonant god of primal life impulse, a vibrant and vital Dionysos/Bacchus in and for our own time—hieratic and glorified. The spiritualized body appears in these direct applications of paint:

Perhaps no red can have that passion unless a body has been painted near it or inside it. Could it be that red is the colour that is continually asking for a body?

(Berger 2000)

For Twombly at this point, all the dualities of form and matter, the one and the many, are collapsed into the poetry of his painting. Seeing *through* the world to its inner workings and movements, Twombly's *poiesis* gives birth to images that themselves continue to move, live, and breathe. Seeing with the flickering and instantaneous eyes of a filmmaker, he creates images that are themselves in motion, transiting, passing through the retina and into the time and space of vision and visibility. Thus, his working forever in series, multiples, and sequences, now makes complete sense for his spiritualizing poetics, tracing the transformations and metamorphoses of vital forms, the instantaneous, mercurial, fleeting breaths and pulsations of the Dionysiac life force as it would manifest to him in successive images temporally registered, recorded and re-framed within altered space-time coordinates, and within different mediums, adding layers and levels of meaningful aesthetic reality.

Almost as an addendum, coda, or perhaps as a small quiet aside or accompaniment to the great 'Bacchus' cycles of 2004-2008, Twombly created a startlingly amazing series of three photographs of flowers in Gaeta in the same year, 2005, as he worked on the eight awe-inspiring 'Bacchus' paintings. The redder than blood-red peonies, at first bunched tightly in a vase, become closer, increasingly larger in form, and blurrier in each of the three successive photographs, until the viewer is completely immersed and engulfed in a burning, pulsating, illuminated color field of flowering fiery flame. With just some slightly-darkened edges around the image, the third overwhelming print of the series entirely absorbs the saturated perceptual plane and vision itself with the drenching power of its pure throbbing redness.

In an essay on his photographs, Anne-Marie Garat comments on Twombly's tendency to frequently present images in a series.

The serial effect, the duplication of similitude in its infinitesimal variations, has the effect of inflecting multiplicity while affirming unfathomable singularity in its problematic isolation, the enigma that every subject belongs to the self.

(Garat in Twombly 2011a, p. 39)

Through his multiplicities of serialized images, in every medium with which he worked, we are able to follow Cy's *inner* vision, and thus travel with him, imaginally, poetically, spiritually, moving ever closer and deeper into the true subject of the images, to their hidden secrets, to the unrepresentable nature and experience of the life-force itself, transforming and revealed through a bliss of abstracted shapes and pure living color.

In a later photographic echo of these red flowers, in 2009 Twombly made another photograph, "Painting Detail (Roses)," in his studio in Gaeta, which again both penetrates and is consumed by the deep flowery petals of burning hot, red color from one of his own 'Rose' paintings. In its centrifugal pull, the photographer, image, and viewer merge and become one in the immediate experience of making and creating. The photographic image is itself, a poetry, in furiously transcendent motion inwards. Twombly often took photographs in his own studio and observed once again portions of his own work, literally through a different lens, reflecting on his reflections. Art duplicates and reflects on itself in these many wondrous series he produced in all mediums. As in the films of Federico Fellini and Ingmar Bergman, when the characters occasionally step out of their roles to comment on their thought, feeling or the cinematic action, Twombly through his overlapping production of paintings, spaces, drawings, sculptures, and photographs, is able to philosophize and meditate poetically and materially on the nature of creation itself, its practice in the world, within the ongoing stream of life. This is an expansively self-effacing conception of art. This is Twombly's *Gesamtkunstwerk*, the transformation of the body of his work and life into art and back again into the lived physical world—now forever changed. The viewer is led to experience an immersion in the oneness of red flower, fire, words, and desire, through an embodied vision, through re-enacting the performance of paint and an active poetizing in the body's rhythms, *and then even further*, in the reflection of this whole process in photography, now captured and come full circle.

In the last decade of his life, Twombly created remarkably few drawings, especially as compared to the prolific output of his drawing practice throughout most of his artistic career until then. In fact, there are no drawings recorded at all after 2008. Among this scant production, however, in 2002 he began to create artist's books, numbering as many as 34 sheets per folio. Every one of them contains almost exclusively *red* blossoms, flowers, *red* squiggles, crimson bursts, meandering lines and *red* lettering. Of the last drawings he was ever to undertake in his life, in 2004, 2007, and again in 2008, there is not one which is not completely some shade of bloody, rusty red, or brilliantly bright red. The very final five drawings he made in 2008 are a stunning revelation, again, of the essence of redness. While the second and third of the sheets are reminiscent of the "Bacchus" folds with their calligraphic swirling spheres, the first, second, and last of these drawings he covers with such intensely tight, bundled acrylic circles of stunning vermillion, that there is almost no white space of paper surface to be seen beneath the throbbing life force and red energies unabashedly and shockingly confronting the viewer (Twombly 2017b, pp. 211-15).

From the 'Bacchus' series onward until the end of his life, all of Twombly's 'late' paintings appear one after the other as to some extent, his 'last paintings' (Pavlouskova 2015). From 2004 until the actually posthumously titled, 'Last Paintings,' "Untitled (Camino Real)," exhibited in 2012, Twombly has purged all traces of blackness, shadow, and *nigredo* from his work. The darkness of depression, melancholy, chaos, destruction, rage, and anger, which had for so long mixed, contaminated, clouded, and obscured the brilliant and bold hues of his redness, is all gone. He has burned and worked his way through his own dark matter. He has *painted* his way over to an 'other side.' And until the end, it is as if his soul and body are joined together in his unique artistic dance. The rhythms of the artist's body and soul seem to be wedded *in* the work, with the soul's redness tincturing and spiritualizing the body itself, while also seeming to give him the actual physical vitality, exuberance and energy needed to take on the many series and cycles of large paintings which he was to still execute until his death in July 2011. Mind and materials appear to have united in the movements of his hand and arm.

In the same way that the 'Bacchus' paintings join the opposites through their use of color, so too does this same series finally appear to meld together the two very different formal impulses which had alternated throughout Twombly's long career in painting. Two seemingly irreconcilable stylistic tendencies with which he had long labored, appear to combine with 'Bacchus' into yet a newer, totally integrated, signature painting style and effortless grace which is to last him until the end of his life. His intellectual and specifically *graphic* affinities towards minimalism, linearity, ritualistic repetitiveness, obsessional detail, serialism, and conceptualism, finally blend with his boldly physical, gesturally assertive, and emotionally impulsive ongoing project of abstract expressionism. Through a lifetime of seeking, Twombly finds his clearest language in an indelible script.

He is no longer writing on or into paintings as much as his paintings themselves have become his writings, his soul's autobiography, the successive pages of his artistic journal, his own discursive language and very particular scriptural form writ large in its own alphabet of emotionally-freighted colors and powerfully inclusive calligraphic forms. He is thinking, feeling and writing in paint, living his life expansively through hand, arm, and fingertips.

Even with the title of the show, 'Bacchus Psilax Mainonmenos,' he announces the conjunction of the two previously polarized epithets into the one god-figure. Bacchus embraces his own 'winged' and 'mad' aspects. The lofty, abstract, distant, ideational and rationally conceptual and scientific methodologies of Apollo merge with the sensuous Mediterranean instinctuality and primitivity of Dionysos/Bacchus. The linear numbering, lettering, notational geometries, conceptual abstractions, and especially the repeated loops, folding spirals and circles come through *with*, and *in* the extending 'Bacchus' series, as the chosen *form* of expression for this highly specific god's final, explicitly explosive appearance in Twombly's long journey through art. The wide, arcing sweeps and draping folds surely continue in his later work, but the momentum of rolling waves, the forces of nature and massed intensities here find their most complete and comprehensive expression. 'Bacchus' comes to an all-consuming, open-ended and passionate resolution and dis-solution. As viewers, we become happily complicit in its endlessness and extensions to infinity. There are no conclusions or destinations, he seems to be saying, only the unrolling way forward. This is Bacchus *now*, the most contemporaneous epiphany of the god, *this* god, in our lifetime. And there are no shores, rocks, or coastlines that break these continuously oncoming, surging waves of color, except for the limits of yet another page, the next sheet, or a further canvas, as it is stretched over the frame or nailed onto the wall and begun, once again, to be worked on.

We are participants and co-creators in Twombly's presentation of this tragic performance of painting, re-membering, and re-creating of Bacchus, the god, making him come alive through language and art. Twombly, the artist, performs the Hölderlinian caesura, the break, rupture, shock, and cut of discontinuity, the jolted awakening of all sublime art. He makes it *new*. As spectators/participants, we literally and imaginatively re-enact these fullest physical extensions of the artist's own body, hand, heart, mind, and arm. We are contained *within* the massive loops he makes, literally. He actually circumscribes our bodies and ourselves, concretely in space, within these elegantly massive, cascading folds of redness. He paints these great wheels of fire that we can enter and ride with, that are still rolling down the road. The great ellipses and circles he creates are both opening, closing, and unbreaking. They are spirals of devotion. Still moving, they continue on. We are both at one with them, and entirely and gratefully, uniquely alone with them, and with the ongoing processes of formation and transformation, the eternally re-creative alchemy of art.

Twombly literally describes his own actual physical limits through the extensions of his arms and through the makeshift, prosthetically lengthened brushes he created specifically for these works; and we are physically and emotionally included in these selfsame sweeping movements, embraced by his art of folding forms. We too exist, within *them*. Within these brilliant folds, we find the true space of our existence. Reaching out to express his limits and boundaries, Twombly transcends them with each successively moving loop, drip, and spatter. The streams of paint all ultimately run where they will, of course; they tend to search and seek out where *they* need to go. All the lines and colors and effort, the many makings of marks, a life lived in art, the multitudes of desires, all flow back towards the earth, back to nature, returning themselves and us to the source and origins of all life.

VIII

Seeing and Being Seen/ The Spaces Between

Twombly's work continues. It goes on. His overarching artistic project since his beginnings in the early 1950s, can be seen as the furthering of an infinite script. His body of work has been drawn from a source of human expression, language and rhythm that is always going on, that is always somehow present and 'sounding,' that we can hear as an audible silence, a landscape and topography of the soul where we live and feel, that is, in fact, *happening now.* This is the realm of the objective psyche, where all the gods and goddesses continually mingle, mix, and match in perpetual joy, delight, and terror. It is the space of the archetypes. The *topos* of what Carl Jung refers to as the 'psychoid' factor is at play here, stretching out to an endless horizon and plunging to a fathomless depth. He refers to this living dimension of the psyche in his later writings as the *unus mundus*, the 'one world,' the unitary reality, non-dual, the momentary intersection of differing points and events on the soul's space-time trajectory and continuum, creating synchronicities that we perceive, 'meaningful coincidences,' and an 'acausal orderedness' and significance that actually speaks to us—and, that in addition, also sees us. It is a window, and opening onto the instantaneous, the sublime, a caesura, rupture, ripple, or gap in the usual fabric of space-time. It stands at the place where all things originate. Twombly paints with this urgency of beginnings. He is always starting anew, re-creating the world in the 'work,' only so that he might begin again.

His art is both the vessel and the medium which contains and conveys a timeless contemporaneity which is always available, though rarely grasped or comprehended. Written as his work to a great extent is, with visible, flowing lines, in the language uniquely particular to the artist, that is, for us, in a foreign tongue, we must still struggle to read it, and/or translate it into our own recognizable vernacular and idiom. As Barthes would say, his work contains a "*secret*: that which concealed in reality can reach human consciousness only through a code, which serves simultaneously to encipher and to decipher that reality" (Barthes 1985, p. 249). These painted, drawn, sculpted, and collaged texts as Twombly's 'code,' are difficult to readily understand, and so we are left to grapple with a strange script. It is the language, essentially, of the unknown, and we are as yet without our Rosetta Stone for decoding it. We are in a *terra incognita*. We are in the present, shocked by the totally contemporary, flung into its midst. We wander in this strangely moving landscape of Twombly's art as outsiders, relative strangers in an alien land, feeling our way step by step over a marvelously expressive and yet challengingly rocky terrain. We have feelings and reactions, but they are ambiguous, uneasy, unclear, indeterminate. We have to grapple with the features and meanings of this idiosyncratic landscape.

This Twomblyan topography, this world that opens before us, despite its impressive immediacy and indisputable presentness, is always, unbeknownst even to itself, pointing and looking way ahead of itself, toward the future. Twombly makes art that is forever out and beyond himself, out in front of himself, and ahead of his time. His work presents a pictorial language of the yet-to-be-known, of the future which is still on the way, arriving, still to come. He is painting into the future of the soul's winding path. While standing solidly, unrecognizably there before us, the works *themselves* simultaneously strain to see into an opaque and murky invisibility somewhere out ahead; and furthermore, they attempt to speak what has heretofore been unspeakable, unsayable. It is a new and incompleted language and music, with its own alphabet, grammar, syntax, logic, tonal scales, and notation. He engages in a kind of automatic writing all his own. He has clearly *named* certain landmarks here and there, even labeled some for us, like Orpheus, Dionysos, Maenads, Bacchus, but the overall text is partial, incomplete, and fragmented, broken off and disjointed, like the different, individually painted panels in a series, separated from one another, with a no man's land of bare gallery or museum wall space between them. They, his works, sometimes themselves seem initially to even stutter and stumble, tripping over their own hesitant meanings, voicing unintelligible sounds, and it is only much later that we may come to realize their fluency, mellifluous beauty and coherence of speech, their elegant articulations and precise connections to what has gone before and comes after, their context, their place in a larger textual and textural world of meaning and *mythopoiesis*. His *oeuvre* is the presentation of an entire mythology. His artistic forays and explorations are thus always way ahead of us, his viewers, as well. Though ultimately just beyond reach, they still manage to satisfy deeply while simultaneously stirring up an eager anticipation and excited promise of things yet to come, an exalted future. *His works both patiently await and reverently, though excitedly, hasten the re-appearances of the gods.* It is a completely activating, facilitating, and energizing art, and yet at the same time, it is also incredibly and quietly receptive, inclusive, and accepting of whatever *will* arrive from the future's distant shores, which brim with exotic and impossible projects, unimaginable hopes, and delirious dreams.

The work appears also as the residue and remains of an arduous process that the artist has undergone throughout his life. It is itself a tremendous landscape of sprawling remnants and ruins. Among other things, it sometimes seems to be a wrestling with the tough, muscular angels and daimons of visual art's long and tortuous history, the shades of Titian, Poussin, Caravaggio, Rembrandt, Turner, Monet, and Pollack. It is a struggle of invocations and incantations, of faith and doubt, as he attempts to call the gods into existence and to name them into being. In the studio, like Plato's mythical demiurge, the archetypal creator-potter, he gives life and shape to the formless matter of his materials, breathing life into found objects. Most of Twombly's sculptures are, in fact, created out of rummaged bits and pieces of debris, discarded junk, and flea-market cast-offs (Nesin 2014). His art is a particular modality of *poiesis*, however, which needs to live, and indeed thrives on the teetering brink between a deeply-rooted presence and an onrushing, entirely uncertain, destabilizing, and chaotic future. He works out of a vortex of abandonment, disappearance, absence, loss, un-knowing, and concealment. His is an art created in times of threat and dis-solution. As we hurtle at full speed through time and space towards vaguely ominous destinations, his *poiesis* slowly and carefully draws from that vertiginously spiraling abyss of non-being which opens up and menaces us with imminent collapse, one work at a time. Grounded in chiasmic depths, he makes just one mark, one piece, materializing one thought, one idea, image, impulse, sensation, and feeling, one after another, collating a *bricolage*, an assemblage, piecing and putting together meanings and things in his and *their* own rhythm.

It is under these disorienting conditions that Twombly continues with the painterly chapters of his artist's panoramic book. Despite working close up, intensely, and immediately, engaging directly and hands-on with materials, he also seems to take the long view. He looks toward, behind, over, and into the vastness of time. His ineffable ongoing script of cascading signs continues page by page, work by work. Lifting paint-saturated brush, stroke after stroke, he creates the gracefully sweeping furls and the swirling, streaking, streaming folds of 'writings,' which rise and fall and scatter and drip to the nearly inaudible strains of a far-away, beckoning song. The calligraphic loopings seem to follow both very ancient and very modern rhythms that only he hears, that he attends to and carries within himself, as a poetry and resonance vibrating in his body. He paints, alternatively, to a music of deep silence as well, creating himself a "language where language ends," a poem, while the work is yet becoming on the outside, in visible form, an "audible landscape," a place, a psycho-geography of the mind which we can also see and hear, because *it appears and sounds* (Rilke 1989, p. 147). It calls to us from the future. His heart pumps out the meter and cadence of his inevitable mark-making movements. As the cardial currents swoosh through his bloodstream and pound in his ears, he rides the rapids and transcribes the lines of feeling onto the canvas, reproducing in rhythmical arcs the pulsating syncopations of his body in space. Inhaling and exhaling the heady scents of his mediums and materials, his work keeps simply moving on. That compelling drive and singular gestural stroke *is* its signal feature, its beat, bop, and swing. Though it sometimes sounds jangling, otherworldly, and strange, it strides forthrightly onward on its own. The late work, especially, does not stop or dawdle anywhere along the way. It is agitated and restless. It is big, rippling, and sinuous, and it needs to move. It is the product of a figure the Greeks revered and hailed as a goddess, *Ananke*, 'Necessity.'

The works present these additive and accumulative accretions of corporeal gestures and marks in such a way that the pieces seem to originate organically. It is his psychical body that we see depicted in dynamic movement—and growth— and evolution. Though his finished pieces are often highly refined, extremely elegant and even sometimes rarified, they steadfastly retain their numerous archaisms, primitivisms, and their characteristic, erotic, dynamically driving and primordially elemental aura of sheerly grounded, bodily human physicality, stains, drops, blood, tears, feces, semen.

Welling up out of ancient origins, whether rough and crude, or stylized and polished, these large pieces all flow *outwardly*. Their vectors flow forth. They move towards the outside. They stream out into the world in ever-widening concentric circles. They become the features and lineaments of the world itself. They become entwined with the visible. They find their homes in the world of visibility. "A painting," Marin says, "is the trace, the index, and the sign both of a fold in the world that has become a seeing body and of a body changed into a world seen" (Marin 1999 p. 172).

As he moves forward and ever more deeply into the materials of his art, Twombly is also always starting over. The point appears to be, however, that he keeps moving toward something, toward a somewhere. In turn, he makes images that move and have the power to move us. We can observe in the works themselves how he concretely and physically moves around and plays with matter and with his different materials. He creates multiple, polyvalent movements so that the materials themselves might fall into place, so that the materials themselves may find *their own* space and inner rhythms. The work appears to finally become image, though, only at the very end, only through once again, his de-creating, his loosening, un-doing and un-making of the materials themselves. Kate Nesin, writing of Twombly's sculptures, says that he seems "to encourage our attention to the materiality" of their surfaces as a way of "*un*finishing them, a way not of fixing but of opening their surfaces (and the things literal or imagined beneath those surfaces)" (Nesin 2015, p. 32). He is like a physicist, chemist, or alchemist, continually conducting experiments in his studio-laboratory, endlessly observing, waiting for the critical moments, just looking, and then suddenly, sometimes furiously, pouncing and engaging with matter in an extremely complicated and sophisticated, or blunt and simple variety of ways. This is his ana-lysis of materials. He re-leases and liberates *their* inner properties. He furthers and midwifes the *telos* of his materials and of matter itself. He is both the medium/mediator/midwife and the master of these dis-solutions.

In the outermost limits of his pictorial language of folding forms, Twombly portrays and describes the clashing valences, impulses and sensations of his physical, material body, in a script, that while attaining completed image and visible form, must wait to be birthed into words, into a language and meaning of the spectator's own making, to be furthered, and dreamed onwards. As he fathoms and unearths the essences of his materials, he simultaneously excavates the stratified layers of his own and the viewer's body, for their historical memories, sensations, wounds, and traumas, as well as for the long-stored and storied soul treasures buried there, sedimented in the cells, muscle, bone, and tissue, deposited throughout all the long centuries of our ancestors' actions, wanderings, and attempts to express this inexpressible.

He traces in the lines and colorful phrasings of his paintings, the movements of his yearning and desiring body. Beyond the appearances themselves, beyond the appearances and forms he leaves on his canvases, he presents and portrays a beyond that exists, that is always becoming, in process, that is also outside of his body, that is, in Rilke's mythopoetic sense, in the air, in space, "as the other/side of the air" (Rilke 1989, p. 147). It is the 'other side' of seeing, and of vision too. He paints the inner lining and the beyond of vision. His works never cease to present that this beyond exists. It is a *topos* that is independent of the artist, or the viewer. He presents the autonomous region and reality of the soul. He taps into the ever-unfolding, ongoing rhythms of the beyond itself. It is the pulse outside of us and *in the world* with which we resonate in these works. But what strenuous exercise, discipline, and practices of looking, seeing, hearing, and attentive listening does it require?

Practically all of Twombly's later, bigger works, from the 2004-8 'Bacchus' cycles, to "III Notes from Salalah" (2005-7), "Untitled" (2005), the six strong "Untitled" (2006) pieces shown at Thomas Ammann Fine Art in 2007, as well as the 13 similar additional "Untitled" pieces, all from 2006, the two 'Part I' sections on canvas and the two pieces on wooden panels, all "Untitled" (2007) from the 'Blooming' series, "Untitled (I-IX)" and the four additional "Untitled" (2008), all with white flowing calligraphy on deep blue grounds, "Camino Real (I-V)" (2009-10), to 'The Last Paintings,' "Untitled (Camino Real) (I-VIII)" (2011), at least 74 very large-scale canvases altogether, are all fairly uniformly, gorgeously painted and lavishingly looping line drawings of an essentially cursive *script*, whose height, width, contiguity, coloration, and serializations of "ruptures, linkages and repetitions" (Bernadac 2013, p.153) are determined almost entirely by variations of purely *rhythmical* gestures. They are his most elaborate continuation of a calligraphic text composed and conducted in varying modulations of forms, colors and connecting sectional pieces which further the unfolding of an ongoing, essentially rhythmical, bodily story. The paintings present continuously rippling, rhythmical story lines. "Without rhythm," Barthes writes, "no language is possible" (Barthes 1985, p. 249). "Rhythm," he says further, "is the genesis of both painting and writing" (In Bernadac 2013, p. 153). "In a unique region of corporeal practice, painting and writing would have begun with the same figurative and nonsemantic gesture that is simply rhythm" (ibid.).

Stefan Zweig, the Austrian writer, in tracing the poet Friedrich Hölderlin's life trajectory from its extremely hopeful and promising beginnings to its tragic finale, writes that "Hölderlin...was continually strengthening his rhythms, which became more and more rustling, impetuous, confused, elemental and stormy" (Zweig 2011, p. 349). Rhythm was everything for the inspired early romantic poet. Sometime around 1805, he told his closest friend, Isaak von Sinclair:

> Spirit is the outcome of enthusiasm, and rhythm can be mastered only by him in whom spirit has quickened. One trained for poesy in the divine sense must recognize the spirit of the highest to be above the law, and must be prepared to sacrifice the law, saying: "Not as I will, but as thou wilt..." Everything is rhythmical; man's whole destiny is a heavenly rhythm, just as every work of art is a unique rhythm.
>
> (ibid., p. 348)

Sadly, what began rhythmically for Hölderlin as "a gently bubbling spring," ended "as a raging torrent" (ibid., p. 349). As rhythm took charge and became autocratic, the poet forgot the warning of his own youthful lines: "Ah, how little we know ourselves,/For within us a god rules!" (ibid., p. 365). He eventually succumbed to the raving dithyrambic god behind the surging rhythms of his being, and the man Hölderlin finally arrived at the end, which he had long since "proclaimed to be the true end of the true poet," and in his own words, was "consumed in the flame, to atone thereby for his failure to control the flame" (ibid., p. 367).

Despite his far-reaching explorations, Twombly, unlike Hölderlin, never strays far from his authentically *human* flame, the sources and grounds, the containing bodily temple of fiery rhythm. In their rolling and looping expressiveness, his late paintings figure the quintessentially *human* movements of the soul, while simultaneously plotting imaginal future directions for the soul's ongoing journey. In these calligraphic rhythmical works, he unifies line and color so that one is enveloped in the delirium and 'miracle' of vision itself. One is caught up in fascination and feels contained in a reciprocal and reversible relationship with the visible itself. Twombly seems to always keep in sensate memory that, "It is first of all by the world that I am seen or thought," as Merleau-Ponty, simply and amazingly states (In Merleau-Ponty 1993, p. 330). We truly exist only as visible beings, from the beginning, being seen by the world.

The human soul, the *psyche* itself, is enabled to move developmentally only through rhythm. The soul is initially activated through the rhythms, moods and modalities, particularly of sounds, grunts, speech, language, and the murmuring of words, inflections, and sentences flitting to and fro in inner space, surrounding the neonate, in the womb. The soul is originally animated only within the maternal matrix. From the very beginning of human life, we first *hear* things. Though invisible, we are spoken to and being seen, imaginally and rhythmically, sought out by words, sensations, wishes, and thoughts. We exist *in utero* contained by the resonant watery medium of amniotic fluids as much as we are held in the particular languages of communicating rhythms, of the mother, the culture, the environment, feelings, reactions, and emotions—all liquidly reverberating within. Throughout both pre- and post-natal infancy, language itself gurgles, pops, bubbles, and bursts all around us. Long before we will 'see' anything, we are listening to *everything*. Before seeing, we are being seen and spoken to, being addressed. Language is experienced as movement, the rustling and rippling movements of breaths in air. It is rhythm that governs and animates all of this new life. All living beings move to the indiscernible and invisible rhythms of an individual destiny, spun out in strands of DNA, nucleotides, cells, and molecules, and woven in the womb. Human being is the manifest expression of Dionysiac *zöe*, the life instinct, in form, creating and generating the pulsating, vital energy of a rhythm necessarily inherent in all growing organisms. Rhythm become form and matter, constitutes us as humans.

What characterizes rhythm for us now, and makes its appearance so fundamental to all nuance, tone, and shading in language and in art, is that it simultaneously touches and enlivens both the body and the soul—at the same time, in the same moment. It unites and conjoins both body and soul, *psyche* and *soma*, into a unitary experience. Rhythm circulates and activates all basic life forms. Rhythm is the glue of the soul, the adhesive that binds, holds and fastens the body and soul, or spirit, together; and like religion, "*ligatures*" human beings, connecting them "to the hidden world of the gods" (Barthes 1985, p. 249). Rhythm *animates* life through the breath. With listening as opposed to hearing, rhythm becomes selective and creative. What distinguishes man from animal, Barthes says, is "the intentional reproduction of a rhythm" (ibid., p. 248). Vocalizations, sounds, words, songs, and praise arise spontaneously from this coalescence of inner rhythms. Rhythm is the insistently beating pulse of the matrix and the *mysterium* out of which all names, sounds, and movements originate. It is the language of the un-nameable. All religious ritual and spiritual practice is guided by rhythm: sitting, standing, walking, chanting, praying, singing, dancing, swaying, bowing. Even with working: hunting, planting, sowing and plowing, weaving, writing, kneading, knotting, and hammering, the body is offering itself up *in rhythm* to the all-encompassing silence of the incomprehensible surrounding it. Since our genesis, the rhythms of body and soul respond to, and are part and parcel of the world and the visible that sees it, accepts it, and envelops it.

In holding together body and soul, rhythm also embraces time and space, unifying *them* into the present. Rhythm draws one into a body that is necessarily rooted in the earth. The present, temporality, and perhaps even time itself, is created through an unfolding sequence of movements and syncopations, of marked and unmarked oscillations which give rise in their turn, eventually, to signs, and much later, to organized sign systems. As language is born out of this shuttling back and forth between rhythms, activity and rest, the to and fro-ing between inner and outer worlds, sounds and space, being and doing, language also carries within itself the potency to transform both time and space through the seed syllables and performative articulations of its creative processes. Words really do make things happen. Words create and make differences. They change us. Language changes the mind. Language has the power to transform our lives. Space and time, insofar as we grasp and define these malleable dimensions, thereby become re-configured, brought into a truly human framework, and they attain a specific 'figure' commensurate with our unique mode of relational being only through language, speech, and words.

Twombly's artistic project until the end of his life appears as the aesthetic enactment of a ritual and rhythmical invoking of the gods into presence, a calling out to them through painting's and mark-making's processes and materials, a beckoning of them into a kind of presencing, manifesting—and visibility, in form. He draws them out. He calls the gods into the realm and dimensions of vision, and through his singular *poiesis*, into the visible. "Every visual something, as individual as it is, functions also as a dimension" (Merleau-Ponty 1993, p. 147). Like his distant, artistically poetic forebears, Hölderlin and Rilke, Twombly appears intent on re-creating our deepest bond with an embodied sense of self, re-establishing our connections with the material and natural worlds, with the *dimensions* of 'things,' and on restituting our transformatively poetic and creative powers as lyrical makers, agents and active do-ers in collaboration with the earth.

Twombly's sublime artistic project since early on has been to facilitate the re-membering and articulation of the members of our own dis-membered though embodied Dionysiac selves. Through art, we re-collect our deepest connections with the mother, *mater*, matter, Mother Nature, and with our own natures, our own natural wilderness places within and without, our own true ground, both inside and outside. In re-claiming our wildness and oneness with the material world, we must also acknowledge and honor the Dionysiac soul spark irradiating the entire body of the natural world, the *anima mundi*, enlivening the objective psyche itself, the *unus mundus*, the one, unitary world in which we dwell, breathe, and move, as in a medium. This realm and dimension of being is the true *human* medium. We swim within a membrane of soul. In realizing the fact that the material world is shot through and through with this psychic, soul substance, we can once again, via *poiesis*, 'creating,' 'making,' 'fabricating' and 'doing,' attempt to make life, the world, and nature, truly *matter*. This compelling mission of totally transfiguring the inner and outer natural worlds is the shared project of both the Hölderlinian and Twomblyan, sublimely Dionysiac artistic endeavors.

The image of Dionysos through both Hölderlin and Twombly, as heralding and re-creating our deepest bond with an embodied sense of self, our connections with the material and natural worlds, and with our transformative and creative poetic powers, is psychologically mirrored and given a theoretical framework in the writings of the Bulgarian-born, French psychoanalyst, Julia Kristeva, with her pioneering concepts of the 'maternal *chora*,' 'ab-jection,' and of '*jouissance*' (Kristeva 1982). The quintessential Dionysiac experiences of ecstasy and enthusiasm are echoed in Kristeva's notion, following Jacques Lacan and Roland Barthes, of *jouissance*, 'joy' or 'joyfulness,' a rapturous and polymorphous "waving and weaving bliss"

(Miller 1990, p. 326). Unlike the beautiful, however, which totalizes, brings comfort and pleasure, and is continuous with the known and accepted culture, the sublime visitation of *jouissance*, "imposes a state of loss…(that) discomforts…(and) unsettles assumptions" (ibid.), *mis en abyme*.

Kristeva claims that in both *jouissance* and abjection, "this crisis of the person…is a state of dissolution," and, it "can be experienced either as suffering or as rapture" (Kristeva 1995, p. 22). *Jouissance*, 'joy,' paradoxically though, arrives through experiences of incompleteness, not-knowing, un-knowing, and may appear whenever the autonomy, substance, and substantiality of our subjectivity is called into question, or is threatened or endangered, when the borders between subject and object cannot be maintained. It is a call, she says, 'out' of one's self. Kristeva writes: "I am solicited by the other in such a way that I collapse" (ibid.). "The point at which Art is found," Kirkeby writes, is precisely "the point where what is intriguing turns dangerous. It is the point of Collapse" (Kirkeby 2012, p. 69). We arrive at that edge, when we can allow ourselves to fall. We let ourselves fall and we continue falling. We are un-done.

The radical duality of Dionysiac art, even within the singular guise of *mainomenos*, in the forms of 'madness' that it brings, unearths the nature of an individual's connection to their earliest infantile states of relationship to, and containment within, a maternal environment. Kristeva aligns *jouissance* and the capacity for joy, with the semiotic disposition and reverie that stems from the earliest symbiotic union with the mother, (as opposed to the developmentally later 'symbolic' phase, the realm of the father). This deeply-rooted, pre-verbal union with the maternal *chora*, the 'nurse,' the innermost space of experience that she conceptually derives from Plato's cosmology in his dialogue, the *Timaeus*, provides a primal grounding in this unnameable, improbable receptacle, that, she says, is anterior to all signs, linguistic, syntactic, or symbolic. The *chora*, the 'vessel' or 'container,' is our original, internally embracing space, the primal maternal holding environment. The "luminous serenity of the unrepresentable" (Kristeva 1980, p. 243) and inexpressible maternal body lies at the basis of all *jouissance* (Adams 1997).

We can thus find in the varying languages, articulations, and expressions of Dionysiac art, however, the distinct capacities to at least attempt to reveal, unveil, or point towards these powerful layers of intra-uterine, as well as transcendent, experiencing:

> At the intersection of sign and rhythm, of representation and light, of the symbolic and the semiotic, the artist speaks from a place where she is not, where she knows not. (S)he delineates what, in her, is a body rejoicing (*jouissant*).
>
> (Kristeva 1980, p. 242)

The sublime artist, in capturing, portraying, or arriving at this state through whatever mediums of *poiesis* are used, breaks through primal repression and returns us to the maternal semiotic *chora*, to this instinctual source and origin of all signifying,

> to the "space" prior to the sign, this archaic disposition of primary narcissism that a poet brings to light in order to challenge the closure of meaning.
>
> (ibid., p. 281)

Jouissance is thus a deeply-felt experience of integration, well-being and wholeness that comes, paradoxically, through a kind of dismemberment, through fragmentation, dissolution, and loosening. It is an anxiety-free bodily joy and a primordial connection to an innermost being, to an original, indivisible sense of self.

It is also the feeling of truly being *seen*, held safely and securely within the maternal gaze, and being loved. When one allows one's self to fall, like Rilke's and Twombly's 'fishes,' we fall into the arms of the 'great mother,' archetypally, internally, and intrapsychically. This matriarchal *numinosum* (Schwartz-Salant 1988, 1988a), Joseph Grotstein refers to psychoanalytically, as the 'background object of primary identification' (Grotstein 1982). He sees it also in a developmental context as a primal psychic structure and an early experiential touchstone of the young child's contact with the timeless and eternal realm of the self. This 'background object of primary identification,' like Kristeva's *chora*,

> corresponds to the most archaic organizing internal object which offers background support for the infant's development…it is one which is awesome, majestic, unseen and behind one. It "rears" us and sends us off into the world. In moments of quiet repose, we sit

on its lap metaphorically. In psychotic illness and in borderline states it is severely damaged or compromised.

(Grotstein 1979, p. 154fn)

This primordial space, gently, provides us with the "soul's true home" (Schwartz-Salant 1988, p. 37), a transcendent though *embodied* sense of self as our native birthright.

As a hard-won psychic state for most people nevertheless, this sense of self is usually only achieved through prolonged ordeals of a ritually initiatory nature, which may entail the terrors of collapse, dis-integration and weakened surrender to the god who could very well tear us apart, the envoy of this Earth Mother, since she is herself ambivalent, split, and of two minds. The threat of actual psychosis looms large during these underworldly psychic journeys. This experience is therefore heralded by Bacchus, Psilax, *and* Mainomenos. He is Her gatekeeper. Dionysos/Bacchus *is* the 'render of souls.' Dionysos/Bacchus, called *Zagreus,* the 'great hunter,' stalks and tracks *us* down. G.W.F. Hegel reminds us that the 'spirit,' which we may think of as whole, light-filled, and unambivalently positive,

> attains its truth only by finding itself in absolute dismemberment. It is not that prodigious power by being the Positive that turns away from the negative... Spirit is that power only to the degree in which it contemplates the Negative face to face and dwells with it. This prolonged sojourn is the magical force which transposes the negative into given-Being.
>
> (In Taussig 2006, p. 170)

George Bataille, in his ongoing philosophical dispute with this line of Hegel's thought, would differ in stating that the force and work of negation in history and in the spirit, is, in fact, radically opposed to achieving either dialectical or redemptive closure. And "to the contrary," as Taussig writes, Bataille would declare that "negation is a sacrifice of the very idea of closure in a continuous face-to-facedness with death and dismemberment" (ibid.). Either way, the 'work,' the *opus,* remains the same: to suffer through and transform dismemberment into *poiesis.*

Twombly's sublime art, has, since his beginnings, been consistently concerned with performatively enacting the lineaments and contours of his own inner confrontations and experiences with the depths of soul. His work in the Dionysiac vein, has always conveyed a languor and rapture, an outward *luxus* and ease, and an ecstasy and jubilation in painterly process. His pieces *also* bear the traces, however, of a fury, a ferocity of intent, of deeply inward victories attained only through an arduous grappling with the daemons of the depths. These images that he makes, that he produces out of the abyss of these processes, most importantly, always *do* things, and *create* effects, rather than re-present or *mean* something specific, or be *about* anything in particular. He has never really attempted to create new images, symbols or representations *per se*, but instead his process has aimed at problematizing the very activities of reference and representation themselves. He has lived and worked out of this deep cleft in his own being. Though clearly he has not seemed to set out to intentionally question or sublate notions of representation, that resultant vector of his work has appeared as a net and powerfully provocative side effect of his major artistic projects. It is his sublime excess. The deeper archetypal background propels his pieces over the top and into the realm of the unknown, into the 'other,' towards the 'outside.' He is constantly interrogating the 'other' within himself, psychically, as well as physically, within his craft and materials, in order to go beyond his own self.

Twombly's art, like Dionysiac psychoanalysis, tragic theatre, and actually our dreams themselves, basically occurring every night of our lives, seeks to first interrupt, radically dis-rupt, and then totally transform our basic representational subjectivity. Rather than conceptualizing meaning, understanding, ideas, or insights, these sublime modalities perform, release, and let loose their already overdetermined meanings. As vehicles for the appearances of Dionysos, these very different aesthetic mediums and forms not only present *mania*, or 'madness,' on both the inner and outer stages of life, they produce and create varying typologies and modalities for *experiencing* a kind of madness itself, *as an actual event*. These works make madness.

Hölderlinian and Twomblyan art stage the dis-articulation, de-construction and dis-organization, not only of the spectator, the spectacle, and of the spectacular relationship itself, they also rupture and smash the specular and speculative nature of the whole enterprise. The entire 'ocularcentric' (Jay 1993), or visually-oriented stance of the subject gets shattered, paradoxically, through an enactment *within the visible*. They stage and perform the death of representation as *mimesis*, the death of representation as the 'imitation' of nature and/or of life. This postmodern, sublime, or Dionysiac art is unwilling to accept imitations.

Tragic theater, Jacques Derrida states, as the "repetition of that which does not repeat itself" (Derrida 1978, p. 250), must always fail in its attempt to represent life as "the non-representable origin of representation" (ibid., p. 234). Writing about Antonin Artaud and quoting from his 'theatre of cruelty,' Dionysiac theatre, Derrida says, "is not a *representation*. It is life itself, in the extent to which life is unrepresentable" (ibid.). He continues:

> This life carries man along with it, but is not primarily the life of man. The latter is only a representation of life, and such is the limit—the humanist limit—of the metaphysics of classical theater. "The theatre as we practice it can therefore be reproached with a terrible lack of imagination. The theatre must make itself the equal of life—not an individual life, that individual aspect of life in which CHARACTERS triumph, but the sort of liberated life which sweeps away human individuality and in which man is only a reflection."
>
> (ibid.)

In his prose *Remarks* on the translation of Sophocles' *Oedipus*, the poet Hölderlin, delineating the quintessence of Greek tragedy, writes:

> For the tragic *transport* is properly empty and the most unbound. Whereby, in the rhythmic succession of representations, in which the *transport* presents itself, *what in (poetic) meter is called the caesura*, the pure word, the counter-rhythmic intrusion, becomes necessary in order to meet the racing alternation of representations at its culmination, such that what appears then is no longer the alternation of representations but representation itself.
>
> (Hölderlin in Lacoue-Labarthe 1989, p. 234)

With this necessary explosion both of representations and of the spectacle, we have come very far indeed from Aristotle's *Poetics*, and perhaps from Freud and Jung as well, on the cathartic nature and function of Greek tragedy, art, dreams, and psychoanalytic practice. There is no longer a *polis* to either perform for, or, ritually, dramatically, or socio-politically attempt to transform. And there is no longer a catharsis, or even a satisfying or soothing representation to be had and/or held afterward. In Hölderlin's and Twombly's modes of *poiesis*, nothing remains. Everything is changed. Nothing can stay the same. Dionysiac art does not allow itself the consolation of representations, but rather strives instead to present and put "forward the unpresentable in presentation itself" (Lyotard 1984, p. 81). It "denies itself the solace of good forms, the consensus of a taste which would make it possible to share collectively the nostalgia for the unattainable" (ibid). All ways of viewing, experiencing and framing spectacle, whether in the '*disreal*' (Lyotard 1989, p. 156) spaces of temple, church, theatre, concert hall, sports stadium, television, computer or video screen, cell phone, tablet, cinema, museum, gallery, or consulting room, are all destroyed, obliterated. Twombly's art takes place outside of the frames.

In concluding his essay on Artaud's theater of cruelty, Derrida states that the art of theater more than any other art should be "the primordial and privileged site" for the "destruction of imitation" (Derrida 1978, p. 234). He continues:

> To think the closure of representation is thus to think the cruel powers of death and play which permit presence to be born to itself, and pleasurably to consume itself through the representation in which it eludes itself in its deferral. To think the closure of representation is to think the tragic: not as the representation of fate, but as the fate of representation. Its gratuitous and baseless necessity.
>
> And it is to think why it is *fatal* that, in its closure, representation continues.
>
> (ibid., p. 250)

As subjects of desire and images, in thrall to illusion and to all the multiply mediated and highly simulated versions of constructed reality surrounding us, we forget that we live within a theatre of representations, within images of images. Dionysiac practices, however, contrary to imitating, repeating, or re-presenting images, illusions or appearances, seek instead to create "new presentations, not in order to enjoy them, but in order to impart a stronger sense of the unpresentable" (Lyotard 1984, p. 81).

The Hölderlinian and Twomblyan languages of art consistently present in word and image, "that there is the non-presentable" (Lacoue-Labarthe 1993, p. 74). The presence of sublimity in their manifold productions, Hölderlin's erstwhile friend, colleague and classmate, Hegel, writes, "makes the matter disappear in which the sublime appears" (Hegel in ibid., p. 85). "This," Lacoue-Labarthe says, "states not merely the metaphysical truth of the sublime, but the sublime truth of metaphysics... The manifestation of the infinite annihilates the manifestation itself" (ibid., p. 86). So that no particular form or image comes into presence. It is already gone. The material art works, poetry, prose, sculpture, drawings, the paintings, all disappear themselves, obliterate and efface themselves in the enactment and experiential explosion of the sublime event.

"We need," according to Kristeva,

> to come as close as possible to the crisis, to accompany it and produce individual works, because that is the predicament we are in, in a kind of pulverization and solitude.
>
> (Kristeva 1995, p. 27)

She says further, that we need to maintain a state of "duality—on one side the most violent fragmentation and abjection, on the other, in the background, an inquiry into the state of the world" (ibid., p. 25). We must thus walk a fine line between the terrors of annihilation and despair, while furthering the constant, circumspect probing and continuous questioning of our situations, which are bound to nevertheless remain inconclusive.

Attempting to interrogate and name this catastrophe and cataclysm we are currently living, both Hölderlin and Twombly have been drawn into the depths of a space where limits and language are lacking. They reach with and through their particular varieties of *poiesis* to penetrate this darkness, this erring around, while shoring their own poetic fragments, words and calligraphic and gestural paintings and assembled sculptures against the world's wreckage, overwhelming absurdity and ruin. Twombly's sculptural expressions in particular are the figurative images, the embodiments and materialized manifestations of these orphaned aspects of ourselves, these human feelings and desires, that like us, are cast-off forms jumbled together, forlorn, alone, and abject.

Naming, and the sublime artists' attempts to name the god who is to come, originate for Kristeva, in the place/space of the *chora*, in the union of subject and predicate, and subject and object. It is the matrix and source for all names and naming, and "a *replacement*," she says, "for what the speaker perceives as an archaic mother" (Kristeva 1980, p. 291). Lodging into pictorial, verbal, or any other kind of language, the experiences of our own instinctual and signifying resources, the modality of our earliest identification with the maternally protective and nurturing space of the *chora*, the artist attempts to produce a specific *jouissance* that traverses "both sign and object" (ibid., p. 242). It is only this performative quality of sublime art that has now in our own time, the capacity to reveal our true and authentic space and place within the folds of *both* the visible *and* the invisible worlds.

This effort at *poiesis* also entails, according to Hölderlin, "the reversal of all modes and forms of representation" (Hölderlin in Santner 2006, p. 94). It is thus a modality of representation and expression which rebels against and resists the foreclosing and totalizing desires of any collective cultural ideology, theory or belief system. It instead produces, establishes and relates with singularities, *a* singularity, the inviolable singularity and irreplaceability of the 'other,' an 'other.' This art creates a space for intimacy with an 'other,' a *rapprochement* and intimacy, perhaps also, with the outside, with what is unconscious, with 'otherness' itself.

It is the *telos* of Dionysiac art to break through primary narcissism and primal repression, to open up and penetrate to an archaic maternal area, to "become the very space where father and mother meet" and thereby arrive at the "space of fundamental unrepresentability toward which all glances nonetheless converge" (Kristeva 1980, p. 249). This is the beatific paradox: that it *is "a space of fundamental unrepresentability toward which all glances nonetheless converge"* (my italics). In this space, which *shows itself* through the world, and envelops us, and is at least as much outside of us and in the world, in *physis* and in matter, as it is inside of us, in *psyche*, we are attempting not only to see and to speak what we are seeing, but we are at the same time being seen, and hearing our own name, our proper name, being spoken or whispered *to us*, however softly or loudly, or alert our listening may be to hear it.

Paul Klee related to a friend once, that:

> "In a forest, I have felt many times over that it was not I who looked at the forest. Some days I felt that the trees were looking at me, were speaking to me...I was there listening..."
>
> (In Merleau-Ponty 1993, p. 129)

Yet feeling so acutely and overwhelmingly for the most part, the *lack* of presence, however, the absence, *nameless* loss and even death of signification, or of 'god,' turns our usual and everyday namelessness at least into something we can, and indeed must, attempt to both mourn and name. The singularity of Friedrich Hölderlin's "poetic courage," Erich Santner says, is, "his capacity to truly dwell within this condition, to freely register the impact of the lack of *'heilige Namen'* ('holy names') *without* thereby positing a death of God" (Santner 2001, p. 44).

Through a thicket of wavering disequilibrium, his life wrenched way out of joint by ravaging madness, Hölderlin proclaims time and again, that poetry must, whatever the cost or circumstances, interpret the world, the gods, and nature itself, to man. In his remarkable poem, *"Dichterberuf,"* "The Poet's Vocation," written in 1800, just before the years of his more precipitous and acute declines, descents, and disappearances into the void, Hölderlin writes:

> But fearless man remains, as he must
> Alone before God, simplicity protects him,
> And he needs neither weapons nor cunning
> Until God's being not there helps him.
>
> (Hölderlin 1972, p. 35)

In this, his final version of the poem, it is precisely god's absence and distance that comes to the aid of man.

Hölderlin's immoveable presence at the inauguration of both modernity and postmodernity for the past two centuries, can be traced back to this valorous heralding and continuous interrogating of what he calls, *'des Tages Engel'*, 'the angel of our times,' as a "primal scene of dispersion and fragmentation" (Santner in Hölderlin 1990, p. 297). It is a time "when the divine is only available in the form of signs to be recollected and interpreted" (ibid.).

Agamben can assign 'a date of birth,' he says, to what he calls this 'poetic atheology,' and it is the day Hölderlin wrote the above last two changed, or 'corrected' verses of "The Poet's Vocation," and therewith proclaimed god's absence in a forcibly sobering sense, as actually, man's salvation. In Agamben's own translation:

> And there is no need for arms and for cunning,
> as long as God's absence aids.

(Hölderlin in Agamben 1999a, p. 90)

This final poetic verse "marks," he writes,

> the point at which the divine and the human alike are ruined, at
> which poetry opens onto a region that is uncertain and devoid of a
> subject, flattened on the transcendental, and which can be defined
> only by the Hölderlinian euphemism, "betrayal of the sacred."

(Agamben 1999a, pp. 90-1)

Through modalities of longing and loss, incompleteness and ruin, Hölderlin's poetry establishes a site, a place for the god who comes and goes, whose absence is our only guarantor of its presence.

> Near and
> Hard to grasp is, the god

(Hölderlin 1984, p.89)

So begins the poem "Patmos" in 1802, perhaps his most powerful evocation of our dispossession and abandonment at the hands of an indifferent deity, the one who in these times of conflagration and holocaust, we know exists, only "because He keeps disappearing" (Michaels 1997, p. 94).

Hölderlin's *poiesis* watches over, preserves and safeguards this absence of meaning. God and man can communicate only in a sacred infidelity. Hölderlin, like Twombly, can only embrace and love the smashed and abandoned ruins that surround us, since these are the only traces we have, the shattered fragments and wrecks of something lost, the tracks and symbols pointing toward an absence, a missing piece, the lost half of the broken *symbolon*. This most particular and painfully obvious aspect of our alienated human condition, Kristeva again, refers to, as the crisis of our 'abjection.' We live in a state in which we are truly neither subject nor object. We are neither subjects nor objects of experience, perception, consciousness, identity, or even awareness or rela-tion. The entire subject/object, self/world, mind/body dichotomy informing the scientific, materialist, positivist, and determinist perspective and tradition from Aristotle, Galileo, Descartes, and Newton, on to the development of technology and industrial production with all of its associated (and dissociated) global, societal, and economic frameworks and practices, is stood on its head. Consensual 'reality' as such is blown up by this quality of experiencing and the appreciation of our fundamental 'ab-jection,' 'being thrown out,' aloneness before god. Kristeva points toward, instead of our Kantian and techno-scientific views, established from the standpoint of the exalted, autonomous or even 'transcendental' subject, to this experiential uncertainty of our 'ab-jection,' to the fact that we are 'ab-ject,' thrown forth, cast off and flung out, beside ourselves, so that we must therefore learn all over again how to move, breathe, and live in this space in-between, without gravity, dis-placed, and yet always falling.

Embracing our *lack* of presence requires that we move even further into realms of *différence*, not-self, non-identity, into dizzying states of dis-integration, dis-solution. In this place where things are unfinished and unresolved, the self apprehended as neither subject nor object, borders, boundaries, rules, limits, and edges fall away. We cannot so easily own, appropriate, identify with, or become this or that thing, idea, image, event, symbol, thought or person, without at the same time, becoming its 'other'—which in itself then also immediately drops off into nothingness and emptiness. Paradoxically, it *is* that radical nothingness or void which is our sole/soul ground. It is precisely in just *this* vertiginously shifting inner earth where we must plant and tend *psyche*, soul. It is our only real ground, the true hopeful *topos* where we may become once more authentically human. Once again, we quote Rilke's Orphic sonnet in this regard, the stanza so often used by Twombly:

> Be—and at the same time know the condition
> of not-being, the infinite ground of your deep vibration,
> that you may fully fulfill it this single time.

(Rilke 1942, p. 95)

As 'ab-ject,' we are of necessity exposed to, and still bound to contain, all of the opposites, all of the warring dualities and contradictions of our riven nature, despair and hope, anguish and rapture, loss and love, and the many others, but in *different* ways than before. Our distinguished sovereignty, as readers and writers, spectators and actors, artists and viewers, as distant interpreters of the world and life in general, must become completely disrupted, and ruptured, by the continuous shocks of discontinuity we are constantly experiencing in both our inner and outer environments. It is Hölderlin's 'time of distress,' a time, as Heidegger says, of '*ständige Unganzheit*,' 'permanent incompleteness,' of "the 'no...longer' of the Gods that have fled and the 'not... yet' of the God to come" (Lacoue-Labarthe 1990, p. 56). The time of the world, the world as picture, and the age of representation as we know it, must come to an end and change. We are ready, waiting, and actively preparing an opening, a clearing, for the gods to return, establishing a location, a *temenos,* and sanctuary for the god to come home.

In his famous poem, "Archaic Torso of Apollo" (1908), Rilke ends with a line which is perhaps the most powerful psychological imperative of the twentieth century: "*Du musst dein Leben ändern*," "You must change your life," or, literally, 'You must make your life other-ed' (Rilke 1989, pp. 60-1). In the penultimate line of that poem, however, in which he is writing of the inner brilliance and dazzling, gleaming light powerfully emanating from an ancient sculpted stone figure, turned 'like a lamp' to an incandescent glow and gaze within the magnificent, fragmented, Hellenistic marble statue of a great rippling muscular torso, 'the translucent cascade of the shoulders' glistening 'like a wild beast's fur,' bursting 'like a star,' 'from all the borders of itself,' he finally states: "for here there is no place that does not see you" (ibid.). This immensely moving stone figure, he says, *sees us*. Though headless, it smiles at us from within itself. This marvelously radiating marble sculpture would not after so many centuries produce such astonishing effects, if it were not *always* looking out at *us*, seeing *us*, whether we are there or not. This defaced torso would not have the power to gaze out at us if it were not in its own way, alive, breathing, and animated by soul. The world, Rilke seems to suggest, is looking back at us, to see what we will do. The world is always looking at us—from within its own ensouled gaze—and will continue to look out and back at us, even long after we will be gone. While *we* may pass away, the world remains.

The world and all that it contains, remains. It persists. It endures. And it becomes significantly touching and poignant for us, in its simplicity, its just 'thereness' and 'suchness,' imbued with memory, meaning, and soul, precisely *because* it precedes *and* supercedes us. We measure our human lives against the world. It has been filled for unimaginably many millennia with soul. The world has been drenched and saturated with vision and *its own* visibility for countless aeons. We human beings are something perishable, small and fragile. We are the fleeting caretakers of this world, just passing through, transiting. The world and its things, objects, people, places, in all of their atmospheres and abjections, remains. It subsists as our source and home, beginning and end, genesis and ultimate destination. It continues to nourish and hold us. The world *is*: "*in order to* be independent of me, is for me *in order to be* without me, to be a world" (Merleau-Ponty 1993, pp. 146-7).

"For here," in this place of fullness, in the presence of *it all*, everything happening all at once, Rilke says, "there is no place that does not see you" (Rilke 1989, p. 61). With this one phrase, Rilke blows up and shatters the aesthetic object-as-object, blasts himself away as the dominating subject as well, and opens us up to an infinitely "new field and logic of encounter," indeed to:

> a new *Werkästhetik*, and a new mode of encounter—a new way of being submitted to the (now dispersed, "serialized") gaze of the object-correlative to it.
>
> (Santner 2006, p. 205)

We are thrown once again out of ourselves, into the world, *ek-stasis*, 'standing outside' of our usual self, possessed by the god of otherness, called and seduced *out* by the other who changes, smashes and obliterates our minds. It is this god Dionysos who allows and makes us lose our 'own' minds, so that we may truly open to self and world. Klee says that, "the painter must be penetrated by the universe and not want to penetrate it" (In Merleau-Ponty 1993, p. 129). We must allow ourselves to be pierced, entered, and to be wounded by the world, by people, by things, by nature, by the 'other.' We must then tend the wound, because it is the only entryway and entrance to our own deepest points within. It is only as 'ab-ject,' flung outside into the 'other,' when we are beside ourselves, that we pass from suffering to joy, from the depths of despond and absence, forlorn, crazed and distraught, into the scintillating presence of both word and world. We are beckoned by the 'other' into language, the repository of soul. It is this 'other' that we seek, this 'other' that names us, that passionately calls to us by our true and proper name, that gives us our voice and voices itself through us. *This* is our original being, our face before we were born. Though it happens only once, it continues to happen. It continues to always *be* happening.

The irrevocable rupture of the sublime is a total explosion. It blows us away. We are gone. It is a "primordial," "permanent" and "never-ending deed" (Schelling in Santner 2001, p. 87). Through this ground-breaking shift, we arrive in a radically altered space, at what Gaston Bachelard calls, "the antecedence of being" (In Weiss 2008, p. 370), the beginning before the beginning. We are continuously being called outside of ourselves, into the world, and into the 'otherness' of the world. It is thus, through this shattering event that we become a person, a self, a not-self, transitory, opened, and fleeting. And it is through this singular instant as well, this transformative trauma, that at least since the initial sparks of consciousness were struck into life, that we and the world *are* en-souled.

Walter Benjamin writes, that "to perceive the aura of an object we look at, means to invest it with the ability to look at us in return" (In Sebald 2011, p. XVI). And Merleau-Ponty adds, that "the prehuman way of seeing things," "*le regard préhumain*," "is emblematic of the painter's way" (Merleau-Ponty 1993, p. 129). This 'prehuman,' or maybe, *most human* gaze, allows us to open to "the autonomous life of things" (Sebald 2013, pp. 168-9). Twombly's paintings and sculptures, as objects animated by soul, represent in all of their ungraspable immanence, "the paradigmatic expression of what we leave behind" (ibid.), that is, the shining beauty of this transient world, everything brilliant, clear, and simply there, existing, animate, bathed in light, life, and wonder, outside of us. In these ordinary things and worldly, everyday objects, tables, trees, stones, paintings, looking out and back at us, "the role of the observer and the observed object are reversed...things look across at us, unblinking, and fix us in their gaze" (ibid., pp. 169-70).

> As many painters have said, I feel myself looked at by the things...
> to be seen by the outside, to exist within it, to emigrate into it, to
> be seduced, captivated, alienated by the phantom, so that the seer
> and the visible reciprocate one another and we no longer know
> which sees and which is seen
>
> (Merleau-Ponty 1968, p. 139)

There are thus "two gazes, one inside the other" (In Merleau-Ponty 1993, p. 287). In this entwining, overlapping, chiasmic intertwining and ensoulment, the reversibility of the gaze seems to indicate that there may be not only 'two gazes,' but a third that contains, connects, and relates the one to the other. Our vision swims like a fish in this third dimension, in the watery medium of soul, held by the viscosity of the visible world and by visibility itself.

Lyotard, again, furthers this experience of reversibility in viewing art:

> There can be no work of art if the seer and the seen do not hold one another in an embrace, if the immanence of one for the other is not manifested and glorified, if the visual organization does not make us feel that our gaze has been seen and that the object is watching.
>
> (Lyotard 1989, p. 224)

In allowing ourselves to be solicited by the gaze of the other that resides in exteriority, in Twombly's 'Bacchus' paintings for example, we risk the formlessness of collapse, and submit joyfully to our own de-centered, dis-appropriated, dis-membered Dionysiac gaze, the loosened looking of psyche's ana-lysis. Dispersed and disseminated throughout this world, our gaze is reciprocally returned to us from every 'other,' and from every thing. We are in "a new open and infinite field" (Santner 2006, p. 206). There is "no place," space, aspect or detail which does not see us, which does not speak to us with our own true name, and to which we "are not called upon to respond" (ibid).

"Psyche as the *anima mundi*, the Neoplatonic soul of the world is," in the words of James Hillman, "already there with the world itself" (Hillman in Polikoff 2011, p. 677). Our Orphic and Dionysiac task as "hearers and a mouth of Nature" (Rilke 1942, p. 67), is, as always, "to hear psyche speaking through all the things of the world, thereby recovering the world as a place of soul" (Hillman in Polikoff 2011, p. 677). The *anima mundi* "as that particular soul-spark, that seminal image, which offers itself through each thing in its visible form" (ibid.), is mediated to us as *event* in sublime art, through *poiesis*, in the words and works of Hölderlin, Rilke, and Twombly.

What we can now perhaps retrospectively begin to see recurring throughout and overarching the vast body of Cy Twombly's diverse and graciously bounteous body of art work, is the paramount value, valence and energetic significance consistently borne and upheld by the *line* itself, the graphism. As the most basic and essential element of his mark-making process, the concretion of visual intensities, we can, of course, see it inscribed in every

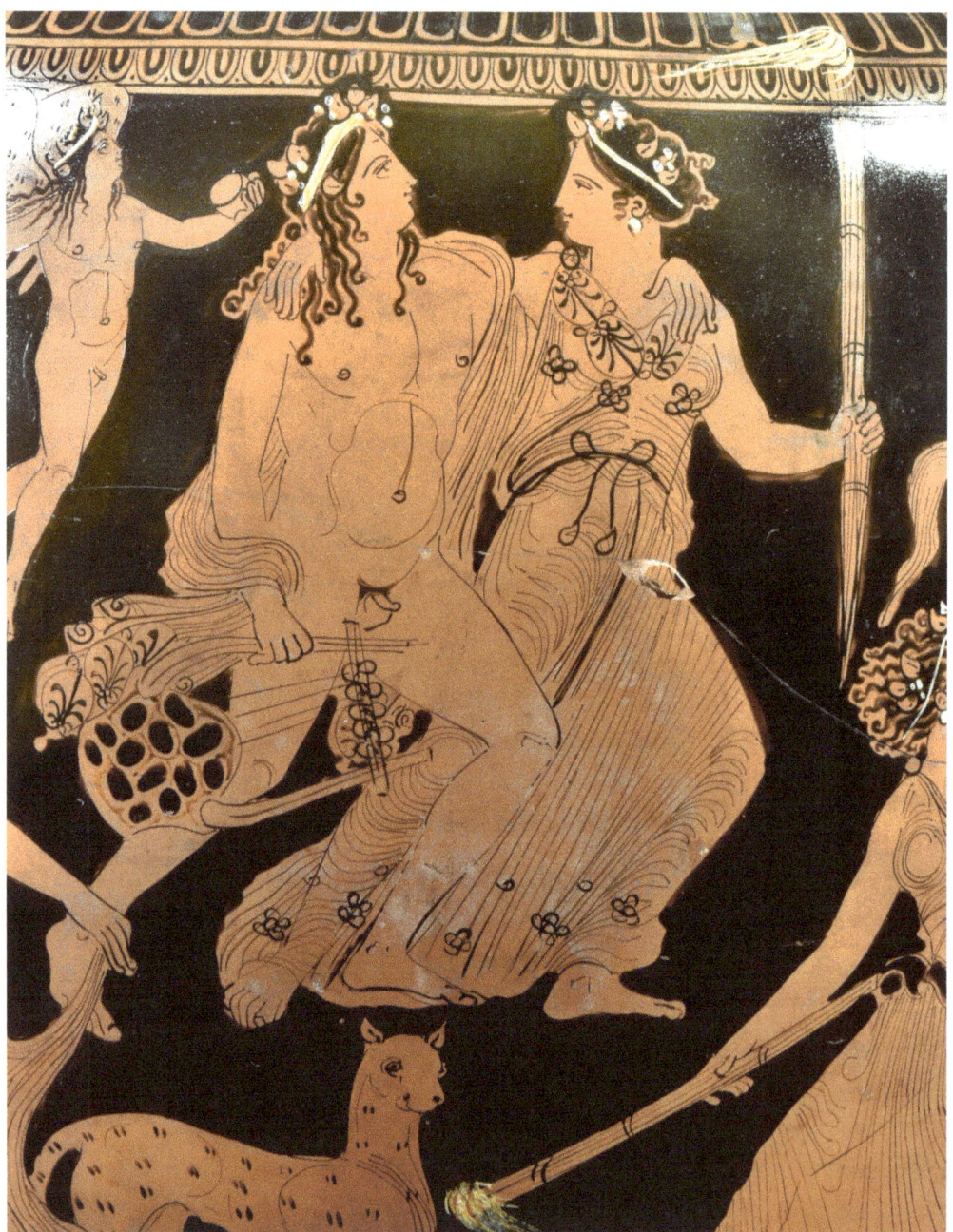

29.   *Dionysos and Ariadne*, detail, c. 400 B.C.

detail, aspect and phase of his multifarious productions. For him, in some sense, it is always about the visible scratch, the lines and their making, the extensions of our eyes and our vision—and also, however, our *limbs*, tracing lines that invisibly connect to our bodies—*and* to our *speech* as well, our voice lines, lines of sound, song, and poetry, suffusing the graphic line with rhythm and movement. Twombly himself always remains and appears in the lines. He is the animator, rhythmical creator and initiating pulsion of the lines. From the earliest, primitive, most directly scrawled slashes, scratches, and gouges of the all-over paintings of the '50s and '60s, through graffiti, words, shapes, signs, letters, and numbers, to the continuously repetitive loops, lines, circles, and fierce thrusting meanders of the 'blackboard paintings,' to the lines of petals, flowers, mandorlas, carts, and ships, all the way to the large, loosely-draped and folding, rolling and majestically cascading sweeps of the later paintings, the line continues to be *the* animating, driving feature and force of his surfaces. The lines themselves *surface*. They show themselves *sur face*. They emerge out of the reciprocally engaged gaze of the artist and his matrix, the material ground of his mediums. They appear and disappear in order to ultimately present themselves on the surfaces of the works.

For Twombly, the line itself, the singular gesture and mark, the visibly pulsating stroke, manifests his thought and passion. It is a rhythm become visible. He elicits from the blank surface, from its hidden realms of emptiness and invisibility, from its infolded inner space, its most interiorized rhythms. The breathing of matter itself is thus given dimensions and allowed to be made visible.

The corporeal rhythms of the world, *its* body, flesh and folds, come to fruition through his aesthetic practice and movements, through this reciprocal dance of mark-making. And the resulting confluences of lines are held there, contained within the space and time of his art works. The supports provide the space for the folds and contours of being to come forth and present themselves. We scan the broadly folding striations, drips, and colored streaks and spatters for the rhythms of his thought—and for our own. We strain to hear his dialogue with mother *materia*. We "must learn the necessity of a scansion that comes to fold and unfold a thought. This is nothing other than the necessity of a rhythm-rhythm itself" (Derrida in Lacoue-Labarthe 1989, p. 3). Twombly's work since the 1950s has materially performed the evolution and "the evocation of a pictorial language of pure, autonomous line: violent graphic gestures of an emotional thinking in search of 'another reality'" (Bastian in Twombly 2014b, p. 21).

Twombly, as we by now well know, loved reading and literature, but perhaps especially, poetry, the lines and the rhythms of poetry. In a recent monograph, Mary Jacobus has elaborated in detail the intimate relationship of Twombly's painting practice with his books, readings, and poetry (Jacobus 2016). They stirred him. And he wrote, drew, and painted the lines, verses, phrases, and stanzas of poetry as inscriptions, across, up, down, and over his own works. Even more frequently, he also freely and purely scribbled lines of his own, broken and unbroken, after, upon and through other lines, crossing out, erasing, effacing—and all as scansions of his own inner poetic rhythms, inspirations and expirations, motivations and memories, all lined as keenly-felt conveyors of feeling and meaning. These are meanings for the most part, however, with most of the 'lines' he actually wrote, which are illegible as 'words,' and essentially nonverbal. They are not explicitly verbal utterances, and yet they *are* and become visible, sounded, and traced in pencil, oil stick, and paint. They have become lines and notations of a Twomblyan music. They are pervaded and inhabited by a distinctly and unmistakeably *Twomblyan* rhythm. All of his work issues from his one body and presents that body in its visibility *and* invisibility. We immediately recognize these inimitable bodily rhythms—in all the works. We can say with some certainty: '*That's a Twombly.*' These lines and marks, gestures and forms, are the meanings of a rhythm, the visual and visible breathings of a rhythm which simply appears. It is there. These artworks are there as their fully-realized manifestations of the rhythms. They stand there before us—breathing. The lines coalesce, as in 'Bacchus,' "Camino Real," or 'The Last Paintings,' "Untitled (Camino Real)", into graceful, flowing fluidities which are scansions of a rhythm and thought made manifest. His lines, from the wide brush stroke, to the discretely small, though nonetheless violent jab, emerge, counterintuitively, from the *depths* of the support, to present on the surface: the *counter-rhythmic caesurae of the invisible.* They burst into the open. His lines themselves dismantle, desystem-atize, deconstruct, and destructure the visible. With disjointed and jagged force, they interrupt the seamless world of the visible, the world of thought, narrative, image, and action, and present in their stead, another, an 'other,' world. It is the world of the in-visible, which is patiently invited, sweetly seduced, cajoled, and finally, brought, carried and urged, through *poiesis,* into being. The work opens up the very possibility of thought and poetry. His lines since the beginnings have traced the antirhythmic counterpoints to the more rhythmical breathings in and out of our usual everyday life processes. Twombly's art brings forth and presents through the presentation of the

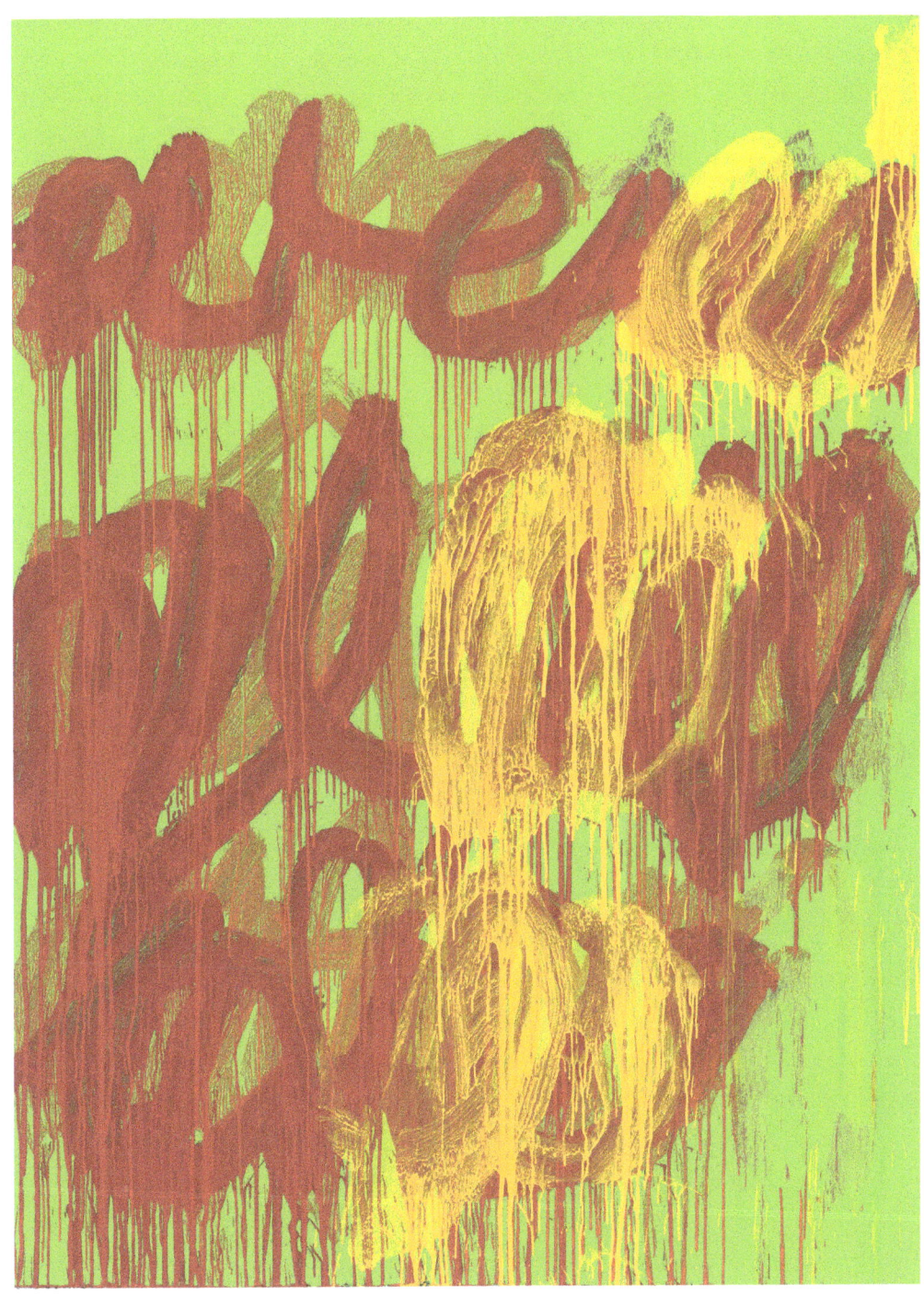

30.   Cy Twombly, *Untitled (Camino Real)*, Part II, 2011.

invisible, an a-rhythmia, a non-rhythmical rhythm which is the breathing and the breath of the invisible itself. The rhythms of his art destroy, undo, and *de-create* our illusions of continuity, sense, and non-sense. Our very sensibilities themselves are undone. His counter-rhythms consistently break through the surfaces. They puncture, punctuate, rupture, tear, shred, and rend the visible, so as to unveil the surge, swell and rhythmical grace of the invisible, the unnameable fullness for which we are born, to which we are destined, and *for* which we are now visible beings in the world, seeing and being seen. "Real singing," Rilke says, "is a different breath" (Rilke 1942, p. 21). "*In Wahrheit singen, ist ein andrer Hauch*" (ibid., p. 20). 'Singing in truth, is another breath.'

The caesura, as performed by Hölderlin, Rilke, and Twombly, is the empty moment when the poem and the painting just stops, when it gets interrupted by the pure transport, the rhythm of the invisible, the original word calling out to us from the depths of its hiddenness and silence. It is what Agamben refers to as the 'end of the poem.' "What is this falling into silence of the poem? What is beauty that falls? And what is left of the poem after its ruin?" (Agamben 1999a, p. 114). The poem ends, he says, with the last line or word as the site and space of the "mystical marriage," the wedding of sound and sense, rhythm and repose, of the semantic and the semiotic, as they collapse together "into silence...in an endless falling. The poem thus reveals the goal of its proud strategy: to let language finally communicate itself, without remaining unsaid in what is said" (ibid., p. 115).

In the end, neither Orpheus nor Dionysos are the true subjects or objects of Twombly's art. These figures and images share with all of us that fundamental aspect of their existence, their *psychic reality*, that they are neither subject nor object. They, too, are abject and separate. They are cast off, abandoned, torn, discarded, fleeting and dispersed. Albeit venerable and legendary, these noble mythologems are traces, memories, and echoes of themselves. They are a resounding phrase, an inexplicable sign, a fragrance, a melody tossed and caught up by a sudden gust of wind, and then gone. Yet they are also, at the very same time, solid, tangible, and powerful, like the terrifying or awe-inspiring images of gods that they are, or even of God. They *are* and ultimately persist and subsist; they last, like stone, metal, gold, a star, the sea, the sun. They have form, duration, and power.

So it is, in life as in art, we begin and end with rhythms. Rilke commences the 'Second Part' of his *Sonnets to Orpheus* with this stanza (II, 1):

> Breathing, you invisible poem!
> World-space constantly in pure
> interchange with our own being. Counterpoise,
> wherein I rhythmically happen.
>
> (Rilke 1942, p. 71)

Breath, our actual breathing, constantly in interchange with the '*Weltraum*,' the 'world-space' in which we live, the world's soul, occurs rhythmically. The world-space is the invisible poem within which we rhythmically happen as living beings. "Our entire existence," as Hölderlin, Rilke's acknowledged predecessor said a century before him, "is rhythm." "Everything is rhythm." "The entire destiny of man" and "every work of art" is a unique, indivisible rhythm (Hölderlin in Agamben 1999, p. 94).

Merleau-Ponty goes so far as to suggest that we take this miracle of rhythmically breathing, inwardly and outwardly, the very words 'inspiration' and 'expiration,' quite literally.

> There really is inspiration and expiration of Being, respiration in Being, action and passion so slightly discernible that it becomes impossible to distinguish between who sees and who is seen, who paints and what is painted.
>
> (Merleau-Ponty 1993, p. 129)

In another translation, this same last line of the philosopher becomes:

> Action and passion so little separable that one no longer knows who is looking and who is being looked at, who is painting and who is being painted.
>
> (In Sebald 2013, p. 197)

Rilke reminds us once again of this too, expansively taking it a step further: "For there is no place at all/that isn't looking at you" (Rilke 1981, p. 147).

In the poem *"An die Musik,"* "To Music" (1918), Rilke attempts to capture the ineffable paradoxes of music: as the "breathing of statues," the "silence of paintings," "You language where all language ends," "You time/standing vertically on... hearts" (Rilke 1989, p. 147). He then, almost in desperation, and diving even deeper, writes of music as 'feeling,' as 'feelings,' as a feeling space, a *'Herzraum,'* a 'heart-space,' which is transformed from something *in* us into something *outside* of us. *Herzraum* becomes *Weltraum*. Heart-space becomes world-space. Rilke says that music is the deepest space *in* us, that rising, grows and forces its way out and away from us (ibid.). And then, ending the poem "To Music," he writes:

> When the innermost point in us stands
> outside, as the most practiced distance, as the other
> side of the air:
> pure,
> boundless,
> no longer habitable.

> (ibid.)

This then, is that moment of de-creation, when, between breaths, we are 'neither this nor that,' *neti, neti,* 'not this, not this.' Or, as it is said also in Sanskrit, *Tvat tvam asi,* 'Thou art that.' When we *are* this and thus, inexorably, *that* also. When we are outside of our selves and can cast and bend our vision so that we actually see and visually touch the sun and the stars. Our gaze spans light years. We exist between these worlds. We are in different places at once, in a separate space. We are here, at one, and yet, contrarily, we are already there, gone, away, scattered, invisibly spent, shared out and exorbitantly splurged amongst the many. We exist in order to stretch apart our farthest practiced bounds and poles, our furthest most disciplined strengths, distances, edges, and contradictions, to create the greatest differences between all the opposing points in us, all so that the god may appear in the space between, in the interval, in the moment, between the moments, between the movements, between breaths, breathless. "For the god," Rilke says, "wants to know himself in you" (ibid., p. 261).

"To work with things," Rilke continues, "is not hubris/when building the association beyond words...Because inside human beings is where God learns" (Rilke 1981, p. 175). Inside human beings is where God will be prepared.

Benjamin, referring to this "Messianic cessation of happening" (In Santner 2001, p. 134) that so rarely occurs, though when it does, needs *us* for it to happen, believes that it is immanent in everything, and that it is also outside, in the world. It *is* the many visages and lineaments of the world itself. It *is* in each thing. It calls us out to recognize, acknowledge, and to honor *it*. This space of the god needs *us* for *its* revelation, valorization, and redemption. The human soul is the place and space, the *topos*, where the work is undergone. It is the clearing in the forest, the temple on the mount, the studio with its materials, the cushion or desk waiting in the corner of the room, where the vessel is tended, the fires kept burning. As much as we desperately need the gods to help us redeem the colossally disturbed and deeply split world order within and without, so, too, do the gods need us to restore the riven opposites within their own divine being. What this presentation of our ordinary and essential humanness through *poiesis* basically and finally manifests, "is an aspect of God which is striving to become conscious of itself—as though the human psyche and matter were the chosen place for God's self-realization" (von Franz 1966, p. 388). Twombly's life-work spread out there before us reveals his attempt to name these gods who still call out to us from their bondage in matter.

In the caesura when the movement stops, in the instant when the music, words, images, or thoughts appear "as if checked in mid-flight for a moment" (Agamben 2002, p. 283), and all the presentations and performances, and all the myriad spectacles and phenomena reveal not what they say, show, mean, or present, but instead their own *and* our own innermost nature and goals, we are loosened, let go, unmoored, set adrift, sailing on a vast, cosmically rocking sea. We know we are both inside *and* outside, carried along by the frail bark of our breath, our continuously rhythmical breathing, inspiring and expiring, moving in and out. We are this one, and this one, as far as we know, only this once. We are, as Rilke says, finally, with the line ending the sonnet to Orpheus I, 3: "A breath for nothing. A wafting in the god. A wind" (Rilke 1942, p. 21).

Appendix I

Excerpted letter from Rainer Maria Rilke to his Polish translator, Witold von Hulewicz, written on November 13, 1925.

"We, of this earth and this today, are not for a moment hedged by the world of time, nor bound within it: we are incessantly flowing over and over to those who preceded us and to those who apparently, come after us. In that widest 'open' world all *are*, one cannot say 'simultaneously,' for the very falling away of time conditions their *existing*. Transience everywhere plunges into a deep being. And so all forms of this earth are not only not to be used in a time-limited way only, but, so far as we are able, to be given place in those superior significances in which we have a part...(I)n an earthly, a deeply earthly, a blissfully earthly consciousness we must introduce what is *here* seen and touched into that wider, that widest circuit...into a whole, *into the whole*. Nature, the things we move among and use, are provisional and perishable; but, so long as we are here, they are *our* possession and our friendship, sharing the knowledge of our grief and gladness, as they have already been the confidants of our forebears. Hence it is important not only not to run down and degrade everything earthly, but just because of its temporariness, which it shares with us, we ought to grasp and transform these phenomena and these things in a most loving understanding. Transform? Yes; for our task is so deeply and so passionately to impress upon ourselves this provisional and perishable earth, that its essential being will rise again 'invisibly' in us. *We are the bees of the invisible. We frantically plunder the visible of its honey, to accumulate it in the great golden hive of the invisible.* The 'Elegies' show us at this work, the work of these continued conversions of the beloved visible and tangible into the invisible vibration, and animation of our (own) nature, which introduces new frequencies into the vibration-spheres of the universe. (Since the various elements in the cosmos are merely different rates of vibration, we are preparing in this way not only new intensities of a spiritual sort but, who knows, new substances, metals, nebulae and stars.) And this activity is singularly supported and urged on through the ever more rapid disappearance of so much of the visible that is not going to be replaced...Animated things, things experienced by us, *and that know us*, are on the decline and cannot be replaced any more. *We are perhaps the last still to have known such things.* On us rests the responsibility of upholding not only the memory of *them* (that would be little and unreliable), but their human and laral worth. ('Laral' in the sense of household gods). The earth has no other way out than to become invisible: *in* us, who with a part of our being participate in the invisible, have (at least) certificates of participation in it, and can increase our holdings in invisibility during our being-here, —*in* us alone can be fulfilled this intimate and continual transformation of the visible into invisibility that is no longer dependent on the being visible and tangible, just as our own destiny continually grows *simultaneously more present and invisible* in us...—All the worlds of the universe fling themselves into the invisible as into their next-deeper reality; *some stars heighten directly in intensity and pass away in the infinite consciousness of the angels, others are dependent on creatures who slowly and laboriously transform them, in whose terror and ecstasy they reach their next invisible realization. We are ...these transformers of the earth; our whole existence, the flights and downfalls of our love, all capacitate us for this task* (beside which, essentially, no other holds)."

(Rilke 1942, pp. 132-36)

Appendix II

From Giorgio Agamben's *Idea of prose*.

> "As threshold, the insignificant name—pure subjectivity—is included in the edifice of joy."

(Agamben 1995, p. 133).

Threshold

Kafka Defended Against His Interpreters

The most diverse legends circulate about the inexplicable. The most ingenious—which was found by the present guardians of the Temple while rifling through the ancient traditions—claims that, being inexplicable, it remains so in all the explanations which have been given and that will continue to be given through the centuries. Indeed, precisely these explanations constitute the best guarantee of its inexplicability. The only content of the inexplicable— and in this lies the subtlety of the doctrine—consists in the command—truly inexplicable: "Explain!" One cannot escape from this injunction because it does not presuppose anything to explain, but is itself the only presupposition. Whatever your response or non-response to its injunction—even your silence therefore—will in any case be meaningful, will in any case contain an explanation.

Our illustrious fathers—the patriarchs—finding nothing to explain, searched their hearts for a way to express this mystery; but for the inexplicable, they found no more fitting expression than explanation itself. The only way—they argued—to explain that there is nothing to explain is to give explanations. Any other stance, including silence, seizes on the inexplicable too clumsily: explanations alone leave it intact.

For the patriarchs, however, who first formulated this doctrine, it had to be inseparably linked to a codicil, which the present guardians of the Temple have dropped. This codicil specified that explanations would not last eternally, and that on a certain day, which they called the "day of Glory," explanations would end their dance around the inexplicable.

Explanations are, in fact, only a moment in the tradition of the inexplicable: they are the moment, to be more precise, which keeps watch over it by leaving it unexplained. Emptied of their content, explanations thus fulfill their task. But at the point where explanations, by showing their emptiness, leave it be, the inexplicable itself is in jeopardy. Only the explanations were, in truth, inexplicable, and the legend was invented to explain them. What was not to be explained is perfectly contained in what no longer explains anything.

(ibid., pp.135-8)

Bibliography

A

Adams, T. (1997). Psychoanalytic framing of the sublime in the creative act. In P. Clarkson (Ed.). *On the sublime in psychoanalysis, archetypal psychology and psychotherapy*. London: Whurr Publishers Ltd.

Adler, G. (1978). *Remembering and forgetting*. London: Harvest. Also in: *Dynamics of the self*. London, Boston: Coventure, Ltd., Sigo Press.

Adorno, T.W. (1992). Parataxis. On Hölderlin's late poetry. In *Notes to literature*, Volume Two. R. Tiedemann (Ed.), S.W. Nicholsen (Trans.). New York: Columbia University Press.

Agamben, G. (1995). *Idea of prose*. M. Sullivan and S. Whitsitt (Trans.). Albany, NY: State University of New York Press.

____. (1999). *The man without content*. G. Albert (Trans.). Stanford, CA: Stanford University Press.

____. (1999a). *The end of the poem. Studies in poetics*. D. Heller-Roazen (Trans.). Stanford, CA: Stanford University Press.

____. (2002). Beauty that falls. In *Cy Twombly: Eight sculptures*. exh. cat., New York and Rome: American Academy of Rome, 1998, p. 5; reprinted in N. Del Roscio (Ed.). *Writings on Cy Twombly*. Munich: Schirmer/Mosel.

____. (2006). Falling beauty. In *Cy Twombly. Sculptures 1992-2005*. S. Moore (Trans.). Munich: Schirmer/Mosel.

Aristotle. (1958). *On poetry and style*. G.M.A. Grube (Trans.). Indianapolis, IN: The Bobbs-Merrill.

Astrachan, G.D. (1992). Orpheus, the lyre player. In *Harvest. Journal for Jungian studies*.V. 38. London: C.G. Jung Analytical Psychology Club.

____. (2013). Analysis as mourning. In *International Journal of Jungian Studies*. V. 5 No. 3, October 2013. Oxon, UK: Routledge, Taylor and Francis.

____. (2017). Orpheus, the praise singer. In *Cy Twombly. Orpheus*. Paris, London, New York: Gagosian Gallery.

Athanassakis, A.N. and Wolkow, B.M. (Trans., Intro. and Notes). (2013). *The Orphic hymns*. Baltimore, MD: The Johns Hopkins University Press.

B

Bailey, C. (1992). *The loves of the gods. Mythological painting from Watteau to David*. New York: Rizzoli Internation Publications Inc.

Barnhart, C.L. (Ed.). (1962). *The American college dictionary*. New York: Random House.

Barthes, R. (1985, 1991). *The responsibility of forms*. R. Howard (Trans.). Berkeley and Los Angeles: University of California Press.

Bastian, H. (1995). In *Cy Twombly. Catalogue raisonné of the paintings*. Volume IV 1972-1995. Munich: Schirmer/Mosel.

____. (2014b). Introduction/Poéte D'Espace. In *Cy Twombly. Catalogue raisonné of the paintings*. H. Bastian (Ed.). Volume VI 2008-2011. Munich: Schirmer/Mosel.

Benjamin, W. (1968). *Illuminations. Essays and reflections*. H. Arendt (Ed. and Intro.), H. Zohn (Trans.). New York: Schocken Books.

Berger, J. (2000). John Berger 1.3.1997. In J. Berger and J. Christie. *I send you this cadmium red: A correspondence between John Berger and John Christie*. Barcelona: ACTAR.

Bernadac, M.-L. (2013). A cycle of paintings by Cy Twombly. S. Miller (Trans.). In *Gagosian Gallery. Summer 2013*. New York: Gagosian Gallery.

Bernstock, J.E. (1991). *Under the spell of Orpheus*. Carbondale and Evansville, IL: Southern Illinois University Press.

Blanchot, M. (1982). *The space of literature*. A. Smock (Trans. and Intro.). Lincoln, London: University of Nebraska.

____. (2003). *The book to come*. C. Mandell (Trans.). Stanford, CA: Stanford University Press.

Boer, C. (Trans.). (1979). *The Homeric hymns*. Dallas, TX: Spring Publications, Inc.

Bontea, A. (2014). Cy Twombly: Painting as an art of thinking. In T. Greub (Ed.). *Cy Twombly. Bild, Text, Paratext*. Paderborn, Germany: Wilhelm Fink.

Bull, M. (2005). Fire *in the* water. In *Cy Twombly. Bacchus Psilax Mainomenos*. New York: Gagosian Gallery.

Burch, R. (1993). On the topic of art and truth: Merleau-Ponty, Heidegger and the transcendental turn. In G.A. Johnson (Ed. and Intro.). *The Merleau-Ponty Aesthetics Reader. Philosophy and painting*. Evanston, IL: Northwestern University Press.

C

Carroll, D. (1987). *Paraesthetics*. New York and London: Methuen.

Cobb, N. (1992). *Archetypal imagination. Glimpses of the gods in life and art*. Hudson, NY: Lindisfarne Press.

Cullinan, N. (2008). Fade to grey: Treatise on the veil. In N. Serota (Ed.). *Cy Twombly. Cycles and seasons*. New York: Distributed Art Publishers, Inc.

____. (2011). *Twombly and Poussin: Arcadian Painters*. London: Paul Holberton Publishing.

D

Daniélou, A. (1979, 1984). *Shiva and Dionysus. The religion of nature and eros*. K.F. Hurry (Trans.). New York: Inner Traditions International, Ltd.

Davenport, G. (Trans. and Intro.). (1980). *Archilochos Sappho Alkman. Three lyric poets of the late Greek bronze age*. Berkeley, Los Angeles, London: University of California Press.

Delehanty, S. (1975). The alchemy of mind and hand. *Cy Twombly: Paintings, drawings, constructions, 1951-1974*, exh. cat., Philadelphia Institute of Contemporary Art,

University of Pennsylvania (Philadelphia, 1975); reprinted in N. Del Roscio (Ed.). *Writings on Cy Twombly*. Munich: Schirmer/Mosel Publishers.

Del Roscio, N. (Ed.). (2002). *Writings on Cy Twombly*. Munich: Schirmer/Mosel Publishers.

Derrida, J. (1978). *Writing and difference*. A. Bass (Trans.). Chicago: University of Chicago Press.

Detienne, M. (1979). *Dionysos slain*. M. Muellner and L. Muellner (Trans.). Baltimore and London: The Johns Hopkins University Press.

____. (1989). *Dionysos at large*. A. Goldhammer (Trans.). Cambridge, London: Harvard University Press.

____. (2003). *The writing of Orpheus*. J. Lloyd (Trans.). Baltimore and London: The Johns Hopkins University Press.

Dodds, E.R. (1951). *The Greeks and the irrational*. Berkeley, Los Angeles, London: University of California Press.

____. (1960). *Euripides Bacchae* (Ed., Intro. and Comm.). Oxford: Oxford University Press.

F

Fagles, R. (Trans.). (1990). *Homer. The Iliad*. B. Knox (Intro. and Notes). London: Penguin Books.

Fierz-David, L. (1988). *Women's Dionysian initiation: The Villa of Mysteries in Pompeii*. Dallas, TX: Spring Publications, Inc.

Froman, W. J. (1993). Action painting and the world-as-picture. In G. A. Johnson (Ed. and Intro.). *The Merleau-Ponty aesthetics reader. Philosophy and painting*. Evanston, IL: Northwestern University Press.

G

Garat, A.-M. (2011). Inner times. In *Le temps retrouvé. Cy Twombly photographe et artistes invités*, vol. II. Arles: Actes Sud/Collection Lambert en Avignon.

Gilmour, J.C. (1990). *Fire on the earth. Anselm Kiefer and the postmodern world*. Philadelphia, PA: Temple University Press.

Grene, D. and Lattimore, R. (Eds.). (1960). *Greek tragedies, v.3*. Chicago and London: The University of Chicago Press.

Greub, T. (2014d). Cy Twombly's "inverted archaeology." In *The essential Cy Twombly*. N. Del Roscio (Ed.). New York: Distributed Art Publishers.

Grotstein, J. (1979). The psychoananalytic concept of the borderline organization. In J. LeBoit and A. Capponi (Eds.). *Advances in psychotherapy of the borderline patient*. New York: Jason Aronson.

____. (1982). *Splitting and projective identification*. Northvale, NJ: Jason Aronson, Inc.

Guthrie, W.K.C. (1952/1993). *Orpheus and Greek religion*. Princeton, NJ: Princeton University Press.

H

Hall, N. (1988). *Those women*. Dallas, TX: Spring Publications, Inc.

Harrison, J.E. (1913). *Ancient art and ritual*. New York: Henry Holt and Company.

____. (1962). *Epilegomena to the study of Greek religions and Themis*. New Hyde Park, NY: University Books.

____. (1980). *Prolegomena to the study of Greek religion*. London: Merlin Press.

Heidegger, M. (1996). *Hölderlin's hymn "The Ister."* W. McNeill and J. Davis (Trans.).Bloomington and Indianapolis, IN: Indiana University Press.

Hillman, J. (1979). *The dream and the underworld*. New York: Harper and Row, Publishers, Inc.

____. (1982). *Anima Mundi*: The return of the soul to the world. In *Spring. An annual of archetypal psychology and Jungian thought*. Dallas, TX: Spring Publications, Inc.

____. (1985). *Archetypal psychology. A brief account*. Dallas, TX: Spring Publications, Inc.

Hochdörfer, A. (2009). "Blue goes out, B comes in." Cy Twombly's narration of indeterminacy. In *Cy Twombly. States of mind*. Munich: Schirmer/Mosel Verlag.

Hölderlin, F. (1972). *Friedrich Hölderlin, Eduard Morike: Selected poems*. C. Middleton (Intro. and Trans.). Chicago, IL: University of Chicago Press.

____. (1984). *Hymns and fragments*. R. Sieburth (Intro. and Trans.). Princeton, NJ: Princeton University Press.

____. (1988). *Friedrich Hölderlin, Essays and letters on theory*. T. Pfau (Trans. and Ed.). Albany, NY: State University of New York Press.

____. (1990). *Hyperion and selected poems*. E.L. Santner (Ed.). New York: Continuum.

____. (1998). *Friedrich Hölderlin. Selected poems and fragments*. M. Hamburger (Trans.). London: Penguin Books.

Hopkins, L. (2014). Twombly's *Hero and Leandro (To Christopher Marlowe)*. In T. Grueb (Ed.). *Cy Twombly. Bild, Text, Paratext*. Paderborn, Germany: Wilhelm Fink.

Horace. (1959). *Satires and epistles. A modern English verse*. S.P. Bovie (Trans.). Chicago, IL: University of Chicago Press.

J

Jacobus, M. (2008). Time-lines: Rilke and Twombly on the Nile. Tate Papers Issue 10, Autumn 2008. www.tate.org. UK/download/file/fid/7313.

____. (2012). *Romantic things. A tree, a rock, a cloud*. Chicago and London: The University of Chicago Press.

____. (2016). *Reading Cy Twombly. Poetry in paint*. Princeton and Oxford: Princeton University Press.

Jay, M. (1993). *Downcast eyes: The denigration of vision in twentieth-century French thought*. Berkeley, CA: University of California Press.

Johnson, G.A. (1993). Structures and painting: "Indirect languages and the voices of silence."

____. Ontology and painting: "Eye and Mind." Both in G.A. Johnson (Ed. and Intro.). *The Merleau-Ponty aesthetics reader. Philosophy and painting.* Evanston, IL: Northwestern University Press.

Jung, C.G. (1948, 1969). On the nature of dreams. In *CW 8, The structure and dynamics of the psyche.* Princeton, NJ: Princeton University Press.

____. (1953, 1968). *CW 12, Psychology and alchemy.* Princeton, NJ: Princeton University Press.

____. (1963). *CW 14, Mysterium coniunctionis.* Princeton, NJ: Princeton University Press.

K

Kahn, C.H. (1979). *The art and thought of Heraclitus.* Cambridge: Cambridge University Press.

Kerenyi, K. (1951). *The gods of the Greeks.* Great Britain: Thames and Hudson.

____. (1959). *The heroes of the Greeks.* Great Britain: Thames and Hudson.

____. (1976). *Dionysos. Archetypal image of indestructible life.* R. Manheim (Trans.). London: Routledge and Kegan Paul.

Kirkeby, P. (2012). *Writings on art.* A. Schnack (Ed. and Intro.), M. Aitken (Trans.). Putnam, CT: Spring Publications.

Klee, P. (1953). *Pedagogical sketchbook.* New York: Frederick A. Praeger, Inc., Publishers.

____. (1961). *Notebooks. The thinking eye,* vol. I. R. Manheim (Trans.), J. Spiller (Ed.). London and Bradford: Percy Lund, Humphries and Co., Ltd.

____. (1964). *The diaries of Paul Klee.* F. Klee (Ed. and Intro.). Berkeley, Los Angeles and London: University of California Press.

Kosinski, D.M. (1989). *Orpheus in nineteenth-century symbolism.* Ann Arbor, MI: UMI Research Press.

Kristeva, J. (1980). *Desire in language. A semiotic approach to language and art.* L.S. Roudiez (Trans. and Ed.). New York: Columbia University Press.

____. (1982). *Powers of horror. An essay in abjection.* L.S. Roudiez (Trans.). New York: Columbia University Press.

____. (1983). Within the microcosm of "the talking cure." In J.H. Smith and W. Kerrigan (Eds.). *Interpreting Lacan.* New Haven and London: Yale University Press, V.6 *Psychiatry and the Humanities.*

____. (1995). Of word and flesh. An interview with Julia Kristeva by Charles Penwarden. In *Rites of passage: Art for the end of the century.* S. Morgan and F. Morris (Eds.). London: Tate Gallery Publications.

L

Lacoue-Labarthe, P. (1989). *Typography. Mimesis. Philosophy. Politics.* C. Fynsk (Ed.). Cambridge and London: Harvard University Press.

____. (1990). *Heidegger, art and politics,* C. Turner (Trans.). Oxford and New York: Basil Blackwell.

____. (1993). Sublime truth. In *Of the sublime: Presence in question.* J. S. Librett (Trans. and Afterword). Albany, NY: State University of New York Press.

____. (1993a). *The subject of philosophy*. T. Tresize (Ed. and Forward). Minneapolis, MN: University of Minnesota Press.

____. (1994). *Musica ficta (figures of Wagner)*. F. McCarren (Trans.). Stanford, CA: Stanford University Press.

____. (1999). *Poetry as experience*. A. Tarnowski (Trans.). Stanford, CA: Stanford University Press.

Larratt-Smith, P. (2014). Psychadelic antiquity. In *Cy Twombly Paradise*. J. Sylvester (Ed.). Mexico City: Fundación Jumex Arte Contemporáneo.

Leeman, R. (2005). *Cy Twombly. A monograph*. London: Thames and Hudson.

Lernout, G. (1994). *The poet as thinker: Hölderlin in France*. Columbia, SC: Camden House, Inc.

Lyotard, J.-F. (1984). *The postmodern condition: A report on knowledge*. G. Bennington and B. Massumi (Trans.). Minneapolis, MN: University of Minnesota Press.

____. (1989). *The Lyotard reader*. A. Benjamin (Ed.). Oxford: Blackwell Publishers Ltd.

____. (1993). Philosophy and painting in the age of their experimentation: Contribution to an idea of postmodernity. In G. A. Johnson (Ed. and Intro.). *The Merleau-Ponty aesthetics reader. Philosophy and painting*. Evanston, IL: Northwestern University Press.

____. (1993a). The interest of the sublime. In *Of the sublime: Presence in question*. J. S. Librett (Trans. and Afterword). Albany, NY: State University of New York Press.

M

Mancusi-Ungaro, C. (2013). Cues from Cy Twombly. In *Cy Twombly Gallery*. J. Sylvester and N. Del Roscio (Eds.). New Haven and London: Yale University Press.

Marin, L. (1999.) *Sublime Poussin*. C. Porter (Trans.). Stanford, CA: Stanford University Press.

McGee, T. G. (1982). *Orfeo* and *Euridice*, the first two operas. In. J. Warden (Intro. and Ed.). *Orpheus. The metamorphoses of a myth*. Toronto and London: University of Toronto Press.

Merleau-Ponty, M. (1968). *The visible and the invisible*. C. Lefort (Ed.), A. Lingis (Trans.). Evanston, IL: Northwestern University Press.

____. (1993). Eye and mind. In *The Merleau-Ponty aesthetics reader. Philosophy and painting*. G. A. Johnson (Ed. and Intro.). Evanston, IL: Northwestern University Press.

Michaels, A. (1997). In L. Ollman. Seeing through nature. *Art in America*, October 1997.

Michaud, P.-A. (2004). *Aby Warburg and the image in motion*. S. Hawkes (Trans.). New York: Zone Books.

Miller, D.L. (1990). An other Jung and an other... In *C.G. Jung and the Humanities*. K. Barnaby and P. D'Acierno (Eds.). Princeton, NJ: Princeton University Press.

Morris, D. (2004). Life, or something like it. In *BOOKFORUM* Summer. New York: ARTFORUM International Magazine, Inc.

N

Nesin, K. (2014). *Cy Twombly's things*. New Haven and London: Yale University Press.

____. (2015). Cy Twombly. In *Gagosian Gallery May-August 2015*. New York: Gagosian Gallery.

Nietzsche, F. (1969). *The birth of tragedy*. W. Kaufmann (Trans.). New York: Vintage Books.

O

Onians, R.B. (1951/1987). *The origins of European thought*. Salem, NH: Ayer Company, Publishers, Inc.

Otto, W.F. (1965, 1981). *Dionysus. Myth and cult*. R.B. Palmer (Trans. and Intro.). Dallas, TX: Spring Publications.

P

Padel, R. (2006). On *Ariadne auf Naxos*. In Glyndenbourne Festival Opera programme. www.ruthpadel.com.

Pavlouskova, N. (2015). *Cy Twombly Late paintings 2003-2011*. London: Thames and Hudson.

Pincus - Witten, R. (1994). Twombly's quarantine. In *Cy Twombly: An untitled painting*. New York: Gagosian Gallery.

Plato. (1973). *Phaedrus and the seventh and eighth letters*. W. Hamilton (Trans. and Intro.). Harmondsworth, Middlesex, England: Penguin Books.

Polikoff, D.J. (2011). *In the image of Orpheus. Rilke. A soul history*. Wilmette, IL: Chiron Publications.

R

Rajchman, J. (1985). The post-modern museum. In *Art in America,* No.10, (October). New York: Brant Art Publications Inc.

Riley II, C.A. (1995). *Color codes*. Hanover, NH: University Press of New England.

Rilke, R.M. (1938). *Translations from the poetry of Rainer Maria Rilke*. M.D.H. Norton (Trans.). New York: W.W. Norton and Co.

____. (1939). *Duino elegies*. J.B. Leishman and S. Spender (Trans.). New York: W.W. Norton and Co.

____. (1942). *Sonnets to Orpheus*. M.D.H. Norton (Trans.). New York: W.W. Norton and Co.

____. (1954). *Selected works. Volume 1 Prose*. G.C. Houston (Trans.). London: The Hogarth Press.

____. (1976) *Rainer Maria Rilke, Poems, 1906-1926*. J. B. Leishman (Trans.). London: Hogarth Press.

____. (1981). *Selected poems of Rainer Maria Rilke*. R. Bly (Trans. and Comm.). New York: Harper and Row.

____. (1984, 1989). *The selected poetry of Rainer Maria Rilke*. S. Mitchell (Ed. and Trans.). New York: Vintage.

____. (1996). *Uncollected poems*. R. Snow (Sel. and Trans.). New York, NY: North Point Press.

Robbins, E. (1982). Famous Orpheus. In J. Warden (Intro. and Ed.). *Orpheus. Metamorphoses of a myth*. Toronto and London: University of Toronto Press.

Ruck, C.A.P. (Ed.). (2014). *Dionysus in Thrace: Ancient entheogenic themes in the mythology and archaeology of Northern Greece, Bulgaria and Turkey*. Berkeley, CA: Regent Press.

S

Santner, E.L. (1986). *Friedrich Hölderlin. Narrative vigilance and the poetic imagination*. New Brunswick and London: Rutgers University Press.

____. (1990). *Stranded objects. Mourning, memory and film in postwar Germany*. Ithaca, NY and London: Cornell University Press.

____. (2001). *On the psychotheology of everyday life. Reflections on Freud and Rosenzweig*. Chicago and London: The University of Chicago Press.

____. (2006). *On creaturely life: Rilke/Benjamin/Sebald*. Chicago and London: The University of Chicago Press.

Saville, J. (2014). An interview with Jenny Saville. In *Gagosian Gallery, February-April 2014*. New York: Gagosian Gallery.

Scavizzi, G. (1982). The myth of Orpheus in Italian Renaissance art, 1400-1600. In J. Warden (Intro. and Ed.). *Orpheus. The metamorphoses of a myth*. Toronto and London: University of Toronto Press.

Schama, S. (2014). Cy Twombly. In *The essential Cy Twombly*. N. Del Roscio (Ed.). New York: Distributed Art Publishers.

Schmidt, K. (2000). Looking at Cy Twombly's sculpture. In *Cy Twombly: Die skulptur/ The sculpture*. K. Schmidt, Ostfildern-Ruit, Germany: Hatje Cantz Verlag.

____. (2011). Immortal-and eternally young: Figures from classical mythology in the work of Nicholas Poussin and Cy Twombly. In Cullinan, N. (Ed.). *Twombly and Poussin: Arcadian painters*. London: Paul Holberton Publishing.

Schulz-Hoffmann, C. (2006). To feel all things in all ways. New sculptures by Cy Twombly. In *Cy Twombly. Sculptures 1992-2005*. Munich: Schirmer/Mosel.

Schwartz-Salant, N. (1988). Before the creation: The unconscious couple in borderline states of mind. In N. Schwartz-Salant and M. Stein (Eds.). *The borderline personality in analysis*. Wilmette, IL: Chiron Publications.

____. (1988a). *The borderline personality: Vision and healing*. Chicago: Chiron.

Sebald, W. G. (2004). *Unrecounted: 33 poems by W. G. Sebald, 33 lithographs by Jan Peter Tripp*. M. Hamburger (Trans.). New York: New Directions.

____. (2011). *Across the land and the water. Selected poems 1964-2001*. I. Galbraith (Trans.). New York: Random House.

____. (2013). *A place in the country*. J. Catling (Trans., Intro. and Notes). New York: Random House.

Schiff, R. (2008) Charm. In *Cy Twombly. Cycles and seasons*. N. Serota (Ed.). New York: Distributed Art Publishers, Inc.

Silverman, H.J. (1993). Cézanne's mirror stage. In G.A. Johnson (Ed. and Intro.). *The Merleau-Ponty aesthetics reader. Philosophy and painting.* Evanston, IL: Northwestern University Press.

Staff, C.G. (2011). A poetics of becoming. The mythography of Cy Twombly. In C*ontemporary art and classical myth.* I.L. Wallace and J. Hirsh (Eds.). Surrey, England: Ashgate Publishing Limited.

Sylvester, D. (2001). Cy Twombly (2000). In *Interviews with American artists.* New Haven and London: Yale University Press.

Sylvester, J. (2008). Sa la lah. In *Cy Twombly. III NOTES FROM SALALAH.* Rome: Gagosian Gallery.

T

Taminiaux, J. (1993). The thinker and the painter. In G. A. Johnson (Ed. and Intro.). *The Merleau-Ponty aesthetics reader. Philosophy and painting.* Evanston, IL: Northwestern University Press.

Taussig, M. (2006). *Walter Benjamin's grave.* Chicago and London: The University of Chicago Press.

____. (2009). *What color is the sacred.* Chicago and London: The University of Chicago Press.

Twombly, C. (1973). *Zeichnungen* 1953-1973. H. Bastian (Ed. and Text). Berlin: Propylaen Verlag.

____. (1979). *Catalogue raisonné des oeuvres sur papier.* Y. Lambert (Ed.). Volume VI 1973-1976. R. Barthes (Text). Milan: Multhipla Edizioni.

____. (1991). *Catalogue raisonné des oeuvres sur papier.* Y. Lambert (Ed.). Volume VII 1977-1982. P. Sollers (Text). Milan: Multhipla Edizioni.

____. (1992). *Catalogue raisonné of the paintings.* H. Bastian (Ed.). Volume I 1948-1960. Munich: Schirmer/Mosel.

____. (1993). *Catalogue raisonné of the paintings.* H. Bastian (Ed.). Volume II 1961-1965. Munich: Schirmer/Mosel.

____. (1994a). *Catalogue raisonné of the paintings.* H. Bastian (Ed.). Volume III 1966-1971. Munich: Schirmer/Mosel.

____. (1994b). Cy Twombly: *An untitled painting.* New York: Gagosian Gallery.

____. (1994c). *Cy Twombly. A retrospective.* K. Varnedoe (Dir). New York: Harry N. Abrams, Inc.

____. (1995). *Catalogue raisonné of the paintings.* H. Bastian (Ed.). Volume IV 1972-1995. Munich: Schirmer/Mosel.

____. (1998). *Cy Twombly: 8 sculptures.* Rome: American Academy.

____. (2000). *Cy Twombly: Die Skulptur/The sculpture.* K. Schmidt (Ed.). Ostfildern-Ruit, Germany: Hatje Cantz Verlag.

____. (2002). *Audible Silence: Cy Twombly at Daros.* E. Keller and R. Malin (Eds.). Zürich: Scalo.

____. (2002 a). *Cy Twombly: Lepanto.* New York: Gagosian Gallery.

____. (2003). *Cy Twombly at the Hermitage: Fifty years of works on paper.* Munich: Schirmer/Mosel.

____. (2004). *Cy Twombly: Fifty years of works on paper*. Munich: Schirmer/Mosel.

____. (2005). *Cy Twombly. Bacchus Psilax Mainomenos*. New York: Gagosian Gallery.

____. (2006). *Cy Twombly. Sculptures 1992-2005*. Munich: Schirmer/Mosel.

____. (2008). *Cy Twombly. Cycles and seasons*. N. Serota (Ed.). New York: Distributed Art Publishers, Inc.

____. (2009). *Catalogue raisonné of the paintings*. H. Bastian (Ed.). Volume V 1996-2007. Munich: Schirmer/Mosel.

____. (2009a). *Cy Twombly. States of mind*. Munich: Schirmer/Mosel Verlag.

____. (2011). *Le temps retrouvé. Cy Twombly photographe et artistes invités*, vol. I. Arles: Actes Sud/Collection Lambert en Avignon.

____. (2011a). *Le temps retrouvé. Cy Twombly photographe et artiste invités*, vol. II. Arles: Actes Sud/Collection Lambert en Avignon.

____. (2011b). *Turner Monet Twombly: Later paintings*. London: Tate Publishing.

____. (2012). *Cy Twombly. The last paintings*. New York: Gagosian Gallery.

____. (2012a). *Cy Twombly drawings. Cat. rais. Vol. 2 1956-1960*. N. Del Roscio (Ed.). Munich: Schirmer Mosel, Gagosian Gallery.

____. (2013). *The Cy Twombly Gallery*. J. Sylvester and N. Del Roscio (Eds.). New Haven and London: Yale University Press.

____. (2013a). Untitled. In *Audible presence. Lucio Fontana, Yves Klein, Cy Twombly*. New York: Dominique Lévy.

____. (2013b). *Cy Twombly drawings. Cat. rais. Vol. 3 1961-1963*. N. Del Roscio (Ed.). Munich: Schirmer Mosel, Gagosian Gallery.

____. (2014). *Cy Twombly. Bild, Text, Paratext*. T. Greub (Ed.). Paderborn, Germany: Wilhelm Fink.

____. (2014a). *Cy Twombly Paradise*. J. Sylvester (Ed.). Mexico City: Fundación Jumex Arte Contemporáneo.

____. (2014b). *Catalogue raisonné of the paintings*. H. Bastian (Ed.). Volume VI 2008-2011. Munich: Schirmer/Mosel.

____. (2014c). *Cy Twombly drawings. Cat. rais. Vol. 4 1964-1969*. N. Del Roscio (Ed.). Munich: Schirmer Mosel, Gagosian Gallery.

____. (2014d). *The essential Cy Twombly*. N. Del Roscio (Ed.). New York: Distributed Art Publishers.

____. (2015). *Cy Twombly drawings. Cat. rais. Vol. 5 1970-1971*. N. Del Roscio (Ed). Munich: Schirmer/Mosel.

____. (2016). *Cy Twombly drawings. Cat. rais. Vol. 6 1972-1979*. N. Del Roscio (Ed). Munich: Schirmer/Mosel.

____. (2016a). *Cy Twombly drawings. Cat. rais. Vol. 7 1980-1989*. N. Del Roscio (Ed.). Munich: Schirmer/Mosel.

____. (2017). *Cy Twombly. Orpheus*. Paris, London, New York: Gagosian Gallery.

____. (2017b). *Cy Twombly drawings. Cat. rais. Vol.8. 1990-2011*. N. Del Roscio (Ed.). Munich: Schirmer/Mosel.

____. (2017c). *Cy Twombly*. J. Storsve (Ed.). Munich: Sieveking Verlag.

____. (2018). *Catalogue raisonné of the paintings*. H. Bastian (Ed.). Vol. VII Addendum. Munich: Schirmer/Mosel.

V

Varnedoe, K. (1994). Inscriptions in Arcadia. In *Cy Twombly. A retrospective*. New York: Museum of Modern Art.

von Franz, M.-L. (1964). The process of individuation. In C.G. Jung (Ed.). *Man and his symbols*. London: Aldus Books Limited.

____. (1966). *Aurora Consurgens*. R.F.C. Hull and A.S.B. Glover (Trans.). London: Routledge and Kegan Paul.

W

Warden, J. (Intro. and Ed.). (1982). *Orpheus. The metamorphoses of a myth*. Toronto and London: University of Toronto Press.

Wasson, R.G., Hoffman, A., and Ruck, C.A.P. (1978). *The road to Eleusis: Unveiling the secret of the mysteries*. New York and London: Harcourt Brace Jovanovich, Inc.

Waters, P. (2006). *The ordinary sublime*. Tallahassee, FL: Anhinga Press.

Weiss, J. (2008). Cy Twombly. Tate Modern. London. In *ARTFORUM*. October 2008. XLVII, NO. 2. New York: Artforum.

Wilhelm, R. and Baynes, C.F. (Trans.). (1950). *The I Ching*. Bollingen Series XIX. Princeton, NJ: Princeton University Press.

Winkler, P. (2013). Just about perfect: A recollection. In *Cy Twombly Gallery*. J. Sylvester and N. Del Roscio (Eds.). New Haven and London: Yale University Press.

Wolin, R. (Ed.). (1993). *The Heidegger controversy: A critical reader*. Cambridge and London: The MIT Press.

Wroe, A. (2011). *Orpheus. The song of life*. New York: The Overlook Press.

Z

Zweig, S. (2011). *Hölderlin, Kleist and Nietzsche. The struggle with the daemon. Master builders of the spirit, Volume 2*. New Brunswick and London: Transaction Publishers.

Acknowledgements

This book is dedicated to my wife Christina, whose openness, generosity of spirit and tireless support is a daily reminder of the renewing power of love.

The initial inspiration for the conceptual scheme of viewing Cy Twombly in the light of Friedrich Hölderlin derives from the writings of Giorgio Agamben. His consistently thoughtful and deeply probing works punctuated and interrogated the development of my own ideas throughout the project.

Since the germinal beginnings of this manuscript as a publishable 'book', I have received invaluable material and archival assistance from the Cy Twombly Foundation, and in particular, from the unflagging availability and willing collaboration of Nicola Del Roscio. Without his continuous efforts and mentorship, this book could not have been realized in its present form. A debt of gratitude is also due to the staff of the Cy Twombly Foundation in New York, Rome and in Gaeta, and at the Fondazione Nicola Del Roscio, and especially to Raffaele Valente, whose studious professionalism made possible the beautiful Cy Twombly images on display.

Warm thanks must also be extended to my first reader, Julie Sylvester, whose unconditional and enthusiastic encouragement set the entire book publication process in motion. Further help at critical junctures has come from Sage Lewis in acquiring images and permissions from a variety of institutions; Joanna Papayiannis in researching ancient art; and Nancy Larsen for typing uncountable drafts of the early chapters dating back to the beginnings of this century. The technical, editing and computer work has been performed brilliantly by Lindsay Rowe Scala in the latter years of the project, and has been painstakingly held together throughout all the phases of this joint creation by my family, Sammy, Benji, and again and again, Christina.

Photography Credits and Copyright Permissions

Page 26, 1. Cy Twombly, *Untitled*, 1984, Gaeta: © Cy Twombly Foundation. Courtesy Archives Fondazione Nicola del Roscio; Page 30, 2. Cima da Conegliano, *Orpheus Playing for the Animals*, c. 1505-10: © Gabinetto Fotografico delle Gallerie degli Uffizi; Page 32, 3. François Perrier, *Orpheus in the Underworld Playing Before Pluto and Persephone*, c. 1647-50, Musée du Louvre: © Art Resource, New York; Page 36, 4. Cy Twombly, *Orpheus*, 1979: © Cy Twombly Foundation. Courtesy Archives Fondazione Nicola del Roscio; Page 38, 5. *Orpheus Singing to the Thracians*, c. 450 B.C., Orpheus Painter, Staatliche Museen zu Berlin, Antikensammlung: © Art Resource, New York; Page 42, 6. Cy Twombly, *Winter's Passage: Luxor*, 1985, Porto Ercole: © Cy Twombly Foundation, Photo credit: Kunsthaus Zürich; Page 45, 7. *Death of Orpheus*, c. 440 B.C., Phiale Painter, Staatliche Antikensammlungen und Glyptothek München: © Art Resource, New York; Page 46, 8. Odilon Redon, *Orpheus*, c. 1903-10, Cleveland Museum of Art; Pages 54-5, 9. Cy Twombly, *Untitled (Say Goodbye, Catullus, to the Shores of Asia Minor)*, 1994, Menil Collection, Cy Twombly Gallery, Houston, Texas: © Cy Twombly Foundation. Courtesy Archives Nicola del Roscio; Page 58, 10. Cy Twombly, *Untitled (Say Goodbye, Catullus, to the Shores of Asia Minor)*, 1994, Menil Collection, Cy Twombly Gallery, Houston, Texas: © Cy Twombly Foundation. Courtesy Archives Nicola del Roscio; Page 70, 11. *Orpheus and Eurydice*, marble relief, Roman copy of 420 B.C. Greek original by Callimachos, Museo Archeologico Nazionale di Napoli: © Art Resource, New York; Page 76, 12. Robert Rauschenberg, *Cy Twombly with a musical instrument*, 1953, Rome: © Robert Rauschenberg Foundation; Page 80, 13. *Dionysos in Ecstasy*, Kleophrades, c. 490 B.C., Staatliche Antikensammlungen und Glyptothek München. Photograph by: Renate Kühling: © Art Resource, New York; Page 96, 14. Cy Twombly, *Dionysus*, 1975: © Cy Twombly Foundation. Courtesy Archives Fondazione Nicola Del Roscio; Page 108, 15. Cy Twombly, *Fifty Days at Iliam, Part IV: Achaeans in Battle*, 1978: © Cy Twombly Foundation. Courtesy Archives Nicola Del Roscio. Photography: Philadelphia Museum of Art; Page 113, 16. *Zeus and Dionysos*, c. 460 B.C., Altamura Painter, Museo Archeologico Nazionale de Spina, Ferrara: © Art Resource, New York; Page 125, 17. *Raving Maenad with Panther and Snake in Hair*, c. 490-80 B.C., Brygos Painter, Staatliche Antikensammlungen und Glyptothek München: © Art Resource, New York; Page 128, 18. Cy Twombly, *Bacchus*, 1981: © Cy Twombly Foundation. Courtesy Archives Nicola Del Roscio; Page 130, 19. Cy Twombly, *Naxos*, 1982: © Cy Twombly Foundation. Courtesy

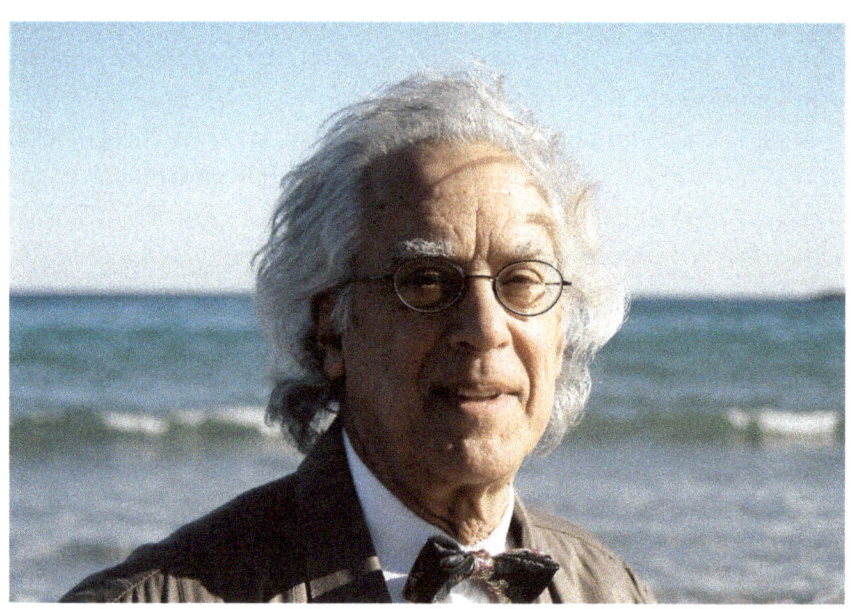

About the Author

Gary D. Astrachan, Ph.D., is a clinical psychologist and Jungian psychoanalyst in private practice in Portland, Maine. He is a faculty member and supervising and training analyst at the C.G. Jung Institutes in Boston and in Switzerland and lectures and teaches widely throughout North America, Latin America and Europe. He is a founding member of the C.G. Jung Center of Brunswick, Maine, and is also an independent curator of contemporary art installations and exhibitions. He is the author of numerous scholarly articles in professional journals and books and writes particularly on the relationship between analytical psychology and Greek mythology, poetry, painting, film, post-modernism and critical theory.